Hermann Gruber

COMPLEXITY OF REGULAR LANGUAGES

On the Descriptional and Algorithmic Complexity of Regular Languages

Hermann Gruber

Bibliografische Information Der Deutschen Bibliothek
Die Deutsche Bibliothek verzeichnet diese Publikation in der Deutschen Nationalbibliografie; detaillierte bibliografische Daten sind im Internet über http://dnb.ddb.de abrufbar.

Gießener Dissertation
Fachbereich Mathematik und Informatik, Physik, Geographie
Justus-Liebig-Universität Gießen (D26) 2009

1. Gutachter: Prof. Dr. rer. nat. Markus Holzer
2. Gutachter: Prof. Dr. rer. nat. Martin Kutrib

Termin der Disputation: 25.09.2009

HARLAND media, Lichtenberg (Odw.) 2010
www.harland-media.de

Gedruckt auf alterungsbeständigem Papier nach ISO 9706 (säure-, holz- und chlorfrei).

Printed in Germany

ISBN 978-3-938363-62-1

Digital ist besser
Tocotronic

Preface

This thesis is a research monograph. As such, it targets at an audience of experts, primarily in the fields of foundations of computer science and discrete mathematics. Nevertheless, already several persons showed interest in understanding at least the main theme of this thesis, but have only little background in mathematics and computer science. This preface can not serve a bluffer's guide to the main body of work, but we try at best to explain at least the central abstractions at an informal level.

The present work deals with mathematical models of computational processes. Several such models exist, each with its own advantages and characteristics. We will concentrate on the simplest of these models, namely on finite automata. An example drawn from everyday life naturally modeled as finite automaton is a vending machine. The observable behavior of a such a vending machine is described as sequence of atomic events. For simplicity, let us assume the possible events are: a coin worth one or two units of money is inserted, in symbols ❶ or ❷, a cup of coffee ∪ is requested and brewed, and alternatively the cancel button © can be hit. Thereafter some coins might be returned, actions for which we introduce the symbols ① or ②. Now the behavior of a correctly operating vending machine is described as a set of sequences made up from these symbols. We expect that most users of the machine will be content with the sequence

$$❶❷①∪❶❶©②❷∪,$$

except possibly for the price of two money units for a cup of coffee. In contrast, the sequence

$$❷∪❶❶©©©①©©©©©$$

is certainly *not* expected to be observed on a machine that operates correctly. We thus model the observable behavior of a vending machine as a set of sequences over some finite alphabet—in our example, this set will contain infinitely many correct sequences, but it will not include all possible sequences. The internal behavior can be modeled as a control unit, which is at each point in time in one of finitely many possible internal states. At this point, we mention that our vending machine always immediately returns overpaid amounts. In this way, we can retain a finite number of states. Otherwise it would be possible to insert arbitrarily large amounts of money before hitting the © button. In order to guarantee that it always returned the correct amount of money, such a machine would require a fairly large memory unit in that case.

A mathematically precise model of a finite state control unit, such as the one found inside the vending machine, is the concept of a *finite automaton*. The set of sequences that form the behavior of a finite automaton is then a *regular language*.[1] This model

---

[1] In everyday life, we conceive the term *language* in a much narrower sense. In computer science, the term is very generously defined: Any set of symbol sequences makes up a (formal) language. There is not too much of interest to say about such a general concept. Thus we study certain interesting families of formal languages, such as the family of regular languages.

draws a clear distinction between the internal realization of the vending machine—the finite automaton—and its externally observable behavior—a regular language.

An advantage of these notions is that once a prototype is developed, the designer may eventually want to replace the internal circuitry by an easer or cheaper one. The users will be content as long as the behavior of the new machine is the same as that of the old one. One part of this thesis is devoted to the question to what extent such simplifications can be automatically computed, while consuming only a reasonable amount of memory and computation time.

The above scenario requires that the desired behavior of the vending machine is specified in the form of a prototype. There is also a more convenient way to specify the desired behavior. The behavior can be described by so-called *regular expressions*. These are a kind of formula that bear some superficial similarity to arithmetical expressions, or the formulas from mathematical logic. For mathematically trained persons, such formulas are often much easier to understand than the complex wiring diagrams of finite automata. The larger part of this thesis deals with questions regarding regular expressions. One such question is the following: Assume we already have a vending machine, but the formula specifying its behavior got lost. The problem is now to reverse-engineer a formula, in the form of a regular expression, from the wiring diagram of the machine. In order to remain understandable, the description of the behavior should of course be as short as possible. From a bird-eye's perspective, this is similar to the process of translating (say) Latin to English. But instead of a description in Latin, we have a formal description in the form of a wiring diagram, and instead of translating it to English for easier understanding, we want to translate it into a regular expression. In both translation tasks, we will encounter sentences and constructs for which there is no direct analogue in the target language. Then we have to think about how to paraphrase these constructs, of course as succinctly as possible. This thesis aims to provide a deeper understanding about how smoothly this task can be accomplished.

We will also seize the strength and limitations of regular expressions as a specification formalism. In the role of a requirements engineer, we often want to combine smaller fragments to specify more complex requirements. Astonishingly, we will find in this thesis that several very simple mechanisms of assembling more complex units cannot be easily described in the language of regular expressions—rather often, such combinations of requirements have to be circumscribed in an extremely cumbersome way. In these cases, practitioners may prefer to use more elaborate formalisms that are more succinct than regular expressions.

We hope that also non-expert readers could catch a glimpse of the material treated in this thesis, and the type of questions addressed. For the expert audience, we hope that this short distraction served as a little *canapé* that wetted their appetite for the technical developments to come in the present thesis.

Collaborations

Some parts of this thesis arose from collaborative work, and we want to acknowledge these contributions. Contributions resulting from joint work with Markus Holzer were presented, partly in preliminary form, at the 10th, 11th, 12th and 13th *International Conference on Developments in Language Theory* [74, 77, 80, 83], at the 8th and 10th installments of the *International Workshop on Descriptional Complexity of Formal Systems* [75, 81], at the 1st *International Conference on Language and Automata Theory and*

Applications [76], and at the 35th *International Colloquium on Automata, Languages and Programming* [79]. The part concerning the conversion of finite automata accepting finite languages into regular expressions is based on joint work with Jan Johannsen, and was presented at the 11th *International Conference on Foundations of Software Science and Computation Structures* [84]. Two of these contributions already appeared, in revised and expanded form, as journal articles [78, 82].

Acknowledgments

I would like to thank all persons who directly or indirectly contributed to this work. Any attempt of listing all contributions will be necessarily incomplete. I hope that at least the most immediate contributors are mentioned. First of all, I would like to thank my advisor, Markus Holzer, not only for his continuous support and advice, but also for his great care at reading a draft of this thesis. In this context, I would also like to thank Irmgard Kellerer, Martina Mensch and Renate Szweda for reading portions of a preliminary draft. I am indebted to Jan Johannsen for sharing his expertise in communication complexity with me, and for becoming enthusiastic about topics outside his main area of research. Thanks also goes to Jeffrey Shallit and Wouter Gelade for sending me preprints of their papers at times these did not appear yet in print. Finally, I thank all of my current and former colleagues for countless inspiring discussions.

Contents

List of Figures

List of Tables

Part I

Getting Started

1 Introduction

Possibly the simplest mathematical model capturing the nature of computation is that of a finite automaton. Admittedly, virtually every computer scientist has taken some courses in which she or he learned about this concept. We start with a short historical survey of the development of the theory of finite automata. Thereafter, we present the main questions addressed and highlight a few of the obtained results.

In the 1940s and 1950s there were many different lines of research that eventually ended up in the same concept, namely that of finite automata. We begin with a very short historical survey of these developments.

Perhaps surprisingly, finite state systems were historically first studied by biologists, rather than by computer scientists or electrical engineers. In the 1940s, McCulloch and Pitts suggested a precursor of the concept of finite automata as a mathematical model of neural activity in nerve nets [139]. A few years later, Kleene [125] introduced a textual specification formalism, the concept of regular expressions. He proved that the sets of sequences that can be described by regular expressions are exactly those that can be described by finite automata. Since that time, this family of languages is known as the regular languages. The definition of (deterministic) finite automata as we know it today was shaped only shortly before by Huffman [105, 106] and Moore [145], whose motivation for studying finite automata was to formalize the behavior of switching circuits. After Kleene's invention of regular expressions, Rabin and Scott [157] introduced another method for describing regular languages, the nondeterministic finite automata. This was such an outstanding conceptual contribution that they later were given the Turing award for this work, the most prestigious prize in computer science [7].

Other lines of research that flowed into the early development of the theory of finite automata came from mathematics, in particular logic and algebra. The dream of having a logical calculus for mechanically proving or disproving mathematical statements dates back to the ideas of Leibniz in the 17th century, and was later formulated precisely by Hilbert [41]. After Gödel had given a negative answer to Hilbert's famous *Entscheidungsproblem* in the 1930s, many mathematicians sought for fragments of arithmetic that were powerful enough to be useful yet weak enough to retain the desirable feature of a decidable theory. Here, Büchi [24], Elgot [57], and Trakhtenbrot [174] identified a decidable fragment of second order logic. As it turns out, this logical theory captures exactly the regular languages. This means that each formula of that theory can be converted into an equivalent finite automaton and *vice versa*. Beside this logical characterization, an algebraic viewpoint proved useful in charting the fine structure of regular languages. It known that Kleene's theorem also allows for an algebraic interpretation in the theory of semigroups, see e.g. [155]. An early success of this approach was Schützenberger's Theorem, which links a basic family of algebras with a basic logical theory: He proved that the aperiodic monoids are equally expressive as first-order logic with total order [166]. A detailed account on the algebraic approach to understanding aspects of regular languages is given in [56]. Last but not least, also in the 1950s, Chomsky was seeking for mathematical models capturing the relevant features of natural language. This led to the definition of the Chomsky hierarchy [31, 32], with the family of regular languages at its lowest level. Notably, although the Chomsky hierarchy was motivated by linguistics, it turned out to be more influential in the field of computer science, cf. [133]. An extensive historical survey about these early developments is given by Mahoney [133].

Fueled by these early successes, the theory of automata saw a golden age in the 1960s and 1970s, and was considered at the time as one of the main interests in theoretical computer science research, cf. [104, 179]. Inside this theory, finite automata became the best known models, cf. [22]. Along with the gained maturity, there had been a significant decrease of interest in research on these topics during the late 1970s. A possible reason is that after several decades of intensive research in the field, it seemed that almost everything interesting about regular languages was known, and only the most difficult problems remained. In a survey appearing in 1980, Brzozowski, one of the pioneers in automata theory, exemplified this view by listing six problems on finite automata [22]. All of these were presumably very difficult, since many excellent researchers had tried to solve them, with little success. Meanwhile, not only that several of these problems have been solved [45, 91, 169], in recent years there appears to be a renewed interest in the theory of finite automata, cf. [180]. This observation is corroborated by many interesting new results on classical questions, see e.g. [13, 86, 101, 118, 162]. The appearance of several recent listings describing old and new open challenges regarding regular languages [30, 59, 104, 181] gives further evidence for such a new momentum.

An attractive feature of regular languages is that the various different characterizations can be effectively obtained, in the sense that one can, in principle, convert automatically between various modes of description e.g. between the abovementioned logical formulas and finite automata. In the 1950s, when most of these *effectiveness* results were first proved, it was unusual to determine the time and memory requirements of such algorithms. Later, along with the growing availability of electronic computers, questions of *efficiency* gained importance: at once, such algorithms proved to be powerful tools in solving real-world problems. Apart from the traditional application domains which marked the origins of regular languages, the latter concept has found widespread use in many areas of computing. Notable examples include traditional applications such as lexical analysis in compiler design [1] and pattern matching in text processing [127]. More recent additions to the list of applications are UML statecharts in software engineering [52], specifications and query languages in XML data and document processing [130, 135], and network intrusion detection in internet packet routing [128].

Part of such applications deals with massive datasets, and there is a growing interest in memory-efficient representations of regular languages, cf. [180]. Such questions were addressed already since the beginnings of automata theory, see e.g. [132, 157]. A systematic study of questions of *descriptional complexity* started in the beginning 1970s, as witnessed by early papers of Meyer and Fischer [143], and of Maslov [136]. Meyer and Fischer compared different models of description, such as different types of automata and regular expressions, while Maslov investigated the effect of language manipulations on the required number of states in deterministic finite automata. Around the same time, the first *computational complexity* results regarding representations of regular languages appeared. Meyer and Stockmeyer showed that increased succinctness of description can render some problems computationally intractable [144]. For deterministic finite automata, efficient minimization is possible, and algorithms solving that problem were developed since the beginning of automata theory [72, 95, 105, 106, 145, 173]. Since it was known that there are cases where the smallest deterministic finite automaton is exponentially larger than the smallest equivalent nondeterministic finite automaton [132], the obvious question was whether we can have similar algorithms for minimizing nondeterministic finite automata. Here the result of Stockmeyer and Meyer implies that minimization of nondeterministic finite automata is computationally hard.

This is of course bad news, and a part of this thesis is devoted to look for ways out. To illustrate the kind of question we are interested in, a part of this thesis is devoted to the computational complexity of the minimization problem of nondeterministic finite automata. Since the problem is hard in the general case, we study special cases on the one hand and approximate solutions on the other hand. Here we continue a line of research that has been studied by different research groups in the past [70, 112, 114, 144]. We announce the solution of several research challenges that were left open by previous investigators. We also investigate various other aspects of minimal nondeterministic finite automata. This includes the comparison of techniques for proving lower bounds, and of different ways to measure the size of a nondeterministic finite automaton. Examples of our results include the following: We show that counting the number of states is essentially different from counting the number of transitions. The minimum number of states can numerically largely differ from the number of transitions, and sometimes it is impossible to minimize both measures simultaneously. We also show that minimizing nondeterministic finite automata is rendered computationally less complex if a finite language is specified explicitly, as a list of words. This setup appears, for example, in computational linguistics [167]. Still, even this severely restricted problem remains computationally intractable (**NP**-hard).

Often we are already content with approximate solutions to such hard problems. In 1993, Jiang and Ravikumar [114] raised the question whether we can obtain an approximate solution in polynomial time, provided the input is specified in a not too succinct manner. In this direction, Gramlich and Schnitger [70] provided some evidence that even weak approximations are impossible to obtain efficiently. Yet there were some technical issues with the result, and these authors posed a few open questions. For instance, they relied on an unusual cryptographic assumption. Most of these issues are resolved by the study presented here. We strengthen their results in several directions: First, we give evidence for hardness of approximation based on the standard assumption, *i.e.*, $\mathbf{P} \neq \mathbf{NP}$. Second, we can show that the problem remains as hard to approximate in the abovementioned use case appearing in computational linguistics. And finally, in several cases we obtain quantitative improvements on the bounds of approximability.

While finite automata are ideally suited for manipulation by computers, regular expressions are the preferred choice to be understood and specified by humans, cf. [141]. This can be explained as follows: just like ordinary arithmetic expressions, regular expressions have a hierarchical structure, which is often more easily perceived than that of a finite automaton. Another advantage is that regular expressions are handy to write down as a formula, thus utilizing only one dimension. In contrast, for finite automata it is even a nontrivial task to find a layout in two dimensions [20]. Still, there are regular expressions that are more difficult to understand than others. A potential source of such perceived complexity is nested application of the Kleene star operator, cf. [141]. This observation led Eggan to the definition of the star height of regular languages in the beginning 1960s [54]. Indeed, already early investigations showed that limiting access to the star operator gives rise to a fine-grained hierarchy inside the regular languages [46, 54, 141]. More precisely, the languages of star height at most k form a strict subset of the languages of star height at most $k+1$, for every integer k. In the decade that followed Eggan's seminal paper, quite a few works investigating regular expressions appeared, see e.g. [35, 36, 46, 92, 140, 141]. All of these were devoted to the concept of star height. The large interest in this concept stemmed from the fact that it was at the time a famous open problem whether the star height of a regular language is computable. Later, in 1980, this question constituted one of Brzozowski's six hard problems mentioned above [22]. The problem was resolved only after 25 years by Hashiguchi [91], with a rather intricate algorithm, cf. [124]. As a structural complexity measure, Brzozowski [22] states that the star height is a rather direct measure of complexity for regular languages.

But the most obvious measure related to the regular expression model is minimum required regular expression size. For that reason, the present thesis is largely concerned with this measure. Properties relating to regular expression size were first subject to systematic study in a paper by Ehrenfeucht and Zeiger in the mid-1970s [55]. In contrast to Eggan's paper introducing star height, that paper did not trigger much follow-up work at the time. It can only be speculated about the reasons for that. One possible reason for this is that the paper appeared at a time of decreasing interest in automata theory. But despite the recently regained research interest in this topic, still very little was known about the descriptional complexity of regular expressions at the time the author started working on this thesis, cf. [59]. In hindsight, this might be due to the lack of suitable techniques for proving lower bounds on regular expression size. Part of this thesis is devoted to the development of tools for proving such lower bounds. At this point, we note that around the same time Gelade and Neven [65] came up with another, quite different, lower bound technique. They to provide answers that partly overlap with results presented in this thesis. One of our tools for establishing lower bounds is based on the insight that if a regular language has sufficiently complex internal structure, then it requires huge regular expressions. More technically, we prove an exponential relation between the star height (*structural* complexity) and minimum expression size (*descriptional* complexity) for the regular languages. In this way, we can harness the rich literature on star height of regular languages to prove descriptional complexity results. The proof techniques developed in this thesis have a wealth of consequences. First, they allow us to study the conversion of finite automata into regular expressions and variations thereof. Second, we can use them to highlight the dynamic aspects of regular expressions, such as the evolution of regular expression size under various language operations. Finally, we are able to answer quite a few open questions regarding regular expressions. This includes not only an open question raised in the 1970s by Ehrenfeucht and Zeiger but also several research challenges proposed more recently by Ellul et al. [59].

We mention in particular the following results: The original proof of Kleene's theorem readily implies that deterministic finite automata over binary alphabets can be converted into regular expressions of size $O(4^n)$. As observed by Ehrenfeucht and Zeiger [55] in the 1970s, we can do better if the given automaton accepts only finitely many words. There we get an upper bound of $n^{O(\log n)}$ on regular expression size. Regarding lower bounds, these authors could only show that size at least $n^{\Omega(\log \log n)}$ will be necessary in the worst case. Consequently, they posed the question of narrowing the gap between the upper and lower bound. We will present a definite answer to their question, as we are able to raise the lower bound to give a tight estimate of $n^{\Theta(\log n)}$ on required size in the worst case. Our new lower bound already applies for binary alphabets. For the general case of infinite languages, the classical bound of $O(4^n)$ remained the best known until present, cf. [59].

Almost 50 years after Kleene's initial discovery, we now devise an improved algorithm, which even attains a bound of $O(1.742^n)$. This is close to optimal, since we also provide a lower bound of c^n, for some constant $c > 1$. We also undertake first attempts at charting the borders of tractability in regular expression manipulation.

The present thesis is organized in three main parts; each of these ends with a summary of the respective technical results. These parts, which constitute the main body of the thesis, are surrounded by an introductory part and a final part. The introductory part will now continue with a short recapitulation of the basic definitions, and, at the very end, the final part discusses possible lines of further research.

2 Basic Notions

The primary aim of this chapter is to fix some basic notions that will be used throughout this work, and to set the stage for the questions we aim to address in this thesis. As we assume that all readers with potential interest in this thesis have a reasonable background in discrete mathematics or computer science, we assume that the reader is familiar with basic mathematical abstractions used in computer science, such as equivalence relations, and with standard asymptotic O-notation in one variable. We furthermore assume the reader is familiar with the most important concepts in the theory of automata, formal languages and computational complexity, such as finite automata or Turing machines and the languages accepted by them, and the most common complexity classes such as **P** and **NP**. Although most relevant concepts regarding regular languages are explicity defined here, the corresponding introductory sections are mostly very terse. We will also make use of concepts from graph theory at various places, but we will not presume any deeper knowledge about graph theory. For thorough introductions into the topics of formal language theory, complexity theory, and graph theory, we refer to [96], [152], and [48], respectively.

2.1 Words and Languages

In formal language theory, the basic objects of study are sets of words over some given alphabet. Here, an *alphabet* is a nonempty finite set, whose elements are abstract entities referred to as *symbols*. A *word* over an alphabet Σ is a finite sequence of symbols from Σ juxtaposed.

Since a symbol can occur multiple times inside a word, a specific occurrence of a symbol inside a word is referred to as *letter*. The *empty word* is the unique word consisting of zero letters, and is denoted by ε. The *length* of a word $w = a_1 a_2 \cdots a_n$ over Σ, with $a_1, a_2, \ldots, a_n \in \Sigma$, is the number n of letters in w and denoted by $|w|$, with the special case $|\varepsilon| = 0$. The *reversal* of the word $w = a_1 a_2 \cdots a_{n-1} a_n$ is the word $a_n a_{n-1} \cdots a_2 a_1$ and denoted by w^R, with the special case $w = w^R$ if $|w| \leq 1$. Given an alphabet Σ, a *formal language* over Σ is simply a set of words over Σ. Often, we will refer to a formal language without explicit reference to an alphabet if the alphabet is known or immaterial.

Besides the usual set operations such as (finite) union and intersection, a basic operation on words and languages is *concatenation*. The concatenation $x \cdot y$ of two words x and y is their juxtaposition xy. Observe that this operation is noncommutative, and that the empty word is the neutral element of the concatenation operation: For every word w, we have $w \cdot \varepsilon = w$ and $\varepsilon \cdot w = w$. This operation generalizes to languages as follows: For two languages L_1 and L_2 over Σ, their concatenation is defined as $L_1 \cdot L_2 = \{\, xy \mid x \in L_1 \wedge y \in L_2 \,\}$. For obvious reasons, we usually omit the operator symbol $\cdot$ and write $L_1 L_2$. Many other operations on words, such as reversal, generalize to languages in a similar fashion: For instance, $L^R = \{\, w^R \mid w \in L \,\}$. The *(left) quotient* of a language L with respect to a set of words W is defined as $W^{-1}L = \{\, y \mid \exists x \in W : xy \in L \,\}$. For better readability, if W consists of a single word w, we also write $w^{-1}L$ instead. Quotients with respect to single words are also called *derivatives*. The *right quotient* of L with respect to Q is defined analogously as $LW^{-1} = \{\, x \mid \exists y \in W : xy \in L \,\}$.

The *iteration*, or *(Kleene) star* is defined as follows: Let Σ be an alphabet and L be a language over Σ. The i-fold concatenation of the language with itself is defined inductively as $L^0 = \{\varepsilon\}$ and $L^{i+1} = L \cdot L^i$ for $i \geq 0$. The iteration, or star, of L is defined as $L^* = \bigcup_{i \geq 0} L^i$. A variant of this operation is the ε-*free iteration*, denoted by L^+, which is defined as $L^+ = \bigcup_{i \geq 1} L^i$. For $i \geq 0$, we will often write $L^{\leq n}$ as a shorthand for the set $\bigcup_{i=0}^n L^i$. For illustration of the star operation, the language Σ^* is the set of all words over Σ; and the *complement* of L is given by $\Sigma^* \setminus L$.

Another interesting language operation is the interleaving of languages, which naturally arises in modeling the observation of two, or more, asynchronous concurrent processes, see [137]. The *interleaving*, or *shuffle*, of two languages L_1 and L_2 over alphabet Σ is

$$L_1 \text{ ш } L_2 = \{\, w \in \Sigma^* \mid w \in x \text{ ш } y \text{ for some } x \in L_1 \text{ and } y \in L_2 \,\},$$

where the interleaving $x \text{ ш } y$ of two words x and y is defined as the set of all words of the form $x_1 y_1 x_2 y_2 \cdots x_n y_n$, where $x = x_1 x_2 \cdots x_n$, $y = y_1 y_2 \cdots y_n$ with $x_i, y_i \in \Sigma^*$, for $n \geq 1$ and $1 \leq i \leq n$, and is denoted by $x \text{ ш } y$. Note that in this definition, some of the subwords x_i and y_i can be empty. Plenty of other language operations have been studied in the literature; for the moment, we shall content ourselves with a final natural example. The *circular shift* of a language is defined as $\circlearrowleft(L) = \{\, yx \mid xy \in L \,\}$. More operations on languages are discussed e.g. in [96, 168].

The most useful class of functions mapping languages to other languages are the *homomorphisms*. A homomorphism ρ is defined by a function $\Gamma \to \Sigma^*$, which maps each symbol from an alphabet Γ to a word over another alphabet Σ. The domain of this map is[1] extended to all words over Γ by letting $\rho(\varepsilon) = \varepsilon$ and $\rho(xa) = \rho(x)\rho(a)$ for each $x \in \Sigma^*$ and $a \in \Sigma$, and to sets of words by letting $\rho(L) = \{\, \rho(w) \mid w \in L \,\}$. For example, let $\Gamma = \{1, 2, \ldots, n\}$ and $\Sigma = \{a\}$. The homomorphism defined by letting $\rho(i) = a^i$ for $1 \leq i \leq n$ maps each sequence $i_1 i_2 \cdots i_k$ to the unique word w over $\{a\}$ with $|w| = \sum_{j=1}^k i_k$ over $\{a\}$. Observe that in this case, for $|w| \geq 3$ we have $|\rho^{-1}(w)| > 1$. An injective homomorphism, that is, a homomorphism ρ with $|\rho^{-1}(w)| \leq 1$ for all w in the range of ρ, is called a *monomorphism*.

An important general class of languages are the *unary languages*, that is, those over a unary alphabet, since there is a natural bijection between sets of natural numbers and unary languages. A unary language $L \subseteq \{a\}^*$ is called n-*cyclic*, if $a^i \in L \iff a^{i+n} \in L$, for every $i \geq 0$. In this case, we call n a *period* of L, and the such period is then referred to as its *minimal period*. We also say L is *cyclic* if it has a (finite) period.

2.2 Regular Languages

Possibly the easiest interesting family of languages over an alphabet Σ is the set of *finite languages*. These can be obtained inductively from $\Sigma \cup \{\varepsilon\}$ by iterated use of the operators concatenation and (finite) union. If we allow in addition the Kleene star as operator, we end up with the set of *regular languages*. Next, we recall some formalisms that allow us to describe exactly the regular languages.

---

[1] Readers with a background in algebra will probably notice that this extension behaves homomorphically with respect to the concatenation operation, hence the name homomorphism.

2.2.1 Regular Expressions

Let Σ be an alphabet. The *regular expressions* over Σ, and the languages they denote, are defined recursively as follows:

- $\emptyset$ is a regular expression and denotes the empty language;

- For $a \in \Sigma \cup \{\varepsilon\}$, the symbol a is a regular expression and denotes the language $\{a\}$,

- if r and s are regular expressions denoting languages R and S, then $(r+s)$, $(r \cdot s)$ and $(r)^*$ are regular expressions denoting the languages $R \cup S$, $R \cdot S$ and R^*, respectively.

The language described by the regular expression r is denoted by $L(r)$.

For convenience, parentheses are sometimes omitted and the concatenation is usually simply written as juxtaposition. The priority of operators is specified in the usual fashion: concatenation is performed before union, and star before both product and union. A language over Σ is called *regular* if it is denoted by some regular expression over Σ. Two regular expressions are called *equivalent* if they denote the same language.

2.2.2 Finite Automata

The concept of a finite automaton is a basic abstraction of a simple computation device. Informally, the characteristic of such an automaton is that it reads an input word from left to right letter by letter, and when the end of the word is reached, it is classified as "accepted" or "not accepted." At any stage of the computation, the automaton is in one of a finite number of states, and the state can be changed only when reading the next input letter. The allowed state changes depend only on the current state and the currently read letter, and are indicated by transitions. Since there are only finitely many such combinations, we also speak informally of a finite control unit. In the following we start with defining the most general model discussed in this work, and then proceed to the definition of various restrictions.

A nondeterministic finite automaton *with ε-transitions* (ε-NFA) is a 5-tuple $A = (Q, \Sigma, \delta, q_0, F)$, where Q is a finite set of states, Σ is a finite set of input symbols, $\delta : Q \times (\Sigma \cup \{\varepsilon\}) \rightarrow 2^Q$ is the transition function, $q_0 \in Q$ is the initial state, and $F \subseteq S$ is the set of accepting states.

For an ε-NFA A, a triple $(p, x, q) \in Q \times (\Sigma \cup \{\varepsilon\}) \times Q$ with $q \in \delta(p, x)$ is called a *transition* of A, which is more conveniently written as $p \xrightarrow{x} q$.

The *computation relation* $\vdash_A \subseteq Q \times \Sigma^* \times Q$ of the ε-NFA A is inductively defined by letting (q, ε, q) in $\vdash_A$ for all $q \in Q$; for all $p, q \in Q$, all words $w \in \Sigma^*$ and all $x \in \Sigma \cup \{\varepsilon\}$, let the triple (p, wx, q) be in $\vdash_A$ if there is a state $r \in Q$ such that both (p, w, r) is in $\vdash_A$ and $r \xrightarrow{x} q$ is a transition of A. For convenience, we also write $p \vdash_A^w q$ to indicate that (p, w, q) is in $\vdash_A$; also, the subscript A is omitted if the automaton A is understood from the context. We also say that the automaton A can go from p to q on reading the word w instead of using the symbolic notation $p \vdash_A^w q$.

The *language accepted* by an ε-NFA A is now defined as

$$L(A) = \{ w \in \Sigma^* \mid q_0 \vdash_A^w f, \text{ for some } f \in F \}.$$

Two finite automata are *equivalent* if they accept the same language. Note that we can always remove all transitions of the form $q \xrightarrow{\varepsilon} q$ without altering the accepted language.

Thus, unless stated otherwise, we will always tacitly assume that the automata under consideration do not have such ε-loops. In a similar manner, we call a state q of a finite automaton A *useful* if there exist words x and y such that both $q_0 \vdash^x q$ and $q \vdash^y f$, where q_0 is the start state and f is an accepting state. We will assume that the finite automata under consideration only have useful states, since all other states can be safely discarded without altering the accepted language.

A *nondeterministic finite automaton* (NFA) is defined like an ε-NFA, but now the transition function has signature $\delta : Q \times \Sigma \rightarrow 2^Q$. Clearly, every NFA is an ε-NFA, but the converse does of course not hold in general. A nondeterministic finite automaton (without ε-transitions) $A = (Q, \Sigma, \delta, q_0, F)$ is *deterministic* (a DFA), if $|\delta(q, a)| \leq 1$, for every $q \in Q$ and $a \in \Sigma$.

We note that many authors define deterministic finite automata instead with the condition $|\delta(q, a)| = 1$, see e.g. [179]. A DFA satisfying this stronger condition is usually called a *complete* DFA. The difference is minor: We could always transform a non-complete DFA into a complete one at the expense of a single additional "dead state." But, for instance, this clashes with the above convention that all states in a nondeterministic finite automaton are useful. Dropping the latter convention would introduce the necessity of dealing with notorious special cases in several definitions and constructions. For instance, we will later introduce notions such as bideterministic or acyclic DFAs, which would become misnomers at once if we required the DFAs to be complete. Thus for reasons of convenience, we stick to the definition as given above, thus also conforming e.g. with [136].

The following theorem is central to the theory of regular languages. For a proof, see any textbook on automata theory, such as [96].

Theorem 2.1. *Let L be a language. Then the following conditions are equivalent:*

- *There exists an ε-NFA accepting L.*

- *There exists a NFA accepting L.*

- *There exists a DFA accepting L.*

- *There exists a regular expression denoting L.*

When we need to specify a regular language, we thus have the choice between several models of description. Note that the proof of the above theorem is effective in the sense that it gives transformation algorithms for each pair of models of description.

2.2.3 The Myhill-Nerode Relation

Yet another way to define regular languages over Σ^* is via an equivalence relation on words in Σ^*. In general, an equivalence relation $\equiv$ on any set S naturally induces a partition of S into a set $S/\equiv$ of *equivalence classes*. For $x \in S$, we use the notation $[x]_\equiv$ to denote the equivalence class containing x. The *index* of an equivalence relation on S is the number of induced equivalence classes.

Now for a language $L \subseteq \Sigma^*$, the *Myhill-Nerode relation* [2] *for L*, denoted by $\equiv_L$, is defined as follows: For $x, y \in \Sigma^*$, we have $x \equiv_L y$ iff for all $z \in \Sigma^*$ holds $xz \in L$ if and only if $yz \in L$. An analogous definition is obtained by replacing both xz and yz with

---

[2]The relation is named after its discoverers, John Myhill and Anil Nerode (cf. [96]).

zx and zy, respectively; but it is not hard to see that the result would be exactly the Myhill-Nerode relation for L^R. That said, we will use the symbol $_L\!\equiv$ to denote the latter equivalence relation for ease of reading. For similar reasons, the equivalence class with respect to $\equiv_L$ (respectively $_L\!\equiv$) that contains $x \in \Sigma^*$ will be denoted by $[x]_L$ (respectively by $_L[x]$).

It is well known that the equivalence classes of this relation are in one-to-one correspondence with the states in the unique (up to renaming of states) state minimal DFA for a regular language[3], and this gives rise to a polynomial-time algorithm for minimizing deterministic finite automata. The proof of this fact, which can be found in [96], gives rise to the following classical theorem:

Theorem 2.2 (Myhill/Nerode). *Let $L \subseteq \Sigma^*$ be a language. Then L is regular iff the Myhill-Nerode relation for L has finite index.*

2.2.4 Complexity Measures for Regular Languages

As mentioned in the previous section, regular languages can be described by regular expressions, or alternatively by various kinds of finite automata. In many contexts, when having two equivalent descriptions of a regular language at hand, the shorter description is the preferred one. We recall next a few definitions for measuring the size of regular expressions and finite automata.

Concerning the descriptional complexity of regular expressions, a variety of different size measures was proposed in the literature [59]. The definition of these measures depends on how the expressions are represented: For instance, if the expression is represented as a parse tree, there is no need to represent parentheses explicitly, but the concatenation operator has to be specified explicitly, contrary to the conventions we introduced above. Luckily, if we disregard obviously redundant expressions, such as subexpressions of the form $\varepsilon + \varepsilon^*$, many different size measures are within a linear factor of each other, see [59] for more details. We will mostly use the following measure as a convenient definition of size:

Definition 2.3. The *alphabetic width* (or *size*) alph(r) of a regular expression r is defined as the total number of occurrences of symbols from Σ in r. For a regular language L, we define its alphabetic width, alph(L), as the minimum alphabetic width among all regular expressions describing L.

According to Ellul et al. [59], this appears to be the most intensely studied variant among the size measures for regular expressions. Incidentally, regular expressions were historically first studied from a different viewpoint, namely *structural* complexity—as opposed to *descriptional* complexity. Of the allowed operators in regular expressions, the star appears to be the most powerful one [141]. Therefore the star height, measuring the nesting depth of stars in an expression, was proposed as a complexity measure already in the early 1960s by Eggan [54].

Definition 2.4. For a regular expression r, the *star height* $h(r)$ is a structural complexity measure inductively defined by:

---

[3] Possibly modulo a single equivalence class: If there exists a prefix $x \in \Sigma^*$ that cannot be completed to any word in L, then the class $[x]_L$ does not correspond to a state in the minimal DFA. Note that all prefixes of this type, if any, are in the same equivalence class.

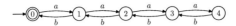

Figure 2.1: A minimal DFA accepting L_4.

- $h(r) = 0$ for $r \in \Sigma \cup \{\emptyset, \varepsilon\}$.

- $h(r_1 \cdot r_2) = h(r_1 + r_2) = \max(h(r_1), h(r_2))$

- $h(r^*) = 1 + h(r)$.

The star height of a regular language L, denoted by $h(L)$, is then defined as the minimum star height among all regular expressions describing L.

For a regular language L, we ideally would like to find a regular expression describing L that is both short and has low star height. The following example shows that these two goals might not be achieved simultaneously (at least not easily).

Example 2.5. Imagine a software buffer supporting the actions a ("add work packet") and b ("remove work packet"), with a total capacity of n packets. Let L_n denote the set of action sequences that result in an empty buffer and never cause the buffer to exceed its capacity. For illustration, a minimum DFA for L_4 is depicted in Figure 2.1.

The two regular expressions

$$\left(a\left(a\left(a(ab)^*b\right)^*b\right)^*b\right)^*$$

and

$$(ab)^* + (ab)^*aa\,(ab + aa(ba)^*bb + bb(ab)^*aa + ba)^*\,bb(ab)^*$$

both describe[4] the language L_4.

Note that the expressions have very different structure. The first is much shorter but has a deeper nesting of stars than the second. Indeed, McNaughton [141]proved in general that $h(L_n) = \lfloor \log(n+1) \rfloor$ so the second, and longer, expression has minimum star height. Although the second expression can be simplified a bit at the expense of symmetry, the author suspects that this language family exhibits a trade-off in the sense that L_n does not admit a regular expression r simultaneously reaching $h(r) \leq \lfloor \log(n+1) \rfloor$ and $\mathrm{alph}(r) \leq 2n$.

As for regular expressions, we introduce measures for the economy of description of finite automata. For each variant of finite automata, two obvious size measures are the number of states and transitions, respectively. The alternative to count the sum of the number of states and transitions, as proposed by Ilie and Yu [110], will not be further discussed here.

Definition 2.6. For a regular language L, the *nondeterministic state complexity* (*nondeterministic transition complexity*, respectively) of L, denoted by $\mathrm{nsc}(L)$ ($\mathrm{ntc}(L)$, respectively) is the minimum number of states (transitions, respectively) among all NFAs accepting L.

---

[4]For readers hesitating to believe this equivalence: A proof of this will have to wait until we discuss an algorithm for converting finite automata into regular expressions in Chapter 10. There a proof will be given in Example 10.3.

The exact analogs of nondeterministic state and transition complexity for ε-NFAs are denoted by $\mathrm{nsc}_\varepsilon(L)$ and $\mathrm{ntc}_\varepsilon(L)$. For the DFA model, the deterministic state complexity (respectively deterministic transition complexity) is denoted by $\mathrm{sc}(L)$ (respectively $\mathrm{tc}(L)$).

2.2.5 Basic Relations between Complexity Measures

Next we briefly review some known results on relations between the introduced complexity measures. A classical result concerns the cost of determinizing finite automata. An upper bound is given by the subset construction given in the seminal paper introducing the model of nondeterministic finite automata [157], and a matching lower bound was found[5] shortly afterwards [132]:

Theorem 2.7. *Let L be a regular language with $\mathrm{nsc}(L) \leq n$. Then $\mathrm{sc}(L) \leq 2^n - 1$. Furthermore, for every $n \geq 1$ there is a language L_n over a binary alphabet showing that this bound is tight.*

This gives an optimal result for comparing the number of states in nondeterministic and deterministic finite automata. The relation between the number of states and transitions in finite automata with and without ε-transitions is sometimes not so clear, although a few things are easily observed: First, recall that the standard algorithm for transforming ε-NFAs into NFAs does not increase the number of states, see [96]. Since NFAs are a special case of ε-NFAs, we have $\mathrm{nsc}_\varepsilon(L) = \mathrm{nsc}(L)$. Thus there is no need to deal with the measure $\mathrm{nsc}_\varepsilon(L)$ separately. Now consider the number of transitions: On the one hand, an n-state finite automaton in which all states are useful has at least $n - 1$ transitions. On the other hand, an ε-free NFA has *a priori* at most $|\Sigma| \cdot n^2$ alphabetic transitions; if the automaton is deterministic, the corresponding bound goes down to $|\Sigma| \cdot n$. These basic observations are summarized in the following lemma:

Lemma 2.8. *Let $L \subseteq \Sigma^*$ be a regular language. Then*

$$\mathrm{sc}(L) - 1 \leq \mathrm{tc}(L) \leq |\Sigma| \cdot \mathrm{sc}(L),$$

and

$$\mathrm{nsc}(L) - 1 \leq \mathrm{ntc}_\varepsilon(L) \leq \mathrm{ntc}(L) \leq |\Sigma| \cdot (\mathrm{nsc}(L))^2.$$

For some of the above inequalities it is easily proved that they are best possible, using very easy witness languages such as $(\Sigma^n)^*$ and a^n, for integers $n \geq 1$. In particular, for alphabets of constant size, deterministic state and transition complexity are always within a constant factor of each other. The power of ε-transitions was studied recently by Hromkovič and Schnitger [99]. They proved that there exist languages L_n such that $\mathrm{ntc}_\varepsilon(L_n) = n$ and $\mathrm{ntc}(L_n) = \Omega(|\Sigma| \cdot n^2/\log n)$. These languages are over a growing alphabet; for binary alphabets they were able to prove a lower bound that still outgrows $\Omega(n(\log n)^c)$ for every constant c. But our current understanding of nondeterministic transition complexity is still rather limited: For instance, we do not know whether there exist infinite families of regular languages L such that $\mathrm{nsc}(L) = n$ but $\mathrm{ntc}(L) = \Omega(|\Sigma| \cdot n^2)$. We will thoroughly investigate this and related questions in Chapter 4.

We now turn to problems of switching the representation between regular expressions and finite automata. Converting regular expressions into equivalent finite automata is a

---

[5]The lower bound in Theorem 2.7 has been rediscovered several times in subsequent years, see [143, 146] and the respective references therein, which point to further independent discoveries.

very old problem, yet still an active area of research, see e.g. [86, 165] for late developments. A classical construction that is found in most textbooks on automata theory shows that regular expressions can be easily transformed into ε-NFAs of linear size, see e.g. [96]:

Theorem 2.9. *Let* L *be a regular language with alphabetic width at most* n. *Then* $\text{ntc}_\varepsilon(L) = O(n)$.

We mention in passing that constructions have been found recently which are more economic than the classical algorithm [110, 86]. The mentioned authors use slightly different size measures for finite automata and regular expressions. A more recent result is that the increase in size is not too drastic either if we want to convert an expression into an (ε-free) NFA. The following upper bound is due to Hromkovič et al. [103]:

Theorem 2.10. *Let* L *be a regular language with alphabetic width at most* n. *Then* $\text{ntc}(L) = O(n(\log n)^2)$.

Schnitger subsequently proved that this bound can be reached for alphabets of growing size, but that the upper bound can be considerably improved for alphabets of constant size [165].

For the other direction, namely converting finite automata into regular expressions, much less was known before this research started. A standard algorithm, known as *state elimination*, can be used to transform a finite automata into a regular expression of size $O(|\Sigma| \cdot 4^n)$. We will study that algorithm in detail in Chapter 10. A somewhat newer result, today also classical, due to Ehrenfeucht and Zeiger, is that such an exponential blow-up can be indeed necessary in the worst case [55]:

Theorem 2.11. *There is an infinite family of languages* L_n, *such that* L_n *can be accepted by an* n-state DFA over an alphabet of size n^2, *but every equivalent regular expression has alphabetic width at least* $\Omega(2^n)$.

Their result prompts the immediate question whether we can do better than the classical algorithm for, say, binary alphabets, by making clever use of the alphabet size. We will study this question and its variations at great depth in Chapters 8 to 10.

2.3 Graphs and Digraphs

A *directed graph*, or *digraph*, $G = (V, E)$ consists of a finite set of vertices V with an associated set of edges $E \subseteq V \times V$. An edge whose start and end vertex are identical is called a *loop*. If G has no loops, then G is called *loop-free*.

If the edge relation of G is symmetric, then G is an *undirected graph*, or simply *graph*. It is often convenient to view the set of edges of an undirected graph as a set of unordered pairs $\{u, v\}$, with u and v in V. If there is no risk of confusion, for an undirected graph G, we refer to the set $\{\, \{u, v\} \mid (u, v) \in E \,\}$ as the set of edges of G, and, abusing notation, denote it by E; it is indeed usual in the literature on undirected graphs to model edges as unordered pairs.

Two vertices in a graph are called *adjacent* if they are connected by an edge; and two edges (u, v) and (x, y) are called *incident* if they share a common endpoint, that is, if $u = x$, $u = y$, $v = x$, or $v = y$. The *neighborhood* $\Gamma(v)$ of a vertex v in a (di)graph is the number of vertices adjacent to v, and its *degree*, denoted by $d(v)$, is defined as the size of its neighborhood. The *average degree* of a (di)graph G is then defined as $\overline{d}(G) = \frac{1}{|V|} \cdot \sum_{v \in V} d(v)$.

A set of pairwise nonadjacent vertices is called an *independent set*. A *(vertex) coloring* of a graph G with k colors is a function $V \to \{1, 2, \ldots, k\}$ assigning to each vertex a color such that no pair of adjacent vertices receives the same color. Clearly, a coloring is equivalent to a partition of the vertex set into independent sets. A graph is called k-*colorable* if it admits a coloring with k colors. The *chromatic number* $\chi(G)$ is the minimum number of colors needed for a coloring of G.

2.3.1 Subgraphs and Connectedness

A digraph $H = (U, F)$ is a *subdigraph*, or simply *subgraph*, of a digraph $G = (V, E)$, if $U \subseteq V$ and for each edge $(u, v) \in F$ with $u, v \in U$, the pair (u, v) is an edge in E. For a subset $U \subseteq V$ of the vertex set of G, the *subgraph induced by* U, denoted by $G[U]$, is the graph $G[U] = (U, E \cap (U \times U))$ naturally obtained by restricting the edge set of G to the domain $U \times U$. When removing a set of vertices U, or a single vertex u, from G, it is often handy to write $G - U$ and $G - u$ to denote the induced subgraphs $G[V \setminus U]$ and $G[V \setminus \{u\}]$, respectively.

A *walk* in a digraph G from vertex u to vertex v is a (possibly empty) sequence of edges $e_1 \ldots e_n$ such that the tail of e_1 is u, the head of e_n is v, and for $1 \leq i \leq n - 1$, the head of e_i is identical to the tail of e_{i+1}. A walk is *closed* if it is nonempty and its start and end vertex coincide; a closed walk on which no vertex is visited more than once is called a *(directed) cycle*, and similarly called a *(directed) path* when such a walk is not closed. A digraph $G = (V, E)$ is *strongly connected* if for every pair of vertices (u, v) of G, there is both a walk from u to v and a walk from v to u. A *tree* is a strongly connected symmetric digraph whose only cycles are those of length two.

A subset $U \subseteq V$ of the vertex set is called a *strongly connected subset*, or *strong subset* if $G[U]$ is strongly connected. Observe in particular that for a vertex u, the set $\{u\}$ is a strong subset iff there is a loop (u, u) in E. A strong subset U is called *nontrivial* if $G[U]$ contains at least one edge, and a strongly connected digraph is said to be *nontrivially strongly connected* if it contains at least one edge. A strong subset which is maximal among the strong subsets with respect to set inclusion is called a *strongly connected component*, or *strong component*, and usually denoted by the letter C.

2.3.2 Bipartite Graphs

A 2-colorable graph $G = (V, E)$ is referred to as *bipartite graph*. A 2-coloring of G naturally partitions the vertex set into two classes $V = X \cup Y$ such that the only edges are between vertices in X and vertices in Y. We refer to the vertices in X as the *left vertices*, and to those in Y as the *right vertices*. It is convenient to orient all edges such that $E \subseteq X \times Y$, thus obtaining a digraph. For this digraph, we use the notation $G = (X, Y, E)$, and in the following we will refer interchangeably to both representations when speaking of bipartite graphs. The definitions given above for general (di)graphs can be recast accordingly for bipartite graphs. For instance, for $U \subseteq X$ and $V \subseteq Y$ we write $G[U, V]$ to denote the subgraph induced by $U \cup V$. An induced subgraph $G[U, V]$ is a *biclique* in G if the edge set of $G[U, V]$ equals $U \times V$. A bipartite graph $G = (X, Y, E)$ whose edge set equals $X \times Y$ is called a *complete bipartite graph*, and is denoted by $K_{m,n}$ if $|X| = m$ and $|Y| = n$. A set of bicliques in G is called a *biclique edge cover* if the union of the edge sets of these bicliques equals E. The minimum number of bicliques needed in order to cover all edges in G is called the *bipartite dimension* of G and denoted by $d(G)$. A *matching* M in a bipartite graph $G = (X, Y, E)$ is a set of pairwise nonadjacent edges, that is, $M \subseteq E$ and $((u, v) \in M \wedge (u', v') \in M) \implies (u \neq u' \wedge v \neq v')$. A matching is *perfect* if all vertices in $X \cup Y$ occur in M. A matching M in G is called $K_{2,2}$-*free matching*, if furthermore

$$(u, v) \in M \wedge (u', v') \in M \implies (u, v') \notin E \vee (u', v) \notin E,$$

that is, the subgraph induced by the vertices occurring in M has no $K_{2,2}$ as subgraph.

Remark. We note that the concept of biclique edge cover can be recast in algebraic terms for studying properties of Boolean matrices, see e.g. [151]. In that context, the term *isolated set* (in a Boolean matrix) is in use to denote $K_{2,2}$-free matchings in bipartite graphs [71].

2.4 Computational Complexity

We assume that the reader is familiar with basic concepts in computational theory such as (non-)deterministic Turing machines, and decision problems viewed as languages accepted by those.

We will assume our Turing machines are equipped with a read-only input tape, and in addition with a single work tape. For (functional) problems requiring output, we assume that they furthermore have an extra write-only output tape. We refer to the latter machines as *transducers*. However, we will mainly be concerned with decision problems whose instances only have yes/no-answers, that is, with languages. As we shall not deal with decidability issues, we assume the following. If a word is in the language accepted by the machine, then the machine accepts, otherwise it rejects; a nondeterministic Turing machine is said to reject a word if all possible computation paths reject.

A variant of Turing machines that allows for communication with an outside source of information is that of an *oracle Turing machine*. Here, any language **A** can serve as an information source, or *oracle*. The oracle Turing machine has a special oracle query tape on which it can write an input x, go to a special query state to ask the question "Is x member of **A**?," and in the next computation step the machine is in a one of two special answer states, indicating whether the answer to the query is "yes" or "no."

A practically motivated analogy to oracle Turing machines might be the following: Suppose we have a provider that offers to compute all queries of the form "Is x member of **A**?." If the provider charges a flat rate for unlimited service[6], which has been already paid in advance, then the computation of such queries does not incur any additional cost to the local machine, apart from the remote procedure call.

2.4.1 Overview of Complexity Classes.

Most complexity classes are defined as the set of languages acceptable by some class of resource-bounded Turing machines. The most commonly studied restrictions on resources concern the time and space needed in terms of the input length, and determinism versus

---

[6]We do not presume that this analogy is "practical" in an economic sense.

nondeterminism. We will assume in the following that all considered languages are over some fixed alphabet Σ.

For a function $f(n)$, the class $\mathbf{DTIME}(f(n))$ is defined as the class of languages acceptable by deterministic Turing machines running in time $f(n)$, where n is the number of bits in the input; and the class $\mathbf{P}$ is defined as $\bigcup_{k\geq 1} \mathbf{DTIME}(n^k)$. This class is important because we consider a problem as *efficiently solvable* if it admits a deterministic polynomial-time algorithm—this is based on the observation that most "natural" languages known to be in $\mathbf{P}$ also admit an algorithm running in time $O(n^k)$, where k is reasonably small. The class $\mathbf{NP}$ is defined analogously to $\mathbf{P}$, but using nondeterministic Turing machines. The space-bounded counterpart for $\mathbf{P}$ is $\mathbf{PSPACE}$, the class of problems permitting an algorithm using only a polynomial amount of space. It is well known that nondeterminism does not add extra computational power to this class, *i.e.*, $\mathbf{NPSPACE} = \mathbf{PSPACE}$, see [152]. The class $\mathbf{PSPACE}$ is in turn included in the class $\mathbf{EXP} = \bigcup_{k\geq 1} \mathbf{DTIME}(2^{n^k})$.

In general, not every complexity class will be closed under all natural language operations. This can give rise to new complexity classes. For instance, we can define for a complexity class $\mathbf{C}$ the set $\mathbf{coC}$ as $\{\, L \mid \Sigma^* \setminus L \in \mathbf{C} \,\}$. On the one hand, we have $\mathbf{P} = \mathbf{coP}$ and $\mathbf{PSPACE} = \mathbf{coPSPACE}$. On the other hand, the equality $\mathbf{NP} = \mathbf{coNP}$ is not known (nor commonly conjectured) to hold, see [152].

Quite a few natural complexity classes lie between $\mathbf{NP}$ and $\mathbf{PSPACE}$. For instance, a language L is in the class $\mathbf{DP}$ if it can be written as $L_1 \cap L_2$ with $L_1 \in \mathbf{NP}$ and $L_2 \in \mathbf{coNP}$. We would like to warn the reader about a common misconception: Note that the class $\mathbf{DP}$ is a common generalization rather than a common restriction of both $\mathbf{NP}$ and $\mathbf{coNP}$. Namely, we would obtain $\mathbf{NP}$ for the *fixed choice* $L_2 = \Sigma^*$, and fixing $L_1 = \Sigma^*$ would result in the class $\mathbf{coNP}$.

The definition of some still more general intermediate classes relies on the notion of time-bounded oracle Turing machines. For an oracle $\mathbf{A}$, define the notions $\mathbf{DTIME}^{\mathbf{A}}(f(n))$ and $\mathbf{NTIME}^{\mathbf{A}}(f(n))$ in the same way as $\mathbf{DTIME}^{\mathbf{A}}(f(n))$ and $\mathbf{NTIME}^{\mathbf{A}}(f(n))$, with the only difference that we replace all occurrences of Turing machines in the definition with occurrences of oracle Turing machines having access to oracle $\mathbf{A}$. In a similar vein, we define the classes $\mathbf{P}^{\mathbf{A}}$ and $\mathbf{NP}^{\mathbf{A}}$. Finally, let $\mathbf{P}^{\mathbf{NP}} = \bigcup_{\mathbf{A}\in\mathbf{NP}} \mathbf{P}^{\mathbf{A}}$ and $\mathbf{NP}^{\mathbf{NP}} = \bigcup_{\mathbf{A}\in\mathbf{NP}} \mathbf{NP}^{\mathbf{A}}$. To conclude, the following chains of inclusions of the mentioned complexity classes are known:

$$\mathbf{P} \subseteq \mathbf{NP} \subseteq \mathbf{DP} \subseteq \mathbf{P}^{\mathbf{NP}} \subseteq \mathbf{NP}^{\mathbf{NP}} \subseteq \mathbf{PSPACE} \subseteq \mathbf{EXP}$$

The class $\mathbf{coNP}$ is not known to be comparable to $\mathbf{NP}$, but we have $\mathbf{P} \subseteq \mathbf{coNP} \subseteq \mathbf{DP}$. By the well-known time hierarchy theorem [90], we know that $\mathbf{P} \neq \mathbf{EXP}$, but currently we cannot rule out that $\mathbf{P} = \mathbf{PSPACE}$. Despite years of extensive effort spent by many researchers, such separation results for complexity classes remain rare [152].

2.4.2 Reducibility and Completeness.

Despite of the still unresolved status of inclusions among complexity classes, we can successfully classify the complexity of many natural problems, both relative to each other and relative to complexity classes. To this end, we recall the concepts of reducibility, hardness and completeness.

Definition 2.12. For two languages $L, M \subseteq \Sigma^*$, we say L is *(many-to-one, polynomial-time) reducible* to M, in symbols $L \leq_m M$, if and only if there exists a polynomial-time bounded transducer f such that for all $x \in \Sigma^*$ holds:

$$x \in L \Leftrightarrow f(x) \in M.$$

Let $\mathbf{C} \supseteq \mathbf{P}$ be a complexity class which is closed under many-to-one polynomial-time reductions. The language M is called $\mathbf{C}$-*hard* for $\mathbf{C}$ (under many-to-one polynomial-time reductions) if all languages in $\mathbf{C}$ are reducible to M. If furthermore M is itself in $\mathbf{C}$ then M is called $\mathbf{C}$-*complete* (under many-to-one polynomial-time reductions).

Indeed the computational complexity of a great deal of problems arising in practice can be classified exactly, in the sense that they can be shown to be complete for one of the complexity classes introduced above. Papadimitriou even states that the computational complexity of a problem cannot be said to be understood completely unless we know that it is complete for the appropriate complexity class [152, p. 166].

To prove such a completeness result, membership in the complexity class under consideration is, more often than not, easily found by devising some straightforward algorithm. Proving that a particular problem L is hard for some complexity class $\mathbf{C}$ can be made an easier task if some similar problem M is already known to be $\mathbf{C}$-hard. Then it suffices to find a reduction f from M to L, since the reducibility relation is reflexive and transitive. The intuition here is that the problem M is at most as difficult as L. In other words, L is at least as difficult as M; and if M is hard then so must be L.

Part II

Nondeterministic Finite Automata

3 Proving Lower Bounds for Nondeterministic State Complexity

The first main part of the thesis will be mainly devoted to questions of algorithmic minimization of NFAs. Before we can address these questions, we have to address a few foundational issues. The first issue, discussed in this chapter, is to examine rigorous techniques for showing minimality of finite automata. As it turns out, for proving minimality with respect to the number of states, there are general-purpose lower bound techniques. Another reasonable objective is to minimize the number of transitions in NFAs, and it is not *a priori* clear whether these two objectives can be achieved simultaneously. This and similar questions relating to nondeterministic transition complexity will be discussed in the next chapter. Building on insights gained on these foundational questions, we will then proceed to investigate computational complexity aspects of NFA minimization problems, thus concluding the first part of the thesis. But let us return to the fundamental question addressed in this chapter:

> How can we determine whether a nondeterministic finite automaton has minimum possible number of states?

The analogous question for the deterministic finite automaton model is answered by the Myhill-Nerode Theorem (Theorem 2.2): The theorem gives a precise characterization of the minimal DFA, which is unique up to isomorphism for each regular language. As a bonus, the minimal DFA can be computed efficiently from a given DFA, which is, under standard assumptions from computational complexity theory, no longer true in the case of NFA minimization, an issue we will discuss in greater depth in Chapters 5 and 6.

In the nondeterministic model, there is no such canonical minimal description, and there are regular languages admitting different state minimal nondeterministic finite automata.

Example 3.1. Consider the finite language $L = \{ab, ac, bc, ba, ca, cb\}$, which has nondeterministic state complexity five—see Figure 3.1.

We have claimed that the two NFAs depicted in Figure 3.1 have the minimum possible number of states. To gain a deeper understanding the power and limitations of the

Figure 3.1: Two non-isomorphic minimal nondeterministic finite automata for the finite language $L = \{ab, ac, bc, ba, ca, cb\}$.

concept of nondeterminism in finite automata, it is crucial to be able to give rigorous proofs for such facts. Next we will study some useful techniques for proving lower bounds on nondeterministic state complexity.

3.1 Two Useful Lower Bound Techniques

A remarkably simple lower bound technique for the nondeterministic state complexity of regular languages is a method put forward first by Birget [14], which is commonly called *fooling set* technique; see also [67, 97] for similar accounts that appeared later. For the convenience of the reader we include a proof of correctness along with the statement of the technique.

Lemma 3.2 (Fooling Set Technique). *Let $L \subseteq \Sigma^*$ be a regular language, and let S be a set of word pairs $S = \{(x_i, y_i) \mid 1 \le i \le n\}$ such that*

1. *$x_i y_i \in L$ for $1 \le i \le n$,*

2. *for $1 \le i, j \le n$, and $i \ne j$, we have $x_i y_j \notin L$ or $x_j x_i \notin L$*

then any nondeterministic finite automaton accepting L has at least n states, i.e., $\mathrm{nsc}(L) \ge n$. Here S is called a fooling set *for L.*

Proof. Let $A = (Q, \Sigma, \delta, q_0, F)$ be any nondeterministic finite automaton accepting the language L. Since $x_i y_i \in L$, there is a state q_i in Q such that $q_0 \vdash^{x_i} q_i$ and $q_i \vdash_A^{y_i} f$ for some $f \in F$. Assume that a fixed choice of q_i has been made for any i with $1 \le i \le n$. We prove that $q_i \ne q_j$ for $i \ne j$. For the sake of a contradiction assume that $q_i = q_j$ for some $i \ne j$. Then the nondeterministic finite automaton accepts both words $x_i y_j$ and $x_j y_i$. This contradicts the assumption that $\{(x_i, y_i) \mid 1 \le i \le n\}$ is a fooling set for the language L. Hence, the nondeterministic finite automaton A has at least n states. $\square$

Example 3.3. Recall that we have claimed in Example 3.1 that the language $L = \{ab, ac, bc, ba, ca, cb\}$ has nondeterministic state complexity five. To prove this fact, it suffices to verify that the five-element set

$$S' = \{(\varepsilon, ab), (ba, \varepsilon), (a, b), (b, c), (c, a)\}$$

is a fooling set for L. This matches the upper bound given by the 5-state NFAs given in Example 3.1.

Unlike the above example, sometimes the fooling set technique is not powerful enough to establish tight lower bounds—we will see examples later in this chapter. Luckily, this easy lower bound technique admits a more powerful generalization. To arrive at this generalization, we first recast the fooling set technique in terms of bipartite graphs.

Lemma 3.4. *$L \subseteq \Sigma^*$ be a regular language. Suppose G is a (not necessarily finite) bipartite graph $G = (X, Y, E)$ with $X, Y \subseteq \Sigma^*$ and $E = \{(x, y) \in X \times Y \mid xy \in L\}$. Then each $K_{2,2}$-free matching in G is a fooling set for L.*

Proof. Immediate from the definition of $K_{2,2}$-free matchings introduced in Chapter 2.3. $\square$

Recall from Chapter 2.3 that the bipartite dimension of a bipartite graph equals the minimum cardinality among the biclique edge covers for G. A more powerful method for proving lower boundsis based on this concept. The technique is a less bulky way of formulating the nondeterministic message complexity method introduced by Hromkovič [97]. In principle, the technique can be tracked back at least to 1970, where a work of Kameda and Weiner [117] on state minimal NFAs appeared. Yet another different viewpoint of the biclique edge cover technique, which however ultimately leads to the same concept, is given by Courcelle et al. [38]. After this historical account on various discoveries, we finally present our own account:

Theorem 3.5 (Biclique Edge Cover Technique). *Let $L \subseteq \Sigma^*$ be a regular language. Suppose G is a (not necessarily finite) bipartite graph $G = (X, Y, E)$ with $X, Y \subseteq \Sigma^*$ and $E = \{(x, y) \in X \times Y \mid xy \in L\}$. If the bipartite dimension of G equals n, then any nondeterministic finite automaton accepting L has at least n states.*

Proof. Let $A = (Q, \Sigma, \delta, q_0, F)$ be any nondeterministic finite automaton accepting L and let $G = (X, Y, E)$ be a bipartite graph satisfying the prerequisites of the theorem.

It suffices to show that the states of A gives rise to a biclique edge cover of size $|Q|$ for the graph G. For each state $q \in Q$ let $H_q = (X_q, Y_q, E_q)$, where the left vertices are given by

$$X_q = X \cap \{ w \in \Sigma^* \mid q_0 \vdash^w q \},$$

the right vertices by

$$Y_q = Y \cap \{ w \in \Sigma^* \mid q \vdash^w f, \text{ for some } f \in F \},$$

and the edges by $E_q = X_q \times Y_q$. We claim that $C = \{ H_q \mid q \in Q \}$ is a biclique edge cover for G. By definition each H_q, for $q \in Q$, is itself a complete bipartite graph. Moreover, each H_q is a subgraph of G: We have $X_q \subseteq X$ and $Y_q \subseteq Y$ by construction, and $E_q \subseteq E$ can be seen as follows: Assume that $x \in X_q$ and $y \in Y_q$. Then the word xy belongs to the language L because $q_0 \vdash^x q$ and $q \vdash^y f$ for some $f \in F$. Hence, (x, y) must be an edge of G. Finally, we must prove that C covers all edges in G. Let (x, y) be an edge in G, for $x \in X$ and $y \in Y$. Then the word xy is in L and since the nondeterministic finite automaton A accepts the language L, there is a state q in Q such that $q_0 \vdash^x q$ $q \vdash^y f$ for some $f \in F$. Therefore $x \in X_q$ and $y \in Y_q$ and the edge (x, y) is covered by the biclique H_q. Altogether this proves that C is a biclique edge cover for G, as desired. $\square$

As observed first in [71, Corollary 2.1], the edges of a $K_{2,2}$-free matching for a graph G must belong to pairwise different bicliques in G, so the maximum size of any $K_{2,2}$-free matching in a graph is a lower bound on its bipartite dimension. Hence the biclique edge cover technique is at least as powerful as the fooling set technique.

Both techniques admit some degree of freedom with respect to the choice of sets of left and right vertices in G. It is not difficult to see that the optimum for both lower bound techniques is attained for the infinite graph $G = (\Sigma^*, \Sigma^*, E_L)$ having $E_L = \{ (x, y) \in \Sigma^* \times \Sigma^* \mid xy \in L \}$. This is rather impractical: For applying these lower bound techniques to a particular regular language, we typically want to choose *finite* sets X and Y of left and right vertices appropriately. Glaister and Shallit propose the following heuristic for the fooling set technique in [67]: Construct a nondeterministic finite automaton $A = (Q, \Sigma, \delta, q_0, F)$ accepting L, and for each state q in Q let x_q be a shortest string such that

$q_0 \vdash^{x_q} q$, and let y_q be the shortest string such that $q \vdash^{y_q} f$ for some $f \in F$. Then choose the set S to be some *appropriate subset* of the pairs $\{(x_q, y_q) \mid q \in Q\}$. According to these authors, the heuristic seems to work well in many cases; this approach of course equally applies to the biclique edge cover technique.

3.2 The Dependency Graph

A drawback of both presented lower bound techniques appears to be that getting a good estimate seems to require conscious thought and "clever guessing." However, we are able to show for the techniques under consideration that this is in fact *not* the case. To this end, we will show that there is a canonical bipartite graph for each regular language, which is independent of the considered method, such that the best attainable lower bound for both the fooling set and the biclique edge cover technique can, in principle, be determined algorithmically. This canonical graph is obtained from the aforementioned infinite bipartite graph by factoring out the equivalence classes induced by the Myhill-Nerode relation $\equiv_L$ and its close relative $_L\!\equiv$, defined in Chapter 2.2.3, from the set of left and right vertices, respectively.

Definition 3.6. Let $L \subseteq \Sigma^*$. Then the *dependency graph* for the language L is defined to be the bipartite graph $G_L = (X, Y, E_L)$, $X = \Sigma^*/\!\equiv_L$ and $Y = \Sigma^*/_L\!\equiv$ and $([x]_L, {}_L[y]) \in E_L$ if and only if $xy \in L$.

It turns out that the dependency graph conveys all necessary information for applying both lower bound techniques in the best possible way.

Lemma 3.7. *Let $L \subseteq \Sigma^*$ be a regular language and $G = (\Sigma^*, \Sigma^*, E_L)$ its associated bipartite graph.*

1. *The maximum size of a fooling set for G is n if and only if the maximum size of a fooling set for the dependency graph G_L equals n.*

2. *The bipartite dimension of G is n if and only if the bipartite dimension of the dependency graph G_L equals n.*

Proof. We only prove the first statement. The second statement can be shown with similar arguments.

Let $S = \{(u_i, v_i) \mid 1 \le i \le n\}$ be a fooling set for the bipartite graph $G = (\Sigma^*, \Sigma^*, E_L)$. By definition any two different edges in S are vertex-disjoint, if S is interpreted as a subset of E_L. Moreover, we find that any two different edges (u_i, v_i) and (u_j, v_j) obey $u_i \not\equiv_L u_j$ and $v_i {}_L\!\not\equiv v_j$. Otherwise the fooling set property is not satisfied. Thus, the idea to obtain the finite bipartite graph that mirrors all relevant properties of G is to replace the vertex sets by the corresponding equivalence classes. This is exactly what is done in the dependency graph.

The construction is done in two steps. Any edge (u_i, v_i) in G can be replaced by (u_i', v_i) whenever $u_i \equiv_L u_i'$. Thus, the "left vertices" in G can be replaced by an essential set of words x_i pairwise nonequivalent with respect to $\equiv_L$. Since L is regular, this set is finite. To conclude the first step, the bipartite graph G' is defined as the subgraph induced by the vertex set (X, Σ^*), where $X = \{x_i \mid 1 \le i \le m\}$ and m is the index of $\Sigma^*/\!\equiv_L$. The fooling set S is updated accordingly. We denote this fooling set by S'. Note that S and S'

are of same size. For the second step we argue as follows: Define the equivalence relation $\sim_X$ on Σ^* by $v \sim_X v'$ if and only if $xv \in L \iff xv' \in L$, for all $x \in X$. We show that this relation is the same as the relation $_L\equiv$. By definition $v \sim_X v'$ implies $v_L\equiv v'$. Conversely, let $v \sim_X v'$. For each $u \in \Sigma^*$ we have $uv \in L \iff [u]_L v \subseteq L$. Thus we conclude $[u]_L v \subseteq L$ if and only if $uv \in L$ iff $uv' \in L$ if and only if $[u]_L v' \subseteq L$. Hence $v \sim_X v'$. This shows that $\sim_X$ is just an alternative formulation of $_L\equiv$, and we can apply a similar replacement procedure as in the first step, now for the "right vertices" in G' using the relation $\sim_X$. This results in a bipartite graph G'', which is defined as the subgraph induced by the vertex set (X, Y), where Y is chosen in a similar way as the x_i's above, but now w.r.t. equivalence relation $\Sigma^*/_L\equiv$. Similarly we modify the fooling set S' and obtain the set S''. It is easy to see that S'' is in fact a fooling set for G'', and that it is of same size as the original fooling set S. This completes the construction. $\square$

The concept of dependency graph of a regular language, and the idea of studying biclique edge covers for this graph, appears perhaps first in the work of Kameda and Weiner [117]. They approach the topic from a rather different viewpoint: In order to give a procedure for finding a state minimal NFA, they define first the dependency graph (in their terminology: the *reduced states map*) based on a pair of minimal DFAs for L and L^R, respectively, and arrive at studying edge covers of the graph with bicliques (in their terminology: *covers by grids*) by inspecting the reverse process of determinization by the subset construction, thus following a perceivably different train of thought than undertaken here.

A closer look at the dependency graph allows to deduce a performance guarantee for the biclique edge cover technique: In fact, this technique can never yield a worse lower bound than the elementary observation that the nondeterministic state complexity of a regular language is always at least logarithmic in its deterministic state complexity.

Theorem 3.8. *Let $L \subseteq \Sigma^*$ be a regular language and G_L the dependency graph for L. Then $2^{d(G_L)} - 1$ is greater than or equal to the deterministic state complexity of L.*

Proof. Let $G_L = (X, Y, E_L)$ and assume that the bipartite dimension of G_L equals k. Then the edge set of G_L can be covered by a set of bicliques $C = \{H_1, H_2, \ldots, H_k\}$. For $x \in X$, let $B(x) \subseteq C$ be the set of bicliques where x occurs as a "left vertex." Without loss of generality, we may assume that $|B(x)| \geq 1$, otherwise the vertex is isolated, and can be removed from the graph without altering the bipartite dimension.

We claim that $B(x) = B(x')$ implies $x \equiv_L x'$, for all $x, x' \in \Sigma^*$. Suppose that $y \in \Sigma^*$ occurs as a "right vertex" in some biclique in $B(x)$. If $B(x) = B(x')$, then both $(x, y) \in E_L$ and $(x', y) \in E_L$. The other possibility is that y does not occur as a right vertex in any biclique from $B(x)$. Then $B(x) = B(x')$ implies that $(x, y) \notin E_L$ and $(x', y) \notin E_L$. By definition of G_L we have $(x, y) \in E_L$ if and only if $xy \in L$. To conclude, if $B(x) = B(x')$, then $xy \in L \iff x'y \in L$, for all $y \in \Sigma^*$, which is the definition of the Myhill-Nerode equivalence $\equiv_L$ of L. Now define $x \sim x'$ with $x, x' \in \Sigma^*$ if and only if $B(x) = B(x')$. This equivalence relation induces at most $2^{|C|} - 1$ equivalence classes, and is a refinement of the Myhill-Nerode relation on X. Thus we have shown that $2^{|C|} - 1$ is greater or equal than the deterministic state complexity of L. $\square$

The above theorem implies in particular that the bipartite dimension of the dependency graph is at least logarithmic in the actual *non*deterministic state complexity. Examples where the technique based on bipartite dimension gives an unsharp lower bound were known for a long time. Possible weaknesses of the biclique edge cover technique were already discussed in Kameda and Weiner's paper [117]. They present an example of a regular language, where, translated into our terminology, the biclique edge cover technique fails to predict the exact nondeterministic state complexity. In that example, the lower bound is off by 1. They attribute the latter result to Shimon Even, at that time visiting Professor at Harvard University. Unfortunately, things can get much worse: In [102, 115] it was shown that the nondeterministic state complexity can be $2^{\Omega(\sqrt{d})}$, where d is the bipartite dimension of the dependency graph. We can further strengthen this result, in showing that this gap can be actually even larger. Thus there is little hope to really improve on Theorem 3.8.

Theorem 3.9. *There is a sequence of unary languages $(L_n)_{n\geq 1}$ such that $\mathrm{nsc}(L_n) = \Omega\left(d^{-1/2} \cdot 2^d\right)$, where d is the bipartite dimension of the dependency graph of L_n.*

Proof. Let $L_n = \{\, w \in 0^* \mid |w| \neq 0 \mod n \,\}$. It is easy to see that the dependency graph of L_n is isomorphic to the $2n$-vertex crown graph $K_{n,n}^-$, obtained from a complete bipartite graph $K_{n,n}$ by removing a perfect matching from the edge set, recall Chapter 2.3 for the relevant graph-theoretic definitions. The bipartite dimension d of $K_{n,n}^-$ was determined in [44, Corollaries 1,2] to be equal to $\sigma(n)$, where

$$\sigma(n) = \min\left\{ k \mid n \leq \binom{k}{\lfloor k/2 \rfloor} \right\}.$$

In particular, this implies $n > \binom{d-1}{\lfloor (d-1)/2 \rfloor}$. By Stirling's approximation of the factorial, we have

$$\binom{d-1}{\lfloor (d-1)/2 \rfloor} = \Omega\left(d^{-1/2} 2^d\right),$$

and we conclude that $n = \Omega\left(d^{-1/2} 2^d\right)$.

It remains to show that there are infinitely many n such that $\mathrm{nsc}(L_n) \geq n$. We show that this is the case, whenever n is a prime number. Thus if we take the sequence $(L_{p_i})_{i \geq 1}$, where p_i is the ith prime number, this will establish the desired result. To this end we argue as follows:

Recall from Chapter 2.1 that a unary language $L \subseteq a^*$ is n-cyclic, if $a^i \in L \iff a^{i+n} \in L$, for every $i \geq 0$, and that the smallest such n is the minimal period of L. In [112, Corollary 2.1] it was shown that if L is a unary cyclic language with minimal period p, where p is prime, then $\mathrm{nsc}(L) = p$. We show that L_n has minimal period n: Clearly, n is a period of L_n. Now assume to the contrary that L_n also has a period m with $m < n$. Then $\varepsilon \notin L_n$ implies $0^m \notin L_n$. But the shortest nonempty word not in the language has length n, a contradiction. Thus the stated claim follows. $\square$

To end this chapter, we finally mention that generalizations of the biclique edge cover technique were investigated recently by Hromkovič et al. [98]. They proved however, that all these generalizations in principle still share the doom of the biclique edge cover technique, as indicated by the above theorem for the latter technique.

4 Minimal NFAs: Number of States and Number of Transitions

After we are armed with proof techniques for establishing optimality with respect to the number of states, it is now natural to ask whether these are enough. After all, if the concepts of nondeterministic state and transition complexity were sufficiently similar, it would be hardly justified to study the transition minimization problem for NFAs on its own right.

But there is some evidence that nondeterministic transition complexity behaves differently. At the very least, is sometimes argued that counting the number of transitions as opposed to the number of states gives a more realistic measure for the amount of memory needed to store a given nondeterministic finite automaton [3, 93, 110, 164]. Nondeterministic transition complexity already appears, under the name *size*, in the landmark paper by Meyer and Fischer [143]. But, to our knowledge, a more systematic study of nondeterministic transition complexity on its own right started only a few years ago. An explanation for this recent rise in interest is an unexpected result by Hromkovič et al. [103] regarding the size of regular expressions and the number of transitions in equivalent NFAs. Despite the apparent lack of maturity of this research area, these few years has seen a notable research activity on nondeterministic transition complexity, see [93, 164] for recent surveys on the topic. In this chapter, we will discuss some at least some aspects in more detail.

4.1 A Trade-off for State versus Transition Minimization

First, we will study to what extent the goals of minimizing the number of states and transitions are compatible. By the basic observations made in Section 2.2.5, for alphabets of constant size, the number of transitions in an n-state minimal NFA is always in $O(n^2)$ and thus also at most quadratic in the nondeterministic transition complexity of the language. Thus minimizing the number of states also gives at least a rough approximation to the minimum required number of transitions.

Can we do essentially better? The best situation we might hope for is that among all state minimal NFAs for a regular language L, we can always find one that simultaneously realizes the nondeterministic transition complexity. Unfortunately, this is far from true: We will show that there are regular languages over a binary alphabet such that every state minimal finite automaton necessarily has $\Omega(t^2)$ transitions, where t is the nondeterministic transition complexity. This phenomenon still occurs in the automaton model with ε-transitions allowed.

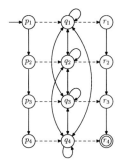

Figure 4.1: The unique state minimal NFA accepting L_4. Transitions labeled with a are indicated by solid arrows and those labeled with b by dashed arrows. A double-headed arrow indicates a pair of transitions with opposed directions.

To this end, we define the following (infinite) languages for $n \geq 1$:

$$L_n = \{\, a^r b a^s b a^t \mid 0 \leq r, t < n \text{ and } s > 0 \,\} \cup$$
$$\{\, a^r b b a^{n-1-r} \mid 0 \leq r < n \,\}$$

We claim that $\mathrm{nsc}(L_n) = O(n)$, that the state minimal NFA is unique up to renaming of states, and has $\Omega(n^2)$ transitions. Figure 4.1 shows this unique automaton in the case $n = 3$. Observe that the subgraph underlying the transition structure connecting the states $q_1, \ldots, q_n$ is a complete directed graph with self-loops, which amounts to n^2 transitions. The precise result on the languages L_n with respect to state and transition complexity reads as follows:

Theorem 4.1. *Let $n \geq 1$. There is a unique (up to the renaming of states) state minimal ε-NFA accepting the language L_n which has $3n$ states and $n^2 + 4n - 2$ transitions.*

For the proof Theorem 4.1, the following restricted variant of the fooling set technique (see Chapter 3.1) is useful, stating that in case the lower bound provided by that technique is tight for a given regular language, then we can infer some properties of the internal structure of any state minimal NFA accepting that language.

Definition 4.2. Assume $L \subseteq \Sigma^*$ is a regular language. A set of word pairs $S = \{\, (x_i, y_i) \in \Sigma^* \times \Sigma^* \mid 1 \leq i \leq n \,\}$ is a *restricted fooling set* for L if

- $x_i y_i \in L$ for $1 \leq i \leq n$,

- both $x_i y_j \notin L$ and $x_j y_i \notin L$, for $1 \leq i, j \leq n$.

The difference to an ordinary fooling set is that the two criteria in the second condition are connected by a logical "and", rather than by a logical "or". Clearly, restricted fooling sets are special cases of fooling sets. So this technique is even less powerful than the fooling set technique for proving lower bounds on nondeterministic state complexity. But in those cases where the technique provides a tight lower bound, this tells us more than just the number of states required by an ε-NFA in order to accept the language:

Lemma 4.3. Let $A = (Q, \Sigma, \delta, q_0, F)$ be an ε-NFA. Assume $L(A)$ allows a restricted fooling set $S = \{(x_i, y_i) \in \Sigma^* \times \Sigma^* \mid 1 \leq i \leq n\}$ of size $|Q|$. Then

- the automaton A is an ε-NFA for $L(A)$ with minimum number of states,

- for $1 \leq i \leq n$, the automaton A has a unique state p_i satisfying

$$q_0 \vdash^{x_i} p_i, \text{ or } p_i \vdash^{y_i} f \text{ for some } f \in F,$$

and for this state p_i furthermore holds

$$q_0 \vdash^{x_i} p_i, \text{ and } p_i \vdash^{y_i} f \text{ for some } f \in F,$$

- if some y_i equals the empty word, then the state p_i defined above is the only accepting state of the automaton.

Furthermore, then the automaton A has no ε-transitions.

Proof. Assume $L(A)$ admits a fooling set S of size $n = |Q|$. Then the first property already follows from Lemma 3.2, since each restricted fooling set is also a fooling set. For the remaining properties, we argue as follows:

For $1 \leq i \leq n$, let L_i denote the set of states $L_i = \{q \mid q_0 \vdash^{x_i} q\}$, and define R_i analogously as $R_i = \{q \mid q \vdash^{y_i} f \text{ for some } f \in F\}$ Clearly, $|L_i \cap R_i| \geq 1$ for each i, since there must exist each a computation along which the automaton A accepts the words $x_i y_i$. Next we claim that for all pairs (i, j) with $i \neq j$ holds $L_i \cap R_j = \emptyset$. Namely, if a state p_i is in $L_i \cap R_i$, then for $j \neq i$, this state can neither be simultaneously in another set R_j nor in another set L_j. Otherwise, the automaton would accept the word $x_i y_j$ or $x_j y_i$, cases which are forbidden in restricted fooling sets. That is, $L_i \cup R_i = L_i \cap R_i$, as desired.

If some y_i equals the empty word, then is clear that

$$R_i = \{q \mid q \vdash^{\varepsilon} f \text{ for some } f \in F\} = F.$$

As the set $L_i \cup R_i$ equals R_i and contains only one state p_i, this state is the only final state.

Finally, for the sake of contradiction, assume that A has an ε-transition $p_i \xrightarrow{\varepsilon} p_j$. Then, as we disallow those ε-transitions that lead a state to back to itself, we have $i \neq j$. We have seen before that $q_0 \vdash^{x_i} p_i$ as well as $p_j \vdash^{y_j} f$, for some final state $f \in F$. But altogether this implies that the automaton accepts the word $x_i y_j$, which is ruled out by restricted fooling sets, contradiction.

$\square$

This technical lemma plays a pivotal role in the proof that follows.

of Theorem 4.1. All words in the language L_n can be written as $xbybz$, with $x, y, z \in \{a\}^*$. Thus it is not hard to see that the state set of every nondeterministic finite automaton can be partitioned into three state sets corresponding to prefixes ending in the x-part, the y-part and the z-part of the set of accepted words. This indeed always a *partition* of the state set, since otherwise the automaton would accept words whose number of occurrences of the symbol b does not equal 2.

We first describe a nondeterministic finite automaton having $3n$ states, which is indeed the unique state minimal nondeterministic automaton, as we shall see later on. The construction is a straightforward generalization of the NFA accepting L_4 as depicted in Figure 4.1.

As suggested above, its state set is split into three classes: We introduce a set of states $P = \{p_1, p_2, \ldots, p_n\}$ such that the word a^{n-1} can be read along the path $p_1 \cdot p_2 \cdots p_n$. These states are used to read the x-parts of the accepted words. Then we have a set of states $Q = \{q_1, q_2, \ldots, q_n\}$ with $\delta(p_i, b) = \{q_i\}$ for $1 \leq i \leq n$. Furthermore, for $1 \leq i \leq n$, let $\delta(q_i, a) = Q$. This ensures that, after the automaton has read the xb-part of the word, and the y-part is not equal to the empty word, it can go to every state in Q on reading $y \in \{a\}^+$. If, however, the y-part equals the empty word, the automaton needs to remember the length of the x-part it has read before, in order to guarantee that $|x| + |z| = n - 1$. We therefore introduce a third set of states $R = \{r_0, r_1, \ldots, r_n\}$, and fix $\delta(q_i, b) = \{r_i\}$ and $\delta(r_i, a) = \{r_{i+1}\}$ for $1 \leq i < n$. Lastly, let p_1 be the start state and r_n be the single accepting state. It is not hard to see that the described automaton indeed accepts L_n, and has exactly $3n$ states and $n^2 + 4n - 2$ transitions.

The rest of the proof consists in showing, with the aid of Lemma 4.3, that every automaton accepting L_n with (at most) $3n$ states must be indeed isomorphic to the automaton constructed above. To this end, let S be the set containing the following $3n$ word pairs: First, all $n + 2$ possible splittings of the word $w = a^{n-1}bb$ into a pair (u, v) such that $uv = w$. Second, all n possible splittings of the word $x = bba^{n-1}$ into a pair (u, v) such that $uv = x$, but this time excluding those two pairs with $u = \varepsilon$ and $v = \varepsilon$. Finally, the $n - 2$ word pairs $(a^{i-1}b, ba^{n-i-2})$, for $1 < i < n$. It is readily verified that this set satisfies the restricted fooling set property for L_n as given in Definition 4.2.

Assume now A is an arbitrary $3n$-state ε-NFA accepting L_n. Then Lemma 4.3 is applicable, and we can infer that A is indeed an NFA, *i.e.*, that it has no ε-transitions. As the automaton accepts the word $w = a^{n-1}bb$, but no subword of w, this word can only be accepted along some computation path of $n + 2$ pairwise different states. Take such a path, and label the states in order of appearance with $p_1, p_2, \ldots p_{n-1}, p_n, q_n, r_n$. The names of the state labels are chosen in a way which will immediately provide the desired isomorphism with the automaton constructed previously. As we will not refer to the previous automaton until the very end of the proof, there will be no risk of confusion. Clearly, p_1 must be the start state of A, and r_n must be an accepting state.

Observe that Lemma 4.3 implies that A has $3n$ states, each defined by some unique computation path, which we will name accordingly: For instance, r_i denotes the unique state s satisfying $s \vdash^{a^{n-1-i}} r_n$, and in a similar way the state satisfying $p_1 \vdash^{a^{i-1}b} s$, which is again unique, is denoted by q_i. Furthermore, the start state of A is p_1 and, by Lemma 4.3, r_n is the only accepting state.

Next, we analyze the structure of transitions in A. To this end, let P denote the set $\{p_i \mid 1 \leq i \leq n\}$, and in a similar manner $Q = \{q_i \mid 1 \leq i \leq n\}$ and $R = \{r_i \mid 1 \leq i \leq n\}$. The only possible transitions between two states in P can be of the form $p_i \xrightarrow{a} p_{i+1}$, since otherwise A would accept a word not in L_n. And all transitions of this form are present in A, as witnessed by the computation

$$p_1 \vdash^a p_2 \vdash^a \cdots \vdash^a p_n,$$

recall the choice of the state names $p_1, p_2, \ldots, p_n$. For similar reasons, the set of all transitions in between states in R_i is given by $\{r_i \xrightarrow{a} r_{i+1} \mid 1 \leq i < n\}$. Furthermore, there cannot be any transitions between a state in P and a state in R in either direction, and if A has an a-transition $s \xrightarrow{a} t$ then s and t are either both in P, both in Q, or both in R.

Regarding the b-transitions in A, we claim that the set of all b-transitions is given by

$$\{\, p_i \xrightarrow{b} q_i \mid 1 \le i \le n \,\} \cup \{\, q_i \xrightarrow{b} r_i \mid 1 \le i \le n \,\}.$$

We have chosen q_i to denote the unique state such that there is a computation $p_1 \vdash^{a^{i-1}} p \vdash^b q_i$ for some state p, and simultaneously a computation $q_i \vdash^b r \vdash^{a^{i-1}} r_1$ for some state r. But this property of the state p coincides with the definition of p_i, and the one for state r coincides with the definition of r_i. Thus, all of the listed b-transitions are in fact present in A. To complete the analysis of the b-transitions, it remains to show that there are no other b-transitions in A. If A has a transition $s \xrightarrow{b} t$, then $s \in P$ and $t \in Q$, or $s \in Q$ and $t \in R$: any other combination would cause A to accept a word whose number of b's does not equal 2. So there remain only two cases to consider. For the first case, assume $p_i \xrightarrow{b} q_j$ is a transition in A for some i, j. As $p_i \in \delta(p_1, a^{i-1})$ and $\delta(q_j, ba^{j-1}) \cap F \ne \emptyset$, the automaton accepts the word $a^{i-1}bba^{j-1}$, and this implies $i = j$. A similar argument holds for the second case.

It remains to classify the set of a-transitions $s \xrightarrow{a} t$ having both s and t in Q. By Lemma 4.3, we know that for every pair (i, j) with $1 \le i, j \le n$, on reading $a^{i-1}b$ starting from p_1, the automaton A has a unique computation path, which furthermore ends in q_i, and that q_j is the only state admitting a computation path leading into an accepting state on reading the word ba^{j-1}. But now there must be a transition $q_i \xrightarrow{a} q_j$, since A accepts the word $a^{i-1}baba^{j-1}$.

Thus we have shown that each ε-NFA A with at most $3n$ states must be isomorphic to the one constructed previously, as desired. The statement of the theorem now follows by counting the number of states and transitions in A. □

The above result sharply contrasts with the following simple observation:

Lemma 4.4. *There is a NFA accepting L_n with $\mathrm{nsc}(L_n) + 1 = 3n + 1$ states and $8n - 1$ transitions.*

Proof. We take the automaton A, remove all n^2 transitions of the form $q_i \xrightarrow{a} q_j$, and add instead a new "loop" state ℓ. Then we add a loop transition $\ell \xrightarrow{a} \ell$, and the transitions $q_i \xrightarrow{a} \ell$ as well as $\ell \xrightarrow{b} r_i$ for $1 \le i \le n$. The result of this construction is illustrated in Figure 4.2 at the language L_4.

It is readily seen that this automaton again accepts L_n and has only $8n - 1$ transitions. □

Essentially the same phenomenon as demonstrated by Theorem 4.1 and Lemma 4.4 was rediscovered later by Domaratzki and Salomaa [51]. As a variation on the theme, they were also able to provide a family of examples where, for each fixed $k \in \mathbb{N}$, the required number of transitions drops from quadratic to linear only after allowing k additional states. Whereas this is not true for the languages above, our examples have the interesting feature that the minimal *deterministic* finite automaton accepting L_n has *even fewer* transitions than the nondeterministic finite automaton constructed in the proof of Lemma 4.4.

Lemma 4.5. *There is a deterministic finite automaton with $4n + 1$ states and $6n + 1$ transitions accepting the language L_n.*

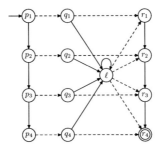

Figure 4.2: An NFA accepting L_4 with one additional state and linear number of transitions. Transitions labeled with a are indicated by solid arrows and those labeled with b by dashed arrows.

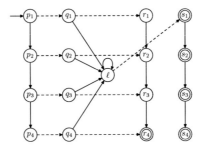

Figure 4.3: A DFA accepting L_4, with a small number of transitions. Transitions labeled with a are indicated by solid arrows and those labeled with b by dashed arrows.

Proof. The proof is by explicit construction of such a DFA. The idea is that the NFA we just constructed in Lemma 4.4 is can be very easily made deterministic; the principle is illustrated in Figure 4.3 at the example of the language L_4.

Formally, the state set of the deterministic finite automaton we construct is partitioned into five classes: the first class consists of states $p_1, p_2 \ldots p_n$, which are are needed to remember the number of as read in the prefix of an accepted word $xbybz$, with $x, y, z \in a^{\leq n}$. These states are arranged in a chain of a-transitions, p_1 being the start state, and $\delta(p_i, a) = p_{i+1}$ for $1 \leq i < n$. The next class has states $q_1, q_2, \ldots, q_n$, which are needed to remember the prefix xb, and we have $\delta(p_i, b) = q_i$ for $1 \leq i \leq n$. In the third class, we have the states $r_1, r_2, \ldots, r_n$ responsible for reading the suffix z of words of the form $xbbz$, where we must ensure that $|x| = n - 1 - |z|$. The transition function reads here as $\delta(q_i, b) = r_i$ for $1 \leq i \leq n$, and $\delta(r_i, a) = r_{i+1}$, for $1 \leq i < n$, and r_n is an accepting state. In the fourth class, we have a single loop state ℓ, with $\delta(q_i, a) = \ell$ and $\delta(\ell, a) = \ell$. The loop state is left once the symbol b is read, after which all valid suffixes $z \in a^{\leq n-1}$ lead to a acceptance. This task is assigned to the states $s_1, s_2, \ldots, s_n$ in the fifth class, all of which are accepting states. Here we have $\delta(\ell, b) = s_1$ and $\delta(s_i, a) = s_{i+1}$ for $1 \leq i < n$. The transition function δ is undefined everywhere else. It is clear that the described automaton is deterministic and accepts the language L_n. We thus obtained a DFA with

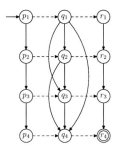

Figure 4.4: The unique state minimal NFA accepting F_4. Transitions labeled with a are indicated by solid arrows and those labeled with b by dashed arrows.

$4n + 1$ states and $6n + 1$ transitions accepting the language L_n, and the proof is complete.
□

In this case, state minimization for nondeterministic finite automata leads to an undesirable complexity with respect to the number of transitions. Moreover, determinization *decreases* the required number of transitions from quadratic to linear. This appears rather counter-intuitive at first glance, since the common perception is that determinization will lead to an undesirable *increase* in size, compare Theorem 2.7.

A similar result can be obtained for the finite languages

$$F_n = \{\, a^i ba^j ba^k \mid i + k + j < n \text{ and } k > 0 \,\} \cup$$
$$\{\, a^i bba^k \mid i < n \text{ and } k = n - i - 1 \,\}.$$

The minimal nondeterministic finite automaton accepting F_n has almost the same structure as the state minimal automaton accepting L_n depicted in Figure 4.1, but the transition structure connecting the states $q_1, q_2, \ldots, q_n$ with each other form a complete *acyclic* digraph instead of a complete digraph—there is an a-transition from q_i to q_j whenever $i < j$. In fact, the following theorem can be proved along the same lines as Theorem 4.1 and Lemma 4.5:

Theorem 4.6. *Let $n \geq 1$. There is a unique (up to renaming of states) state minimal nondeterministic finite automaton accepting the finite language F_n which has $3n$ states and $\frac{n(n-1)}{2} + 4n - 2$ transitions. On the other hand, F_n can be accepted by a trim deterministic finite automaton with $5n - 2$ states and $8n - 8$ transitions.*

4.2 Nondeterministic State and Transition Complexity

The above results show that minimizing the number of states and transitions are of fundamentally different nature. We now address a related question, namely: how does nondeterministic state complexity compare, in the worst case, to nondeterministic transition complexity? The difference to the previous question is that now the number of transitions is not conditioned on the requirement that the NFAs under consideration should be state minimal, and the minimum number of states and the minimum number of transitions may be realized by a pair of NFAs having completely different structure.

Recall that, for alphabets of constant size, Lemma 2.8 gives a trivial quadratic upper bound on the size of this gap. Here we show, by a counting argument, that this quadratic bound can be almost reached, already for binary alphabets, and even if we allow ε-transitions!

Lemma 4.7. *Assume $L \subseteq \{a,b\}^{\leq n}$. Then $\mathrm{nsc}(L) < \frac{3}{\sqrt{2}}\sqrt{2^n}$.*

Proof. Let $\ell = \lfloor (n-1)/2 \rfloor$ and $m = \lceil (n-1)/2 \rceil$. We construct a nondeterministic finite automaton $A = (Q, \{a,b\}, \delta, p_\varepsilon, F)$, where $Q = P_1 \cup P_2$ (the union is disjoint) with $P_1 = \{\, p_w \mid w \in \{a,b\}^* \text{ and } |w| \leq \ell \,\}$ and $P_2 = \{\, q_w \mid w \in \{a,b\}^* \text{ and } |w| \leq m \,\}$, the set $F = \{q_\varepsilon\} \cup \{\, p_\varepsilon \mid \varepsilon \in L \,\}$, and the transition function is specified as follows:

1. For all $w \in \{a,b\}^{\leq \ell - 1}$ and $x \in \{a,b\}$, the set $\delta(p_w, x)$ contains the element p_{wx}.

2. For all $w \in \{a,b\}^{\leq m-1}$ and $x \in \{a,b\}$, the set $\delta(q_{xw}, x)$ contains the element q_w.

3. It remains to connect the states in P_1 to those in P_2. To this end, observe that each nonempty word w in $L \setminus \{\varepsilon\}$ admits a unique decomposition as $w = uxv$ where x is a single letter, and the lengths of u and v are such that $|u| = \lfloor (|w|-1)/2 \rfloor$ and $|v| = \lceil (|w|-1)/2 \rceil$. For each word $w = uxv$ decomposed in that way, we let $\delta(p_u, x)$ contain the element q_v.

This completes the construction of the nondeterministic finite automaton. It is easy to see that for the number of states in A, we have

$$|P_1| + |P_2| = 2^{\ell+1} - 1 + 2^{m+1} - 1 < \frac{3}{\sqrt{2}}\sqrt{2^n}.$$

It remains to show that $L(A) = L$. Note that every state p_w in P_1 is only reachable by the word w from the initial state p_ε, and that for every state q_w in P_2 there is only one path leading to the final state q_ε. So every transition leading from P_1 to P_2 is responsible for the acceptance of exactly one word in L. This proves the stated claim. $\square$

Next we show that, in some precise sense, almost all languages L with $L \subseteq \{a,b\}^{\leq n}$ require a much larger number of transitions than $O(\sqrt{2^n})$. We note that a similar but numerically weaker statement is proved, for a different purpose, in [70].

Lemma 4.8. *For $n \geq 8$, the number of languages over $\{a,b\}$ that can be accepted by nondeterministic finite automata with ε-transitions having at most $\frac{2^n}{4n}$ transitions is bounded above by*

$$\sqrt{2^{2^n}} = o\left(\left| \left\{ L \mid L \subseteq \{a,b\}^{\leq n} \right\} \right| \right).$$

Proof. For the proof it will be more convenient to bound the number of languages acceptable by nondeterministic finite automata with ε-transitions having at most $\frac{2^n}{4n}$ "edges" instead—by an edge, we mean an edge in the underlying digraph of the automaton. As an edge can be labeled with more than one alphabet symbol, there are always at least as many transitions in the automaton as edges in the underlying graph.

Combining two arguments given in [50] and [70], there are at most $7\binom{s^2}{t}(2s-1)+1$ languages over a binary alphabet that can be accepted by nondeterministic finite automata with ε-transitions with exactly s states and exactly t edges: there are $\binom{s^2}{t}$ ways to place t edges between pairs of states, and every such edge may be labeled with one of the 7 nonempty subsets of $\{\varepsilon, a, b\}$. Either the initial state q_0 is accepting or not, and we can assume that the other accepting states are labeled $q_1, q_2, \ldots, q_k$ with $0 \le k \le s-1$. If no final state is selected, only one language can be accepted, namely the empty language.

If we bound only the number of edges from above, observe that the number of states needed can exceed the number of edges needed by at most 1. Moreover, if a language can be accepted by a nondeterministic finite automaton with at most t edges, then it can also be accepted by an automaton with exactly t edges and exactly $t+1$ states: In case exactly t edges are needed in order to accept the language, we can just add as many additional useless states as needed to the automaton without changing the accepted language. Otherwise, the language can be accepted by an automaton with exactly $t' < t$ edges and $t'+1$ states. We then add as many useless (nonaccepting) states as needed, and for each such state we extend the transition function by adding an edge leading from the start state to the newly added useless state, in order to get a total number of t edges and $t+1$ states without altering the accepted language. Thus we obtain an upper bound of $7(2t+1)\binom{(t+1)^2}{t}+1$ on the number of these languages. Using $\binom{m}{k} < m^k/k!$ and $\log k! > k \log k - \frac{3}{2}k$, we find that

$$\log\binom{(t+1)^2}{t} < 2t\log(t+1) - t\log t + \frac{3}{2}t < 2t\log t,$$

for $t \ge 8$, and the number of languages under consideration is at most $7(2t+1)t^{2t}+1$. Setting $t = 2^{n-2}/n$, we find that for $n \ge 8$ this number is smaller than

$$\frac{7(2^{n-1}/n+1)}{(4n)^{2^{n-1}/n}}2^{2^{n-1}}+1 < 2^{2^{n-1}}.$$

This proves the stated claim. $\qquad\square$

Now we are ready for establishing a large gap between nondeterministic state and transition complexity in the ε-NFA model; since $\mathrm{ntc}_\varepsilon(L) \le \mathrm{ntc}(L)$ for each regular language L, the lower bound of course also applies for the model of NFAs without ε-transitions.

Theorem 4.9. *For every $k \ge 34$, there is a set T of finite languages over Σ such that for every $L \in T$ holds*

$$\mathrm{nsc}(L) < k, \quad but \quad \mathrm{ntc}_\varepsilon(L) > \frac{k^2}{c \cdot \log k},$$

for some constant $c \le 72$. Moreover the cardinality of T is of order $2^{\Omega(k^2)}$.

Proof. Let n be the unique integer such that $\frac{3}{\sqrt{2}}\sqrt{2^n} < k \le 3 \cdot \sqrt{2^n}$. Then by our choice of n holds $\log k > \frac{1}{2}n + \log\frac{3}{\sqrt{2}} > \frac{1}{2}n$ and $k^2 \le 9 \cdot 2^n$.

Next consider the languages that are subsets of $\{a, b\}^n$. By Lemma 4.8, for $n \ge 8$, there are more than $2^{2^n} - \sqrt{2^{2^n}}$ subsets of $\{a, b\}^n$ that cannot be accepted by ε-NFAs having at most $\frac{2^n}{4n}$ transitions. The lemma is applicable for $k \ge 34$, since $\frac{3}{\sqrt{2}}\sqrt{2^8} < 34$. Let these languages form the set T. Then we have, for $k \ge 34$, that

$$|T| > 2^{2^n-1} \ge 2^{k^2/9-1} = 2^{\Omega(k^2)}.$$

In contrast, for every $L \in T$ holds $\mathrm{nsc}(L) < \frac{3}{\sqrt{2}}\sqrt{2^n} < k$ by Lemma 4.7. But any nondeterministic finite automaton accepting a language $L \in T$ has more than $\frac{2^n}{4n}$ transitions, even if ε-transitions are allowed, and $\frac{k^2}{\log k} < \frac{9 \cdot 2^n}{1/2n} = 72 \cdot \frac{2^n}{4n}$, which gives the desired lower bound. $\qquad\square$

In [51], it is reported that a similar result for ε-free nondeterministic finite automata was proved independently by J. Kari. We also note that Domaratzki and Salomaa obtained a (weaker) lower bound for the gap between nondeterministic state and transition complexity by more constructive means [51]: They give an explicitly defined family of languages where $\mathrm{nsc}(L_n) = O(n)$, but $\mathrm{ntc}(L_n) = \Omega(n^{3/2})$.

5 Computational Complexity of NFA Minimization

After we have discussed lower bound techniques for the size of nondeterministic finite automata, and also have compared different means of measuring that size, we are now ready to address the problem of how to obtain such small NFAs. Following the classical approach of classifying the computational complexity of algorithmic problems by means of their decision versions [63], we investigate in this chapter the following decision problem:

> Given an integer k, encoded in unary[1], and a description of a regular language, what is the computational complexity of deciding whether there exists an NFA with at most k states accepting that language?

We can of course study variations on this question such as minimizing the number of transitions or ask for a small regular expression in place of an NFA. Instead, we want to focus in this chapter on the effect which succinctness of the input representation can have on the computational complexity of the minimization problem. Stockmeyer and Meyer [172] showed that the above decision problem is **PSPACE**-complete if the input is specified as NFA, and Jiang and Ravikumar [114] proved that the problem remains still as hard when given a DFA:

Theorem 5.1. *Given an integer k and a DFA or NFA A, deciding whether there exists an equivalent NFA with at most k states is* **PSPACE**-*complete.*

It is not hard to see that the computational complexity of the problem drops if we restrict our attention to an appropriate subclass of regular languages, e.g. the finite languages: The equivalence problem restricted to NFAs accepting finite languages is **coNP**-complete [172]. Thus, a nondeterministic polynomial time bounded Turing machine with access to an **NP**-oracle can nondeterministically guess an NFA with at most k states, and use the oracle to decide whether the guessed NFA is equivalent to the given one; the described computation path accepts iff this is the case. This gives an upper bound of $\mathbf{NP^{NP}}$, irrespective of whether the input is given as a DFA or NFA.

5.1 Computational Complexity for Given Explicit Description

Is the complexity of NFA minimization for finite languages actually lower than this, e.g. can we do it in **NP**? We will show that the answer is yes if the input is given

---

[1]Since we are usually not interested in NFAs which are even larger than the given description, we can safely assume that k is encoded in unary. We also note that all of the following arguments can be easily adapted to the case of binary encoding.

more explicitly, as a list of words. That setup has found applications in computational linguistics [167]. Another setup where the problem is in **NP** is when we search for a small NFA for representing a Boolean function, and the input is specified as a truth table; the question of determining the complexity of this problem was raised recently in [70]. More precisely, to each n-bit Boolean function $f : \{0,1\}^n \rightarrow \{0,1\}$, where $n \geq 1$ is some natural number, we can naturally associate a finite language as follows:

$$L_f = f^{-1}(1) = \{ x_1 x_2 \ldots x_n \in \{0,1\}^n \mid f(x_1, x_2, \ldots, x_n) = 1 \}.$$

Theorem 5.2. *Given an integer k and a finite language L, specified as a set of words $\{w_1, w_2, \ldots, w_n\}$ (or given $L = f^{-1}(1)$ as a truth table of an m-bit Boolean function f), deciding whether there exists a NFA accepting L having at most k states is* **NP***-complete.*

Proof. Of course, a truth table for L can be easily transformed (in time polynomial in 2^m) into a list containing all words in L. Membership within **NP** for the latter representation can be seen as follows. Building a trie (i.e., a prefix tree) from the list of words results in a finite automaton of size linear in the size of the list. Since this trie is indeed a deterministic finite automaton, also a NFA C accepting the complement $\Sigma^* \setminus L$ can be constructed in polynomial time, using the standard construction for complementing DFAs, see [96].

Thus, a nondeterministic polynomial-time bounded Turing machine can nondeterministically guess the description of a NFA A with at most k states, and test if $L(A) \cap L(C) = \emptyset$. If this test fails, then $L(A) \not\subseteq L$, and the Turing machine rejects. Otherwise it proceeds by simulating the automaton A on the inputs $w_1, w_2, \ldots, w_n$ one by one, and if A accepts all of the words, then also $L \subseteq L(A)$, and the Turing machine accepts.

We will prove in Chapter 6, Theorem 6.6 that the problem is **NP**-hard for input specification as truth table—actually, we will prove a stronger result, which also comprises the approximability of this problem. This will readily give a corresponding hardness result for the case L is specified as a set of words. $\square$

5.2 Computational Complexity for Given DFA or NFA

However, the NFA minimization problem becomes **DP**-hard if the input is specified as a finite automaton, even if we restrict the input format to deterministic finite automata. Recall that **DP** is the class of decision problems, or equivalently, languages, that can be written as the intersection of a language in **NP** and a language in **coNP**. We note again that this is different from requiring that a language should be both in **NP** and in **coNP**: for instance, **DP** contains all languages in **NP** $\cup$ **coNP**. Assuming[2] **NP** $\neq$ **coNP**, the latter is of course a proper superset of **NP**. Regarding the technical question of how to establish **DP**-hardness of a particular problem under consideration, we use the following lemma:

Lemma 5.3. *Let L_1 be an* **NP***-hard language and L_2 a* **coNP***-hard language, and let L_3 be another language. If there is a polynomial-time computable, two-parameter function $f(\cdot, \cdot)$ such that for all input pairs (x, y) holds*

$$f(x, y) \in L_3 \text{ if and only if both } x \in L_1 \text{ and } y \in L_2,$$

---

[2]This assumption is commonly believed to be true among complexity theorists, indeed a stronger assumption is very common, namely that the so-called "polynomial hierarchy" does not collapse, cf. [152].

*then L_3 is **DP**-hard.*

Proof. The essential part is to prove that the set of pairs

$$P(L_1, L_2) = \{\, (w, x) \mid \text{both } x \in L_1 \text{ and } y \in L_2 \,\}$$

is **DP**-hard. For then, by transforming the function f with parameters x and y into a one-parameter function, which maps each string encoding a pair (x, y) to the value of $f(x, y)$, we easily get a polynomial time reduction from $P(L_1, L_2)$ to L_3. This will complete the proof once we have shown that the set $P(L_1, L_2)$ is **DP**-hard.

To this end, we have to prove nothing less than that every language $M \in$ **DP** is polynomial-time reducible to the set of pairs $P(L_1, L_2)$. We proceed as in the proof of [152, Thm. 17.1], where a similar statement is shown. All we know about the language M is that we can write it as $M = M_1 \cap M_2$, for some $M_1 \in$ **NP** and some $M_2 \in$ **coNP**. We can infer something about the sets M_1 and M_2: Since L_1 is **NP**-hard, the set M_1 is reducible to L_1 via some polynomial-time reduction r_1. Similarly, since L_2 is **coNP**-hard, the set M_2 is reducible to L_2 via another polynomial-time reduction r_2. Now the desired reduction from M to $P(L_1, L_2)$ is simply given by

$$r : w \mapsto (r_1(w), r_2(w))\,, \text{ for each input } w.$$

Then $r_1(w) \in L_1$ and $r_2(w) \in L_2$ holds, if and only if both $w \in M_1$ and $w \in M_2$. The former condition is equivalent to the requirement $(r_1(w), r_2(w)) \in P(L_1, L_2)$, while the latter is clearly equivalent to saying $w \in M$. $\qquad\square$

We use this kind of reduction for the proof of the main result of this chapter:

Theorem 5.4. *Given an integer k and a DFA accepting a finite language, deciding whether there exists an equivalent NFA having at most k states is **DP**-hard.*

Proof. Given a pair (G, Φ), with G a non-2-colorable planar graph and Φ a DNF formula, that is, a Boolean formula in disjunctive normal form[3], we construct in polynomial time an integer k and a DFA A accepting a finite language, such that $\mathrm{nsc}(L(A)) \leq k$ iff both G is 3-colorable and Φ is a tautology. Since the corresponding decision problems for G and Φ are **NP**-complete [63, Problem GT 4] and **coNP**-complete [63, Problem LO 8], respectively, with the aid of Lemma 5.3 this will imply the desired **DP**-hardness result.

The outline of the proof is as follows: We give two polynomial time reductions $f : G \mapsto (r, B)$ and $g : \Phi \mapsto (s, C)$, each of which constructs in polynomial time an integer and a DFA accepting a finite language, such that $\mathrm{nsc}(L(B)) \leq r$ iff the chromatic number of G equals 3 and $\mathrm{nsc}(L(C)) \leq s$ iff Φ is a tautology. Then we construct the DFA A which accepts the marked concatenation $L(B)\$L(C)$, where $\$$ is a new alphabet symbol. Since we use a special marker for concatenation, it is clear that the DFA A can be constructed in polynomial time. Also, $\mathrm{nsc}(L(A)) = \mathrm{nsc}(L(B)) + \mathrm{nsc}(L(C))$ since any NFA accepting this language can be decomposed along the $\$$-transitions into two disjoint NFAs accepting $L(B)$ and $L(C)$, respectively. Clearly, if G has chromatic number 3 and Φ is a tautology, then $\mathrm{nsc}(L(A)) \leq r + s$.

---

[3]Recall that a Boolean formula Φ is in *disjunctive normal form* (DNF) if it is a disjunction of conjunctions of literals, that is, if Φ is of the form $\Phi = \bigvee_i \bigwedge_j t_{ij}$, where each literal t_{ij} denotes a, possibly negated, occurrence of a Boolean variable.

In order to establish the converse, we have to take extra care: Our reductions have to ensure that in *any case*, both $\text{nsc}(L(B)) \geq r$ and $\text{nsc}(L(C)) \geq s$ holds. Only with this additional condition, we obtain: If $\text{nsc}(L(A)) > r + s$, then necessarily $\text{nsc}(L(B)) > r$ or $\text{nsc}(L(B)) > s$ and thus G is not 3-colorable or Φ is not a tautology.

Therefore the proof will be completed once we have established the following two claims:

Claim 5.5. There is a polynomial-time computable function f that, given a non-2-colorable planar graph G, constructs an integer r and a DFA B accepting a finite language, such that

- $\text{nsc}(L(B)) \leq r$ iff G is 3-colorable, and

- in any case, $\text{nsc}(L(B)) \geq r$.

Claim 5.6. There is a polynomial-time computable function g that, given a DNF formula Φ, constructs an integer s and a DFA C accepting a finite language, such that

- $\text{nsc}(L(C)) \leq s$ iff Φ is a tautology, and

- in any case, $\text{nsc}(L(C)) \geq s$.

Proof of Claim 5.5. The construction of a DFA with the desired features proceeds in several steps: Recall from Chapter 2.3 that the bipartite dimension of a bipartite graph G', denoted by $d(G')$, is the minimum number of bicliques needed in order to cover all edges in G'. The associated decision problem was shown to be **NP**-complete by Orlin [151, Theorem 8.1] and also appears in Garey and Johnson's list of **NP**-complete problems [63, Problem GT 18]. Orlin gives a polynomial-time reduction that, given an arbitrary graph G with m edges, constructs a bipartite graph G' such that $d(G') = m + \chi(G)$. Of course this reduction also works for our restriction where G is a non-2-colorable planar graph. This restriction has the following feature: the Four Color Theorem [5] implies that every planar graph is 4-colorable,[4] so that $d(G')$ is equal to $m + 3$ if G is 3-colorable, and to $m + 4$ otherwise.

We feed the result G' into another reduction: Amilhastre et al. [3, Lemma 1] observe that if we interpret the edge set of a bipartite graph $G' = (X, Y, E')$ as a set of words $L \subseteq X \cdot Y$, then a biclique edge cover of size k for G naturally gives rise to a NFA with a single initial state, a single final state and k additional states, and *vice versa*. Here, the additive term 2 comes from the start state and the final state, which do each not correspond to a biclique. Thus the minimum number of states needed by an NFA for accepting L equals $d(G') + 2$. From that list of words, we can construct in polynomial time a DFA B accepting that set, and we fix the parameter r as $r = m + 5$. Since $\text{nsc}(L(B)) = d(G') + 2$, since Orlin's construction gives $d(G') = \chi(G) + m$, and since the chromatic number of a non-2-colorable planar graph always equals either 3 or 4, we obtain $r = m + 5 \leq \text{nsc}(L(B)) \leq m + 6 = r + 1$. Thus the reduction shares all of the desired properties, and the proof of Claim 5.5 is complete. $\qquad\square$

Proof of Claim 5.6. The second reduction is more complicated and relies on a definition of a special language L commonly specified by multiple DFAs—similar to a construction described in [114].

---

[4]As discussed by Appel and Haken [5], their original proof contained several errors. Due to its sheer volume, a full verification of that proof appears to be infeasible, cf. [158]. Therefore, Robertson et al. [158] devised a simplified proof, and Gonthier [68] later gave a fully formalized and correct proof, checked with an automated theorem proving software.

From the formula Φ, having variables $x_1, x_2, \ldots, x_n$ and m clauses, we construct in polynomial time DFAs $A_1, A_2, \ldots, A_m$ such that A_i accepts the set of assignments $t = t_1 t_2 \cdots t_n$ satisfying the ith clause. Then $\bigcup_i L(A_i) = \{0,1\}^n$ if and only if Φ is a tautology. Note that constructing a DFA for this union of languages would already solve the tautology problem, since equivalence of a pair of DFAs can be decided in time polynomial in the size of the larger automaton. So we have to use a different encoding[5].

Without loss of generality, we assume that the state set of every DFA A_i reads as $Q_i = \{q_{i0}, q_{i1}, \ldots, q_{in}\}$, and for each j, there is a word w_{ij} of length j such that A_i is in state q_{ij} after reading w_{ij}. We also assume that $Q_i \cap Q_j = \emptyset$ for $i \neq j$. The language $P(i,j)$ is defined as the set of words which could be accepted by A_i if q_{ij} was redefined as the only accepting state, that is

$$P(i,j) = \{\, w \in \{0,1\}^{\leq n} \mid q_{i0} \vdash_{A_i}^w q_{ij} \,\}.$$

We introduce a new symbol a_i for each automaton A_i, and a new symbol b_{ij} for each state q_{ij} in $\bigcup_{i=1}^m Q_i$. In addition, we have new symbols $c_1, c_2, \ldots c_n$, and d. Define the language $P(i)$ as a marked version of the language accepted by A_i:

$$P(i) = \bigcup_{j=0}^n (a_i \cdot P(i,j) \cdot b_{ij});$$

and define B_j as the set of all special b-symbols whose second index is j:

$$B_j = \{\, b_{ij} \mid 1 \leq i \leq m \,\}.$$

Then the auxiliary language R is defined as the set

$$(\{0,1,c_1\}\{0,1,c_2\} \cdots \{0,1,c_n\}\{d\}) \cup \bigcup_{j=1}^n (\{0,1,c_1\}\{0,1,c_2\} \cdots \{0,1,c_j\}B_j).$$

Lastly, we define the language L as the union

$$L = R \cup \{0,1\}^n \cup \bigcup_{i=1}^m (P(i) \cup a_i L(A_i)).$$

The role of R is basically to assert that all strings of the form xb_{ij} with $x \in \{0,1\}^j$ are in L, and the marker symbols c_j ensure any NFA accepting L needs $n-1$ states in addition to those needed to accept the set $\{0,1\}^n \cup \bigcup_{i=1}^m (P(i) \cup a_i L(A_i))$.

Given $A_1, A_2, \ldots, A_m$, it is easy to construct in polynomial time a DFA with $n+1$ states accepting $\{0,1\}^n$, a DFA with $n+2$ states accepting R, and a DFA with $2 + m(n+1)$ states accepting $\bigcup_{i=1}^m (P(i) \cup a_i L(M_i))$. By the well-known product construction, a DFA accepting the union of these three languages can be obtained in polynomial time, and this union equals L.

We will now show that the size of the minimal NFA accepting L has in any case at least $s = 2 + m(n+1) + n$ states, and that this lower bound is exact if and only if Φ is a tautology.

---

[5]We note that the difficulty arises only as we need to encode the instance into a DFA; for NFAs or regular expressions, the reduction would be a rather simple exercise, compare [63, Chapter 3.3, Exercise 10].

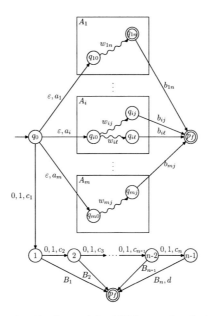

Figure 5.1: Sketch of construction for a minimal NFA accepting L_Φ in case Φ is a tautology. The two final states labeled p_f are actually a single state.

If Φ is a tautology, then the s-state NFA sketched in Figure 5.1 accepts L. To prove that $\mathrm{nsc}(L) \geq s$, we use the fooling set technique from Lemma 3.2:

For each $i \in \{1, 2, \ldots, m\}$ and each $j \in \{1, 2, \ldots, n\}$, choose some word w_{ij} in $P(i,j)$, and define the set of pairs $S = S_1 \cup S_2$ with

$$
\begin{aligned}
S_1 &= \{\,(a_i w_{ij}, b_{ij}) \mid 1 \leq i \leq n \text{ and } 1 \leq j \leq m\,\}, \quad \text{and} \\
S_2 &= \{\,(x, y) \mid xy = c_1 c_2 \cdots c_n d\,\}.
\end{aligned}
$$

We claim that S is a fooling set of size s for L; thus $\mathrm{nsc}(L) \geq s$.

It is readily observed that $xy \in L$ for all pairs $(x, y) \in S$. Next, we note that the word $a_i w_{ij} b_{i\ell}$ is in L if and only if $j = \ell$. Of course, if $j = \ell$ then $a_i w_{ij} b_{i\ell} \in L$. Assume now $i \neq \ell$. Since the word begins with a_i and ends with $b_{i\ell}$, it is not in L, or it is in $P(i) \cup a_i \cdot L(A_i)$. It is clear that $w_{ij} \in P(i,j)$. Any word in $P(i)$ ending with $b_{i\ell}$ is in $a_i \cdot P(i, \ell) \cdot b_{i\ell}$, so $w_{ij} \in P(i,j) \cap P(i, \ell)$. But automaton A_i is deterministic, so $P(i,j) \cap P(i, \ell) = \emptyset$ if $j \neq \ell$, and thus $a_i w_{ij} b_{i\ell} \notin L$. Thus, the subset S_1 has the fooling set property.

We turn to the elements in S_2: Let $w = c_1 c_2 \cdots c_n d$. Obviously, the word $w = w \cdot \varepsilon = \varepsilon \cdot w$ is in L, but ww is not. And none of the words $a_i w_{ij} w$, or $w b_{ij}$ are in L, so we can add the pairs (ε, w) and (w, ε) to S_1 to form a larger fooling set. Next, note that no proper subword of w is in L, so S_2 for itself also has the fooling set property for L. To see that all the remaining pairs in S_2 can be added to S_1, observe that $a_i w_{ij} y$ cannot be in L if y ends with the letter d.

Now assume Φ is not a tautology, and let t represent a truth value assignment such that Φ evaluates to the truth value "false." Decompose t as $t = uv$ with $0 < |u| < n$.

We claim that $S \cup \{(u,v)\}$ (the union is disjoint) is still a fooling set for L: For sake of contradiction, assume this is not the case. Since $uv \in \{0,1\}^n$ and hence in L, there must exist some other pair $(u',v') \in S$ such that uv' and $u'v$ are both in L.

We first consider the case that (u',v') is in S_2: In this case, $u'v' = w$ for $w = c_1 c_2 \cdots c_n d$. If $|u'| > 0$, then $u'v$ begins with c_1, and any word in L beginning with c_1 must not end with a symbol in $\{0,1\}$. But $u'v$ has this form. If $|u'| = 0$, then $u'v$ takes on the form $c_1 c_2 \cdots c_n dv$ for a nonempty word v, and this word is clearly not in L either.

So (u',v') must be in S_1 and thus of the form $(a_i w_{ij}, b_{ij})$, with both $a_i w_{ij} v$ and $u b_{ij}$ in L. We can deduce that $w_{ij} v$ must be in $L(A_i)$, since the word $a_i w_{ij} v$ begins with a_i. And u must be in $P(i,j)$, since the word $u b_{ij}$ ends with b_{ij}. Since A_i is deterministic and w_{ij} is also in $P(i,j)$, we have $w_{ij} \equiv_{L(A_i)} u$, where $\equiv_{L(A_i)}$ is the Myhill-Nerode relation for $L(A_i)$, which we encountered in Chapter 2.2.3. But together with $w_{ij} v \in L(A_i)$ this implies, by definition of that relation, that the word uv is also in $L(A_i)$. Since A_i accepts precisely all truth assignments satisfying the ith clause, the accepted word $t = uv$ must be a satisfying assignment for the DNF formula Φ, contradicting our original assumption on t.

Thus, if Φ is not a tautology, then L admits a fooling set of size $s+1$, and $\mathrm{nsc}(L) \geq s+1$ in this case. This completes the proof of Claim 5.5. □

Having established both claims, the proof is now completed. □

Remark. As a technical note, we mention that the reduction in Claim 5.5 has the desirable feature that the optimum value is always either r or $r+1$. If we would have a similar property in a reduction establishing Claim 5.6, it would be rather straightforward to prove the problem **coDP**-hard as well. Yet we were not able to find such a reduction to date.

Since the DFAs used in the proof of Theorem 5.4 have a rather simple structure, and we could as well construct equivalent regular expressions (without stars) in polynomial time. In this way, we obtain as a simple corollary **DP**-hardness results for finding a minimum state NFA also for the other usual input formats:

Corollary 5.7. *Given an integer k and an NFA or regular expression denoting a finite language, deciding whether there exists an equivalent NFA having at most k states is* **DP***-hard.*

Apart from the restriction to finite languages, another popular field of study, especially for understanding what circumstances can render a certain problem hard, is to consider languages over a unary alphabet. We briefly summarize known analogous complexity results for the restriction of the NFA state minimization problem to unary languages: Similar to the case of finite languages, the equivalence problem for unary NFAs is no longer **PSPACE**-complete, but **coNP**-complete [172]; An analogous argument as outlined at the beginning of the chapter for the case of finite languages thus gives an upper bound of **NP^{NP}**. For a lower bound, given a unary NFA, deciding whether there exists an equivalent NFA with only one state is **coNP**-hard [172]. We note that when a DFA is given, the computational complexity of the problem might be different: Observe that the states of a unary DFA are arranged along a simple path that is followed by a cycle. We call such a DFA cyclic, if this path is empty. At least for case where a unary cyclic DFA is given, the problem is in **NP** [112]. On the negative side, even in this case there is evidence that there is no polynomial time algorithm [112], although that evidence is weaker than an **NP**-hardness result.

6 Approximation Complexity of NFA Minimization

In the previous chapter, we have seen that already very restricted versions of the NFA minimization problem are computationally hard. Thus it appears reasonable to look for approximation algorithms.

If $\mathbf{P} = \mathbf{PSPACE}$ (respectively $\mathbf{P} = \mathbf{NP}$), then of course all minimization problems whose decision version is in $\mathbf{PSPACE}$ (respectively in $\mathbf{NP^{NP}}$) can be not only approximated, but optimally solved in polynomial time. Until the above questions are solved, we can prove negative results on approximability only under additional hypotheses such as $\mathbf{P} \neq \mathbf{NP}$.

The issue of determining the approximation complexity of NFA minimization was raised by Jiang and Ravikumar [114]. The recent work by Gramlich and Schnitger [70] contains negative results on approximability when the given language is specified as a DFA, namely that the number of states and transitions cannot be approximated within a factor better than $n^{1/2}/(\log n)^{O(1)}$ for state minimization and better than $n/(\log n)^{O(1)}$ for transition minimization, already for binary alphabets.

But these results were obtained under a certain cryptographic assumption,[1] asserting that some problems are sufficiently hard on average, which is much stronger than familiar worst-case assumptions such as $\mathbf{P} \neq \mathbf{NP}$. While their result shows that obtaining only very moderate approximation guarantees would require a major breakthrough in algorithm design, such an assumption does not fit nicely into the usual framework of inapproximability results. Thus a natural question posed by the authors of [70] is whether we actually need such strong assumptions, or whether we can prove similar results assuming only $\mathbf{P} \neq \mathbf{NP}$.

Another issue raised in [70] is to determine the complexity accordingly when the input is specified explicitly, as a truth table, instead of a finite automaton. We will resolve both questions in one shot, by proving an inapproximability result for truth table input, solely based on the assumption $\mathbf{P} \neq \mathbf{NP}$. It is understood that the problem only gets harder when the specification is a finite automaton instead of a truth table.

Finally, we will turn our attention to the case of unary languages. Here, we report a positive result concerning the approximability for DFA input. In contrast, we show that for NFA input, the problem is not approximable at all. This was already known for alphabets of size at least two [70]. The latter two results provide a partial and an optimal resolution, respectively, of two further research problems raised in [70].

---

[1] For the interested reader: The assumption they use is that the non-uniform complexity class $\mathbf{L/poly}$ contains strong pseudorandom functions, see [70] for the precise definitions.

6.1 Basic Notions in Approximation Complexity

We briefly recall some basic notions in approximation complexity. The used notation is mostly standard, compare [8, 63].

A *minimization problem* $\Pi = (I, \text{sol}, m)$ is specified by a set I of *problem instances*, together with a set $\text{sol} = \text{sol}(x)$ of *(feasible) solutions* for each instance $x \in I$ and a function m that assigns to each instance-solution pair a *solution value* $m(x, s)$, which is a nonnegative integer measuring the quality of that solution for instance x. A minimization problem is called *nonconstructive*, if the solutions and the solution values are identical.

The *optimum value* for instance x, denoted by $\text{opt}(x)$, is the minimum solution value among all feasible solutions for x. Given a solution s for instance x, its *performance ratio* is defined as $R_\Pi(x, s) = m(x, s)/\text{opt}(x)$.

An *approximation algorithm* for Π with performance ratio c is a polynomial time algorithm that computes for each instance x a solution s such that $R(x, s) \leq c$ always holds. Here the performance ratio may be a constant, or a function of the input size. If problem Π admits an approximation algorithm with performance ratio c, we say Π is c-approximable.

For *maximization problems* these notions are defined analogously; generally we talk about *optimization problems*, a term which comprises both minimization and maximization problems.

Remark. In principle, the above definitions must be stated more rigorously. For instance, it is required that the set I of problem instances can be recognized in polynomial time. Such details will not be an issue in the course of our investigation. Thus, for simplicity of exposition, we abstain from making the above definitions mathematically precise. The details of how this is done are found in [8].

As for decision problems, there is a notion of reducibility and completeness in the setup of approximation complexity.

A wide variety of different notions of such reducibilities has been proposed in the literature, see e.g. [39]. Our weapon of choice is the C-reduction introduced in [170]:

Definition 6.1. Let Π and Π' be two optimization problems. A *continuous reduction*, or *C-reduction* from Π to Π' consists of two polynomial-time computable functions f and g such that:

- The function f maps each instance x of Π to an instance $f(x)$ of Π'.

- The function g maps each solution s for $f(x)$ back to a solution $g(x, s)$ for x whilst increasing the performance ratio by at most a linear factor:

$$R_\Pi(x, g(x, s)) \leq c \cdot R_{\Pi'}(f(x), s),$$

for some constant $c > 0$.

The function f in a C-reduction can blow up the size of the instance by a polynomial factor, which can have a quantitative effect on what we can deduce about the approximability of the problem. For two input size measures $|x|_\Pi$ and $|y|_{\Pi'}$, we say that a given C-reduction has *input expansion* $(\beta(n), |\cdot|_\Pi, |\cdot|_{\Pi'})$ if for all instances x of Π holds $|f(x)|_{\Pi'} \leq \beta(|x|_\Pi)$. Here we assume $\beta : \mathbb{N} \to \mathbb{Q}^+$ is a monotonically increasing function. For notational convenience, we will usually just write $|y|_{\Pi'} \leq \beta(|x|_{\Pi'})$ instead of $(\beta(n), |\cdot|_\Pi, |\cdot|_{\Pi'})$.

Lemma 6.2. *Let $b : \mathbb{N} \to \mathbb{Q}^+$ be a monotonically increasing function, and let $\Pi = (I, \text{sol}, m)$, $\Pi' = (I', \text{sol}', m')$ be two minimization problems. Assume Π' is approximable within $b(|y|_{\Pi'})$, for all $y \in I'$, and there is a C-reduction from Π to Π' with input expansion $|x|_\Pi \leq a(|y|_{\Pi'})$. Then Π is approximable within $O(b(a(|x|_\Pi)))$, for all instances x of Π.*

Proof. Assume $A'(y)$ is a polynomial-time algorithm approximating Π' within a factor of $b(|y|_{\Pi'})$. We give a polynomial-time algorithm $A(x)$ for Π based on A' with the desired performance ratio as follows: Given an instance x of Π, A uses the C-reduction to compute an instance $f(x)$ of Π'. Then A' computes $s' = A'(f(x))$, and finally $g(f(x, s'))$ yields a solution s for x. The properties of the reduction then ensure that the performance ratio of s with respect to x fulfills

$$R_\Pi(x, s) \leq c \cdot R_{\Pi'}(f(x), s') \leq c \cdot b(|f(x)|_{\Pi'}) = O(b(a(|x|_\Pi))),$$

and the proof is completed. $\qquad\square$

Next we define a notion of completeness for approximation complexity classes. Observe that the notion of C-reducibility is reflexive and transitive. We write $\Pi \leq_C \Pi'$ if there is a (sequence of) C-reduction(s) from Π to Π'. An optimization problem is in the class **NPO**, if its corresponding decision version is in **NP**. The class **NPO** falls apart into classes of problems with respect to their degree of approximability: An **NPO** problem belongs to the class **APX**, if it is c-approximable for some constant c. Similarly, the problem belongs to the class **poly-APX**, if it is $f(n)$-approximable for some $f(n) \in n^{O(1)}$. Here n denotes the size of the instance. Similar classes, such as **log-APX** and **exp-APX**, can be defined analogously. An optimization problem Π is **poly-APX**-complete (with respect to C-reductions) if both Π is in **poly-APX** and every problem in **poly-APX** is C-reducible to Π.

6.2 Approximability for Given Explicit Description

Our aim in this section will be to prove bounds on the limits of approximation for the NFA minimization problem in the case where the input is a finite language specified explicitly, in the form of a truth table or of a list of words.

In order to get lower bounds on approximability, the biclique edge cover problem is a natural candidate to reduce from. One reason is that minimum biclique edge covers are, at least to some extent, tied to nondeterministic state complexity, as outlined in Chapter 3, and the other reason is that the problem is very hard to approximate: By combining a recent inapproximability result for the chromatic number problem by Zuckerman [182] with a C-reduction from the minimum clique partition problem to the biclique edge cover problem by Simon [170], one immediately sees that the latter is not approximable within $|V|^{1/5-\varepsilon}$. But that is not yet the end of the story, since we can improve the latter reduction, and get a stronger hardness result:

Theorem 6.3. *For all $\varepsilon > 0$, the biclique edge cover problem cannot be approximated within $|V|^{1/3-\varepsilon}$ or $|E|^{1/5-\varepsilon}$, unless $\mathbf{P} = \mathbf{NP}$.*

Proof. Let the clique partition number $\overline{\chi}(I)$ of a graph I be defined as the smallest number k such that the vertex set of I can be covered by at most k cliques. The associated decision problem is **NP**-complete [63, Problem GT15], and, being a simple reformulation

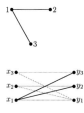 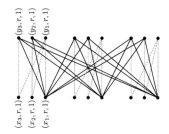

Figure 6.1: The original graph I (top left), the bipartite graph I_B (lower left), and the subgraph of G induced by the vertices in row r (right), consisting of $t = 3$ copies of I_B. The induced subgraph $G[X_{1,r}, Y_{1,r}]$ forms a biclique.

of the graph coloring problem, not approximable within $|V|^{1-\varepsilon}$, for all $\varepsilon > 0$, unless $\mathbf{P} = \mathbf{NP}$ [182]. We briefly recall the construction by Simon [170, Theorem 5.1a] for reducing the graph coloring problem to the biclique edge cover problem.

For an undirected graph $I = (V, E)$ with $V = \{v_1, v_2, \ldots, v_n\}$, we construct its bipartite version $I_B = (X_B, Y_B, E_B)$ by choosing as set of left vertices $X_B = \{x_1, x_2, \ldots, x_n\}$ and $Y_B = \{y_1, y_2, \ldots, y_n\}$ as set of right vertices, and letting $(x_i, y_j) \in E_B$ if and only if $i = j$ or $\{v_i, v_j\} \in E$. An edge (x_i, y_j) is called ascending if $i < j$, descending if $i > j$, and horizontal if $i = j$.

The biclique edge cover instance $G = (X, Y, \mathcal{E})$ consists of t^2 copies (the number t to be fixed later accordingly) of I_B, which we think of as being arranged in a $t \times t$ grid; and the bipartition of the vertex set is inherited from I_B. The ith left (right, respectively) vertex in copy (p, q) is denoted by (x_i, p, q) $((y_i, p, q)$, respectively). Two vertices (x_i, p, q) and (y_j, r, s) in different copies are connected by an edge if: either they are in the same row, i.e., $p = r$, and (x_i, y_j) is an ascending edge in E_B, or they are in the same column, i.e., $q = s$, and (x_i, y_j) is a descending edge in E_B. Accordingly, we say that an edge in $\mathcal{E}$ connecting vertices (x_i, p, q) and (y_j, r, s) is ascending if $i < j$, descending if $i > j$, and horizontal if $i = j$.

In [170], it is noted that if there is a system of s bicliques covering all horizontal edges in $\mathcal{E}$, then a partition of I into at most s/t^2 cliques can be constructed in polynomial time from this system, and

$$\overline{\chi}(I) \leq d(G)/t^2. \tag{6.1}$$

Conversely, each partition of I into r cliques corresponds to a system of rt^2 bicliques which cover all the horizontal edges in $\mathcal{E}$, and maybe some non-horizontal edges. However, note that the rt^2 bicliques do not necessarily cover all edges involving only vertices of a single copy of I_B: As an example, consider the partition of the graph I given in Figure 6.1 into $r = 3$ cliques.

To cover the remaining edges, we can do somewhat better than proposed in the original reduction from [170]: For $x_i \in X_B$, define $X_{i,p}$ as the set of ith left vertices in the copies of I_B which are in row p, and define $Y_{i,p}$ as the set of right vertices y in row p such that $((x_i, p, q), y)$ is an ascending edge in $\mathcal{E}$. It is not hard to see that the induced subgraph $G[X_{i,p}, Y_{i,p}]$ is a biclique which covers all ascending edges in row p incident to x_i, see Figure 6.1 for illustration by example.

By proceeding in this way for each row and each left vertex x_i in X_B, all ascending edges in G can be covered using no more than tn bicliques. The descending edges in G can be covered by tn bicliques in a similar manner. Thus

$$d(G) \leq t^2 \cdot \overline{\chi}(I) + 2tn, \tag{6.2}$$

which can be reformulated as

$$\frac{1}{t^2 \cdot \overline{\chi}(I)} \leq \frac{1}{d(G) - 2tn}. \tag{6.3}$$

Suppose now C is a biclique edge cover for G of size s. Then we can construct a clique partition for I of size s/t^2 in polynomial time from C, see [170] for details. For the performance ratio of this solution, which is given by $\frac{s/t^2}{\overline{\chi}(I)}$, Inequality (6.3) immediately yields an upper bound of

$$\frac{s/t^2}{\overline{\chi}(I)} \leq \frac{s}{d(G) - 2tn}. \tag{6.4}$$

To establish a C-reduction, our goal is to obtain a linear upper bound on the performance ratio $\frac{s/t^2}{\overline{\chi}(I)}$ in terms of the performance ratio $\frac{s}{d(G)}$. This can be achieved by choosing $t = 4n$: Since for every instance I of the clique partition problem the inequality $\overline{\chi}(I) \geq 1$ trivially holds, Inequality (6.1) yields $d(G) \geq t^2$, or, equivalently,

$$2tn = \frac{1}{2}t^2 \leq \frac{1}{2}d(G). \tag{6.5}$$

Putting this into Inequality (6.4), we can conclude

$$\frac{s/t^2}{\overline{\chi}(I)} \leq \frac{s}{d(G) - 2tn} \leq 2\frac{s}{d(G)}, \tag{6.6}$$

thus giving the desired linear upper bound.

So we have established a C-reduction with input expansion $|X| \leq O(|V|^3)$. The desired hardness result regarding the measure $|X|$ follows by Lemma 6.2. Estimating the number of edges in $\mathcal{E}$, we have at most $t^2|E_B|$ edges inside the individual copies of I_B, per row at most $\binom{t}{2}|E_B|$ edges in between different copies of I_B that share the same row, and per column the same bound applies for edges in between different copies that share the same column. Summing up the second and third bound over all rows and columns, respectively, we obtain altogether an upper bound of $t^2|E_B| + 2t \cdot \binom{t}{2}|E_B| = O(|V|^5)$, so this is equally a C-reduction with input expansion $|\mathcal{E}| \leq O(|V|^5)$. The claimed inapproximability result regarding the number of edges follows again by Lemma 6.2.

Finally, we note that Inequality (6.1) implies that $d(G) \geq t^2 = \Omega(|X|^{2/3})$, since $|X| = \Theta(n^3)$ and $t = 4n$. $\qquad \square$

To get our inapproximability result for the NFA minimization problems, we need a slightly strengthened version of Theorem 6.3. This will be established by the following lemma.

Lemma 6.4. *The graph coloring problem is C-reducible to a set of restricted instances of the graph coloring problem, where each instance $G' = (V', E')$ is promised to have chromatic number $\Omega(\log |V'|)$. The input expansion of this reduction is quasi-linear, i.e. $|V'| \leq |V| \log |V|$.*

Proof. Let $k = \log |V|$. For a given instance G of the graph coloring problem, define G' as the graph obtained by replacing each vertex in G with a k-clique; that is, G' is the lexicographic product of G with a k-clique. This construction clearly runs in polynomial time and has the desired input expansion. To establish that it is also a C-reduction, it suffices to give a polynomial-time algorithm to transform a coloring with $k \cdot c$ colors of G' into a c-coloring of G'. Such an algorithm is implied by a constructive proof of the equality $\chi(G') = k \cdot \chi(G)$ given in [66]. $\qquad\square$

We now establish a slightly stronger version of Theorem 6.3:

Lemma 6.5. *For all $\varepsilon > 0$, the biclique edge cover problem cannot be approximated within $|V|^{1/3-\varepsilon}$ or $|E|^{1/5-\varepsilon}$, unless $\mathbf{P} = \mathbf{NP}$. This also holds for a set of restricted instances that are promised to have bipartite dimension at least $\Omega(|V|^{2/3} \log |V|)$.*

Proof. We feed the restricted instances of the graph coloring problem constructed in the proof of Lemma 6.4 into the reduction from the proof of Theorem 6.3. Correctness clearly carries over; and chaining the reductions from Lemma 6.4 and Theorem 6.3 gives a slightly larger input expansion of $|X| \leq O(|V| \log |V|)^3$ and $|\mathcal{E}| \leq O(|V| \log |V|)^5$, thus losing a polylogarithmic factor in approximation hardness. But since the given bounds on approximability are of the form $|V|^{1/3-\varepsilon}$ and $|E|^{1/5-\varepsilon}$ for all $\varepsilon > 0$, it is easy to see that weakening the inapproximability result by a polylogarithmic factor has no effect. For instance, for each constant $\varepsilon > 0$, we have $(\log |V|)^{O(1)} \leq |V|^{\varepsilon}$ for $|V|$ large enough, and thus the inapproximability gap remains at least $|V|^{1/3-2\varepsilon}$ for any constant ε arbitrarily close to zero, which is the same result as before.

The desired lower bound on the bipartite dimension of the problem instances readily follows from Inequality 6.1. $\qquad\square$

Now we are ready to establish our first inapproximability result for NFA minimization. In the proof of the following theorem, we crucially rely on the particular structure of the biclique edge cover instance we constructed during the proof of Theorem 6.3.

Theorem 6.6. *Given a truth table of size N for a Boolean function f, no polynomial-time algorithm can approximate the number of states of a state minimal nondeterministic finite automaton accepting L_f with performance ratio $N^{1/6-\varepsilon}$, for all $\varepsilon > 0$, unless $\mathbf{P} = \mathbf{NP}$.*

Proof. We use the function f to encode the edges in the graph $G = (X, Y, \mathcal{E})$ from the proof of Theorem 6.3, and use the notations defined therein. Recall X consists of vertices of the form (x_i, p, q), where x_i is in X_B, p denotes a row index and q a column index, and similar for y_j, that is, (x_i, p, q) and (y_j, p, q) both belong to same the copy of I_B. Without loss of generality we assume $V = \{0, 1\}^m$ for some m. The $t = 4n$ addresses each for rows and columns can be respectively encoded in binary using a fixed length code of length $\log t = m + 2$. Throughout the rest of the proof, $c_1, c_2, \ldots, c_t$ denote the words encoding the t column addresses in order, and in a similar manner, $r_1, r_2, \ldots, r_t$ the row addresses in order. We then encode[2] the edges $((x, p, q), (y, a, b))$ in $\mathcal{E}$ as $x r_p c_q (r_a c_b)^R y$, and define L_f as the set of all codewords corresponding to an edge in $\mathcal{E}$. In the following, we will use the term "edge" to denote a word encoding an edge in $\mathcal{E}$ as there is no risk of confusion.

---

[2] Some readers might be amazed about this particular choice of encoding. These are hereby informed that both proofs of Claims 6.7 and 6.8 do crucially rely on features of the chosen encoding.

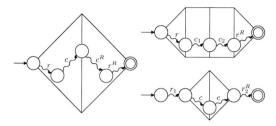

Figure 6.2: Schematic drawings of the nondeterministic finite automata accepting M (left), M' (top right), and M'' (bottom right).

Claim 6.7. The nondeterministic state complexity of L_f is bounded below by the bipartite dimension of G.

Proof. We apply the biclique edge cover technique introduced in Chapter 3.1 to give a lower bound for $\mathrm{nsc}(L_f)$. Let $\Gamma = (A, B, E_{L_f})$ be the bipartite graph given by $A = B = \{0,1\}^{m+2(m+2)}$, and $E_{L_f} = \{(u, v) \in A \times B \mid uv \in L_f\}$. By an obvious bijection holds $d(G) = d(\Gamma)$, and the latter gives a lower bound for the nondeterministic state complexity of L_f. This completes the proof of Claim 6.7. $\qquad\square$

Claim 6.8. Given a biclique edge cover of size at most s for G, we can construct in polynomial time an NFA accepting L_f having at most $O(s) + O(|X|^{2/3} \log |X|)$ states.

Proof. We establish the claim by constructing, given a biclique edge cover of size at most s for G, a union of sufficiently small NFAs accepting the language L_f.

For the horizontal edges in $\mathcal{E}$, we give a construction inspired by the proof of Theorem 6.3. Let $\{(X_j, Y_j) \mid 1 \le j \le s/t^2\}$ be a set of at most s/t^2 bicliques covering all horizontal edges in $I_B = (X_B, Y_B, E_B)$. For the jth biclique, we define an auxiliary language H_j as $H_j = X_j \cdot M \cdot Y_j$, where $M = \{rc(rc)^R \mid r, c \in \{0,1\}^{m+2}\}$ is the language ensuring that the row and column address of $x \in X_j$ is the same as the row and column address of $y \in Y_j$. As there are no horizontal edges between different copies of I_B, the language M ensures that the union of languages $\bigcup_j H_j$ contains all codewords corresponding to horizontal edges in $\mathcal{E}$, and is a subset of L_f. Each H_j can be described by a nondeterministic finite automaton having $O(t^2)$ states: As all words in the sets X_j and Y_j have length m, each of them can be accepted by an NFA with $O(2^{m/2}) = o(t)$ states. The language M can be accepted by a NFA with $O(2^{2(m+2)}) = O(t^2)$ states. A schematic drawing of such an automaton is given in Figure 6.2. And a standard construction for nondeterministic finite automata yields an automaton with $O(t^2)$ states for the concatenation of these languages. Finally, the union of these languages can be accepted by an NFA having $O(t^2 \cdot (s/t^2)) = O(s)$ many states. We use a similar matching language as M to construct an NFA accepting a subset of the codewords of $\mathcal{E}$ which in particular contains all ascending edges. This time, the language has to ensure that the the left and the right vertex share the same row address, that is $M' = \{rc_1 c_2 r^R \mid r, c_1, c_2 \in \{0,1\}^{m+2}\}$, and this language can be accepted by an NFA with only $O(t \log t)$ states, see Figure 6.2 for illustration.

Following the idea in the proof of Theorem 6.3, the graph G has for every row p and every vertex $x_i \in X_B$ a biclique $G[X_{i,p}, Y_{i,p}]$ containing only ascending edges. As we have an ascending biclique for each $x_i \in \{0,1\}^m$, it is more economic to share the states needed for addressing. Thus, a part of the automaton is a binary tree, whose root is the start state and whose leaves address the nodes in X_B. That is, after reading a word x of length m, the automaton is in a unique leaf of the binary tree. In a symmetric manner, we construct an inverted binary tree whose leaves address the nodes in Y_B, and whose transitions are directed towards the root, which is the final state of the automaton. It remains to wire the copies of the automaton accepting M' into these two binary trees appropriately, using no more than $|X_B|$ copies of it: Each leaf x_i of the binary tree, addressing some node in X_B, is identified with the start state of a fresh copy of the NFA. The transitions entering the final state of this copy are replaced with transitions entering the inverted binary tree at the appropriate address. This completes the description of the construction for an NFA that accepts a subset of $\mathcal{E}$ which includes all ascending edges, whilst having only

$$O(|X_B| + |Y_B| + |X_B| \cdot t \log t) = O(|X|^{2/3} \log |X|)$$

states—recall that $|X| = \Theta(t^3)$ and $|X_B| = |Y_B| = \Theta(t)$.

For the descending edges, we carry out a similar construction, this time using the language $M'' = \{\, r_1 cc^r r_2 \mid r_1, c, r_2 \in \{0,1\}^{m+2}\,\}$ ensuring that the column addresses match, see again Figure 6.2 for illustration. Then a similar construction gives a compact NFA describing the codewords of a set of edges including all descending edges in G. Finally, the union of all these languages can be described by an NFA with the desired upper bound on the number of states. This completes the proof of Claim 6.8. □

The upper bound $O(s) + O(|X|^{2/3} \log |X|)$ given by Claim 6.8 does not suffice by itself to establish a C-reduction from the graph coloring problem to our problem. But by proceeding as in the proof of Lemma 6.5, we can ensure that any biclique edge edge cover for G has cardinality at least $\Omega(|X|^{2/3} \log |X|)$, while increasing the input expansion of the C-reduction only by a polylogarithmic factor.

On these instances, Claim 6.8 transforms a biclique edge cover of size at most s into an NFA of size $O(s)$ accepting L_f, and together with Claim 6.7, this establishes a linear relation between the optimum solution values. Altogether, this gives a C-reduction from the graph coloring problem with input expansion $N \leq |V|^6 (\log |V|)^{O(1)}$, where the polylogarithmic factor is due to the reduction given in the proof of Lemma 6.5, which ensures that the bipartite dimension of the biclique edge cover problem instances is large enough. □

For transition minimization we encounter the following situation.

Theorem 6.9. *Given a truth table of size N for a Boolean function f, no polynomial-time algorithm can approximate the number of transitions of a transition minimal nondeterministic finite automaton accepting L_f with performance ratio $N^{1/6-\varepsilon}$, for all $\varepsilon > 0$, unless* **P = NP.**

Proof. We can mimic the proof of Theorem 6.6 if we are able to establish counterparts of Claim 6.7 and Claim 6.8 with respect to the number of transitions.

Claim 6.10. The nondeterministic transition complexity of L_f is bounded below by the bipartite dimension of G minus 1.

Proof. Immediate from the inequality $\mathrm{ntc}(L) \geq \mathrm{nsc}(L) - 1$ for each regular language L. □

For an upper bound on $\mathrm{ntc}(L_f)$, we take a closer look at the NFA constructed in the proof of Claim 6.8.

Claim 6.11. Given a biclique edge cover of size at most s for G, we can construct in polynomial time an NFA accepting L_f having at most $O(s) + O(|X|^{2/3} \log |X|)$ transitions.

Proof. The number of transitions in the NFA accepting $H_j = X_j \cdot M \cdot Y_j$, can be seen to be in $O(|V|^2)$ transitions. There the number of transitions is dominated by those needed in order to accept M. But for this language, Figure 6.2 depicts the structure of an automaton whose number of transitions is linear in the number of states. The other matching languages M' and M'' can be also accepted by automata whose number of transitions is linear in the number of states.

In the construction for the ascending edges, the remaining point to verify is that that the wiring of the copies of the automata accepting M' into the two binary trees mentioned in the proof of Claim 6.8 does not require too many additional transitions. The construction requires to replace each transition that would end in the final state of the automaton accepting M' with several transitions ending in the appropriate leaves in the inverted binary tree. Note that the number of transitions entering the final state of the automaton accepting M' is exactly 2, and each of these is replaced with transitions ending in at most $|Y_B|$ many leaves. Thus the number of additional transitions is at most $2|Y_B| - 2 = O(t)$, and this is linear in the number of transitions already present in the automaton accepting M'. Essentially the same argument holds for the wiring of the automaton accepting M'' into the two binary trees. This establishes the second claim. □

As in the proof of Theorem 6.6, this gives a C-reduction from the graph coloring problem with input expansion $(O(n^6(\log n)^{O(1)}), |V|, N)$. □

In case the input is specified as a list of words instead of a truth table, we get an improved inapproximability result because the finite language we used in the above reduction allows a more compact description if we specify it as a list of words, rather than as a truth table:

Theorem 6.12. *Given a list of words of total length N specifying a finite language L over a binary alphabet, no polynomial-time algorithm can approximate the number of states of a minimum state nondeterministic finite automaton accepting L with performance ratio $N^{1/5-\varepsilon}$, for all $\varepsilon > 0$, unless $\mathbf{P} = \mathbf{NP}$. The same bound applies when minimizing the number of transitions instead of the number of states.*

Proof. The language L_f defined in the proof of Theorem 6.6 based on the bipartite graph $G = (X, Y, \mathcal{E})$ contains $|\mathcal{E}| = O(2^{5m})$ words, each of length $6m + 8$. The inapproximability results are obtained with the same reduction as in the proof of Theorem 6.6 and Theorem 6.9, but instead of a truth table of size $O(2^{6m})$, we now construct a list of words of total length $O(m2^{5m}) = O(\log(|X|) \cdot |X|^{5/3})$, and the inapproximability ratio changes accordingly.

□

Remark. We established C-reductions from the graph coloring problem to various NFA minimization problems. While strong inapproximability results for the graph coloring problem are known, the author is not aware of any published proof that the graph coloring problem is **poly-APX**-hard. For the somewhat similar clique problem [63, Problem GT19], **poly-APX**-hardness follows from one of the main results of [121], together with a few technicalities explained in [29, Lemma 21] (attributed to M. Sudan) and [175, Theorem 3.22]. In [121], it is furthermore claimed that the clique and graph coloring problems are mutually reducible, yet that claim is not elaborated upon any further. Notice that the standard gap preserving reduction from the clique problem to the graph coloring problem, see e.g. [182], preserves the gap between optimum values, but there seems to be no obvious way to turn this argument into a C-reduction. Clearly, together with the results presented above, **poly-APX**-hardness of the graph coloring problem would immediately imply **poly-APX**-completeness for all of these NFA minimization problems.

We conclude this section by showing that two simple approaches can be used to obtain nontrivial approximations for truth table specifications:

Theorem 6.13. *(i) Given a truth table of size $N = 2^m$, specifying an m-bit Boolean function function f, then there is a polynomial-time algorithm approximating the number of states of a state minimal nondeterministic finite automaton accepting L_f within a factor of $O(N^{1/2}/\log N)$. (ii) When considering transition minimization the performance ratio changes to $O(N/(\log N)^2)$.*

Proof. First we note that nondeterministic state and transition complexity are both at least $m = \log N$, except when L_f is empty. For state minimization we use the construction used in Chapter 4 for the proof of Lemma 4.7, to obtain an NFA with $O(N^{1/2})$ states. This construction can be implemented to run in time polynomial in the number of words in L_f. For transition minimization, a result by Champarnaud and Pin [26] states that the minimal DFA accepting a language in $\{0, 1\}^m$ always has at most $O(2^m/m) = O(N/\log N)$ states and transitions. From this the stated bounds easily follow. □

We remark that the given constructions for minimizing the number of states and transitions are of rather different nature.

6.3 Approximability for Given DFA

In this section, we consider the case where the input is specified as a DFA. Since a list of words can be readily transformed into a decision-tree-like deterministic finite automaton without increase in size, the same bound on approximability as in Theorem 6.12 for state and transition minimization holds, namely $n^{1/5-\varepsilon}$, for all $\varepsilon > 0$. If we allow alphabets of growing size $O(n)$ and consider state minimization, that bound can be improved as follows:

Lemma 6.14. *Given a n-state deterministic finite automaton A accepting a finite language over an alphabet of size $O(n)$, no efficient algorithm can approximate the number of states of a state minimal nondeterministic finite automaton accepting $L(A)$ with performance ratio $n^{1/3-\varepsilon}$, for all $\varepsilon > 0$, unless $\mathbf{P} = \mathbf{NP}$.*

Proof. We can again use the reduction given by Amilhastre et al. in [3, Lemma 1], which we already used in the proof of Theorem 5.4, where we analyzed the classical computational complexity of the present problem:

If we interpret the edge set of a bipartite graph $G = (X, Y, E)$ as a set of words $L \subseteq X \cdot Y$, then a biclique edge cover of size k for G naturally gives rise to a $k + 2$-state NFA, and *vice versa*. Since every language of this form can be described by a DFA with state set Q

of size at most $|X| + 2$, this gives a C-reduction with input expansion $|Q| = O(|X|)$, and the approximability bound follows with Theorem 6.3.

$\square$

Remark. Notice that the proof of the above lemma offers no clues at all about the (computational or approximation) hardness of transition minimization.

On the positive side, we can prove approximation guarantees if we consider *unary* languages specified by a DFA. Next we describe an approximation algorithm, which, for a given DFA accepting a unary language, constructs in polynomial time an equivalent NFA whose size is at most quadratic in the size of a minimum equivalent NFA. A similar result was obtained by Gramlich [69] for the further restriction to unary cyclic languages. This subclass of the unary regular languages was defined in Chapter 2.1. Our algorithm extends the basic approach due to Gramlich [69] to the non-cyclic case. For the proof of this approximation guarantee, we collect first some known facts about unary finite automata.

It is not difficult to see that a unary DFA consists of a path starting in the initial state, followed by a cycle of one or more states. Following the usual notational convention introduced by Chrobak [33], the *size* of a unary DFA is the pair (λ, μ), where $\lambda \geq 1$ and $\mu \geq 0$ denote the number of states in the cycle and in the path, respectively. The following characterization of minimal unary DFAs is found e.g. in [154]:

Theorem 6.15. *A unary DFA of size (λ, μ) accepting the language L is minimal if and only if the following two conditions are met:*

1. *For any maximal proper divisor d of λ, there exists an integer h with $0 < h < \lambda$ such that $a^{\mu+h} \in L$ if and only if $a^{\mu+h+d} \notin L$, and*

2. *$a^{\mu-1} \in L$ if and only if for all $k > 0$ holds $a^{\mu+k\cdot\lambda-1} \notin L$.*

As a corollary, we obtain:

Corollary 6.16. *Assume A is a minimal unary DFA of size (λ, μ). Then both λ and μ are minimal parameters among all DFA accepting L, i.e., there is no equivalent DFA of size (λ', μ') with $\lambda' < \lambda$ or $\mu' < \mu$.* $\square$

For unary NFAs, Chrobak [33] suggested a normal form generalizing the one for DFAs. A unary NFA in this normal form consists of a path that starts in the initial state and one or more mutually disjoint cycles. The behavior of such an automaton is almost everywhere deterministic, except for the last state on the path component: Here the automaton branches nondeterministically into one state for each of the cycles. A unary NFA of this form is said to be in *Chrobak normal form*. The size notation (λ, μ) for DFAs naturally carries over to NFAs, but now λ refers to the total number of states belonging to cycles. Next, we recall the main result of Chrobak[3] relating nondeterministic state complexity and unary NFAs in Chrobak normal form from [33].

Theorem 6.17. *For every n-state unary NFA, there is an equivalent NFA in Chrobak normal form of size (n, μ) and an equivalent DFA of size (λ, μ) with $\lambda = 2^{O(\sqrt{n \log n})}$ and $\mu = O(n^2)$.*

---

[3]The original proof contains an error, which was discovered and mended in [60]

Now we are ready to prove the announced approximability result.

Theorem 6.18. *There is a polynomial-time algorithm which, given a DFA of size (λ, μ) accepting a unary language L, constructs an equivalent NFA which has $O(\sqrt{\mu} + \log \lambda)$ times the size of the minimum state NFA—and this ratio guarantees a size in $O(\mathrm{nsc}(L)^2)$.*

Proof. We begin with a description of the algorithm: Without loss of generality, we assume that the given DFA is a minimal DFA. Our algorithm first constructs a minimal DFA of size $(\lambda, 0)$ accepting the derivative $L' = a^{-\mu}L$, which is cyclic and of minimal period λ. This can be easily done by "chopping the tail" of the DFA. Gramlich [69] shows that the problem under consideration is approximable within $O(\log \lambda)$ in the special case where the input is a cyclic DFA of period λ. In this way, we can construct an NFA A' in Chrobak normal form accepting L' of size at most $\ell = \mathrm{nsc}(L') \cdot O(\log \lambda)$ in time polynomial in the size of the input. By prepending the tail, which had been chopped, before the start state of A', and changing the starting point of the tail into the new start state of the resulting, we obtain an NFA A, which is the desired result.

The above construction assumes that when chopping tail, the tail maintains all accepting states on it. Then the the constructed NFA A accepts L. Clearly this algorithm runs in polynomial time. It remains to argue that the algorithm achieves the desired performance ratio. In the case $\mu = 0$, the described algorithm coincides with the one given by Gramlich [69] and gives the performance ratio $O(\log \lambda)$. Thus, the claimed performance ratio is correct in this case.

For the case $\mu > 0$, we will prove first that each NFA in Chrobak normal form accepting L has at least μ states which are not part of any cycle, which we will refer to as the tail length of the automaton. For the sake of contradiction, assume C is an NFA in Chrobak normal form accepting L whose tail length is $\mu' < \mu$. The determinization procedure given in the proof of [33, Theorem 4.4] shows that an equivalent DFA of size (λ', μ') can be constructed from C, for some λ'. But this DFA still accepts L, contradicting Corollary 6.16.

Thus the NFA A constructed by the above algorithm is in Chrobak normal form, is of size (ℓ, μ), and the parameter μ is minimal among all automata in Chrobak normal form. By Theorem 6.17, this implies that $\mu = O(\mathrm{nsc}(L)^2) = \mathrm{nsc}(L) \cdot O(\sqrt{\mu})$. Since $\ell = \mathrm{nsc}(L') \cdot O(\log \lambda)$, the last step in establishing the equation $\ell + \mu = \mathrm{nsc}(L) \cdot O(\sqrt{\mu} + \log \lambda)$ is to show that $\mathrm{nsc}(L') = O(\mathrm{nsc}(L))$:

Let $n = \mathrm{nsc}(L)$. Again by Theorem 6.17, we deduce that there is an NFA in Chrobak normal form of size (n, m) for some tail length m. An NFA accepting $a^{-m}L$ in Chrobak normal form of size at most $n + 1$ is obtained from this automaton by replacing the states in the tail with a single start state and connecting it to the cycles appropriately.

We claim that $\mathrm{nsc}(a^{-m}L) = \mathrm{nsc}(L')$. Surely we have $m \geq \mu$, since we observed before that μ is the minimum possible tail length among all NFAs in Chrobak normal form accepting L. Thus, for some $x \geq 0$, the quotient $a^{-m}L$ can be written as

$$a^{-m}L = a^{-x}(a^{-\mu}L). \tag{6.7}$$

As $L' = a^{-\mu}L$ is a unary cyclic language with period λ, it also holds $a^{-m}L = a^{-x+k\lambda}(a^{-\mu}L)$, for all $k \in \mathbb{Z}$. For k large enough, $-x + k\lambda > 0$, and we obtain another quotient equation, namely

$$a^{-\mu}L = a^{-k\lambda+x}(a^{-m}L). \tag{6.8}$$

Thus the languages $a^{-\mu}L$ and $a^{-m}L$ are mutual quotients.

Now a basic result [58, Theorem 26] about the nondeterministic state complexity of quotients is that for each unary regular language L and each unary word w, we have $\mathrm{nsc}(w^{-1}L) \leq \mathrm{nsc}(L)$. Together with Equations (6.7) and (6.8), which imply that the languages are mutual quotients, we immediately obtain

$$\mathrm{nsc}(a^{-\mu}L) \leq \mathrm{nsc}(a^{-m}L) \leq \mathrm{nsc}(a^{-\mu}L),$$

hence $\mathrm{nsc}(L') = \mathrm{nsc}(a^{-m}L)$ as desired.

Finally, since μ is equals the minimum tail length among all NFAs in Chrobak normal form accepting L, with Theorem 6.17, we observe that $O(\sqrt{\mu} + \log \lambda) = O(\mathrm{nsc}(L))$. □

6.4 Approximability for Given NFA

We turn to the question of approximability when the input is given as NFA. Here, Gramlich and Schnitger [70] showed that the situation is hopeless in the case of alphabets of size at least two:

Theorem 6.19. *Given an n-state NFA over binary alphabet, it is impossible to approximate the nondeterministic state complexity of the accepted language within a factor of $o(n)$, unless* **P** = **PSPACE***.*

The proof of that theorem is robust in the sense that the same result holds when the objective is transition minimization:

Corollary 6.20. *Given an NFA with n transitions over binary alphabet, it is impossible to approximate the nondeterministic transition complexity of the accepted language within a factor of $o(n)$, unless* **P** = **PSPACE***.*

Still along the same lines, Gramlich and Schnitger obtained a corresponding hardness result for the problem of minimizing regular expressions:

Corollary 6.21. *Given a regular expression of size n over binary alphabet, it is impossible to approximate the alphabetic width of the described language within a factor of $o(n)$, unless* **P** = **PSPACE***.*

When restricting to unary languages, they obtained a somewhat weaker bound on the limits of approximability, namely a bound of $\sqrt{n}/\ln n$. For constructive approximability, that is, if we require to construct an equivalent NFA instead of merely estimating the nondeterministic state complexity, their bound improves to $n^{1-\delta}$ for each $\delta > 0$ (unless **P** = **NP**).

Here we optimally determine the approximability of the problem for given unary NFA: Again the problem is not approximable within $o(n)$, as in the case of binary alphabets—of course the hardness assumption must be adjusted to $\mathbf{P} \neq \mathbf{NP^{NP}}$, or equivalently $\mathbf{P} \neq \mathbf{NP}$, since, as previously explained, the minimization problem for this restriction is in $\mathbf{NP^{NP}}$.

Theorem 6.22. *Given an n-state NFA accepting a unary language L, it is impossible to approximate $\mathrm{nsc}(L)$ within a factor of $o(n)$, unless* **P** = **NP***.*

Proof. Our proof is an adaptation of the classical proof of the fact that the problem of determining whether a unary NFA accepts the universal language $\{a\}^*$ is **coNP**-hard [172]. For convenience and ease of notation, we outline the modified construction completely, not just the modifications.

This proof is by a reduction from the **coNP**-complete unsatisfiability problem for 3SAT-formulas in conjunctive normal form [63, LO2]: Given Φ as the conjunction of clauses $C_1, C_2, \ldots, C_m$ in the variables $x_1, x_2, \ldots, x_n$, where each clause is the disjunction of at most 3 literals, it is **coNP**-complete to determine whether Φ is unsatisfiable. This problem remains **coNP**-hard if we require that no clause has more than one occurrence of each variable, and that the last clause is of the form $C_m = (x_n)$, where x_n is a variable occurring only in C_m. For reasons that will become later obvious, on this point we differ from the classical reduction. Now the core idea of the original construction is to find a suitable unary representation of truth assignments in $\{0,1\}^n$ for the variables $x_1, x_2, \ldots, x_n$. Let $p_1, p_2, \ldots, p_n$ be n distinct primes (to be fixed later), among which p_n is the largest and p_{n-1} is the second largest one. Define the function $r : \mathbb{N} \to \mathbb{N}^n$ as

$$r(x) = \begin{pmatrix} x \mod p_1 \\ x \mod p_2 \\ \vdots \\ x \mod p_n \end{pmatrix}.$$

If $r(x) \in \{0,1\}^n$, we call x a *representation*. According to the Chinese Remainder Theorem [89], every y in $\{0,1\}^n$ has a unique representation $r^{-1}(y)$ when reduced modulo $\prod_{i=1}^{n} p_i$.

We will define a language L_Φ which is equal to $\{a\}^*$ if and only if Φ is unsatisfiable. First, let $\overline{R_i} = \{\, a^k \mid k \mod p_i \notin \{0,1\} \,\}$. Then we have

$$\overline{R} = \{\, a^k \mid k \text{ does not represent an assignment} \,\} = \bigcup_{i=1}^{n} \overline{R_i},$$

and an NFA accepting this language can be constructed in time $O(n \cdot p_n)$. Next, observe for a clause C with variables, say, x_1, x_2, x_3, there is a unique assignment a_1, a_2, a_3 to these variables such that the clause is not satisfied. Thus the language of all representations x such that $r(x)$ does not satisfy C is given by

$$L(C) = \bigcap_{i=1}^{3} \{\, a^k \mid k \mod p_i = a_i \,\}.$$

Also, an NFA accepting L_C of size $p_1 \cdot p_2 \cdot p_3$ can be constructed in time polynomial in p_n.

Finally, we define the language L_Φ as $\bigcup_{i=1}^{m} L(C_i) \cup \overline{R}$. It can be readily seen that L_Φ is a cyclic language, and that $L_\Phi = \{a\}^*$ if and only if Φ is unsatisfiable.

Given the list of primes and the formula Φ, we can construct an NFA accepting L_Φ in time polynomial in $p_n \cdot m$, whose states are arranged in a union of cycles. Moreover, if p_n is used to represent the special variable x_n, then among the cycles of the constructed NFA, there needs to be only a single one whose length is a multiple of p_n, namely for the language $\overline{R_n} \cup L(C_m)$. The latter language has period p_n. So we can assume that the size of this automaton equals $N = p_n + O(m \cdot p_{n-1}^3)$. Now we fix the primes $p_1, p_2, \ldots, p_{n-1}$ to be the first $n-1$ primes. By the prime number theorem holds $p_{n-1} \leq 2n \ln n$ for n

large enough [89], thus these primes can be found in time polynomial in n. Now comes the second point where we deviate from the classical reduction: We want to achieve that the size of p_n predominates in the size of the constructed NFA, so we set p_n to be the first prime greater than $m(p_{n-1})^3$. Bertrand's Postulate (see [89] for a proof) asserts that $p_n \leq 2m(p_{n-1})^3$, and thus p_n can also be found in time polynomial in $m \cdot n$. We conclude that for the size of the constructed NFA holds $N = \Theta(p_n)$.

Clearly, if Φ is unsatisfiable, then $L_\Phi = \{a\}^*$, and $\mathrm{nsc}(L_\Phi) = 1$. For the other case, the classical construction was analyzed in [70, Lemma 19]. There it was shown that the minimal period of L_Φ is at least $\frac{1}{2}\prod_{i=1}^{n} p_i$, provided L_Φ is not universal—the proof was given in the setup where the involved primes to represent the truth assignments are the first n primes, but the proof is valid for any set of n distinct primes. As L_Φ is cyclic, its nondeterministic state complexity is bounded below by the largest prime power dividing its minimal period [112, Corollary 2.1]. Thus $\mathrm{nsc}(L_\Phi) \geq p_n = \Omega(N)$ in this case, where N is the number of states of the given NFA.

Now assume there is a polynomial time algorithm approximating the size of a minimal equivalent unary NFA within $o(N)$, where N is the number of states of the given NFA. Then this algorithm could be applied to decide whether $\mathrm{nsc}(L_\Phi) = o(p_n)$, thus solving a **coNP**-hard problem in polynomial time, which implies **P** = **NP**. □

This last proof also works, with obvious modifications, if the input is specified as a regular expression, and/or if we want to approximate the minimum number of transitions or the size of a minimum equivalent regular expression, hence we obtain the following as simple corollaries:

Corollary 6.23. *Given an NFA with n transitions accepting a unary language L, it is impossible to approximate $\mathrm{ntc}(L)$ within a factor of $o(n)$, unless* **P** = **NP**. □

For regular expression minimization, the statement reads as follows:

Corollary 6.24. *Given a regular expression of size n denoting a unary language L, it is impossible to approximate the minimum alphabetic width $\mathrm{alph}(L)$- within a factor of $o(n)$, unless* **P** = **NP**. □

We omit the statements for various other cases, such as of given regular expression over unary alphabet, and objective to estimate the nondeterministic state complexity.

7 Summary of Results on NFA Minimization

We close this part with a short summary of our results on minimum nondeterministic finite automata. In contrast to the DFA model, NFAs with minimum number of states, or transitions, do not admit a nice characterization, so we have to resort to estimates. We started our investigation in Chapter 3 with presenting two lower bound techniques, a simple one, which is rather easy to apply and often gives good enough results, and a more sophisticated one, which is more difficult to apply but proved useful at various places in subsequent chapters. We also saw that we cannot expect too much from these techniques: also the more powerful technique can have an exponential relative error. We remark that this observation was strengthened in a new study, where Hromkovič et al. investigated seemingly promising generalizations of this proof technique, but they found examples witnessing that these techniques again can only attain poor guarantees on relative error [98].

All these methods concerned the number of states in NFAs, so we also looked at the relation between number of states and transitions in this automaton model. There we showed that state and transition minimization are rather different problems, and the two can even be opposite goals. Then we proved that transition complexity can be much larger than state complexity. Here, of course, much larger does not mean exponential, since there is a trivial quadratic upper bound for constant size alphabets. We mention that the question of whether such a quadratic bound can be reached is wide open: Our lower bound was based on a counting argument, and proof techniques giving superlinear lower bounds for concrete families of witness languages are rare, and the few existing ones appear to be rather specialized. In this context, the works of Domaratzki and Salomaa [51], and of Hromkovič and Schnitger [99] are worth mentioning as they prove such superlinear lower bounds. Futher pointers to the literature on this topic are found in two recent surveys by Holzer and Kutrib [93] and by Salomaa [164].

We then turned to the computational complexity of NFA minimization. As we have seen, varying the input representation and/or the restriction to subfamilies of the regular languages gives rise to a rich panoply of NFA minimization problems. In the tables below, we summarize known and new complexity and approximability results regarding various NFA minimization problems.

It is worth mentioning that another line of research we did not touch upon concerns the NFA minimization problem for finite automata with restricted nondeterminism: For example, unambiguous finite automata are restricted nondeterministic finite automata, where every accepted word has at most one accepting computation—and possibly several other computations that do not lead to a final state. Since DFAs are easily seen to be unambiguous, this automaton model also describes all regular languages. While unambiguous finite automata can still allow exponential space savings over DFAs, see e.g. [143], the equivalence problem of unambiguous finite automata can be decided in polynomial time [171], and the complexity of the unambiguous finite automaton minimization problem is **NP**-complete [114], and thus probably less complex than the **PSPACE**-complete NFA minimization problem. This prompted researchers to investigate the minimization problem for classes of automata whose nondeterministic choices are still further restricted, hoping to find a model of finite automata that can offer space savings over the deterministic model while also admitting minimization in polynomial time. However, it turns out that even the slightest nondeterministic extensions of the deterministic model will render the resulting minimization problem intractable, i.e. **NP**-complete, see [16, 134]. Several recent surveys covering this and related developments are available, see e.g. [93, 94, 100].

So, what can be done at all about the NFA minimization problem from a practical viewpoint? There is the exact exponential algorithm by Kameda and Weiner [117], but this algorithm is commonly considered impractical as it uses exponential space, cf. [109]. To date we are not aware of any implementation of that algorithm. Nevertheless a few heuristics for reducing the size of a given NFA are available [25, 109, 111], which run in polynomial time. All of these attempt to generalize the Myhill-Nerode relation. Recall that the equivalence classes of the latter relation correspond to the states in the state minimal DFA. The common idea is to find a generalized notion of similarity among states, such that similar states can be merged into a single state. State merging may result in very poor performance in the worst case [85, 131]. At the very least, preliminary experiments indicate that such heuristics can sometimes effectively shrink the given NFAs [25, 111].

NFA → NFA

Instance : NFA A, integer k.

Solution : Number of states of a smallest NFA equivalent to A.

Complexity : **PSPACE**-complete, also for transition minimization [172].

Approximability : Not approximable within $o(n)$ unless $\mathbf{P} = \mathbf{PSPACE}$ [70]; same applies for transition minimization and smallest equivalent regular expression, and also when given regular expression instead of NFA.

DFA → NFA

Instance : DFA A, integer k.

Solution : Number of states of a smallest NFA equivalent to A.

Complexity : **PSPACE**-complete [114], for transition minimization **NP**-hard (Theorem 5.2).

Approximability : Unless $\mathbf{P} = \mathbf{NP}$, not approximable within $O(n^{1/3-\varepsilon})$ for growing alphabet size (Theorem 6.14) and within $O(n^{1/5-\varepsilon})$ for fixed alphabet size (Theorem 6.12), for all $\varepsilon > 0$. Under certain cryptographic assumption not even approximable within better than $n^{1/2}/(\log n)^{O(1)}$ [70]. For transition minimization, the inapproximability bound is $n^{1/5-\varepsilon}$ (Theorem 6.12), and under cryptographic assumption even $n/(\log n)^{O(1)}$ [70].

Acyclic DFA → NFA

Instance : Acyclic DFA A, integer k.

Solution : Number of states of a smallest NFA equivalent to A.

Comment : Contained in $\mathbf{NP^{NP}}$ (also for given NFA) but $\mathbf{DP}$-hard (Theorem 5.4), for transition minimization **NP**-hard (Theorem 5.2).

Approximability : Unless $\mathbf{P} = \mathbf{NP}$, not approximable within $O(n^{1/3-\varepsilon})$ for growing alphabet size (Theorem 6.14) and within $O(n^{1/5-\varepsilon})$ for fixed alphabet size (Theorem 6.12), for all $\varepsilon > 0$. For transition minimization, approximability bound is $n^{1/5-\varepsilon}$, for fixed or growing alphabet size (Theorem 6.12).

List of words → NFA

Instance : Finite language L as a list of words, integer k.

Solution : Number of states of a smallest NFA accepting L.

Comment : **NP**-complete, also for transition minimization (Theorem 5.2).

Approximability : Unless $\mathbf{P} = \mathbf{NP}$, not approximable within $O(n^{1/5-\varepsilon})$ (Theorem 6.12), for all $\varepsilon > 0$. Same bounds apply to transition minimization.

Truth table → NFA
Instance : Truth table describing an m-bit Boolean function f, integer k.
Solution : Number of states of a smallest NFA accepting $L_f = f^{-1}(1)$.
Comment : **NP**-complete, also for transition minimization (Theorem 5.2).
Approximability : Unless $\mathbf{P} = \mathbf{NP}$, not approximable within $O(n^{1/6-\varepsilon})$ (Theorem 6.6), for all $\varepsilon > 0$, where $n = 2^m$ denotes input size. Same bounds hold for transition minimization. Approximable within $O(n^{1/2}/\log n)$, respectively $O(n/\log n)$ for transition minimization (Theorem 6.13).

Unary DFA → NFA
Instance : Unary DFA A, integer k.
Solution : Number of states of a smallest NFA equivalent to A.
Comment : Contained in $\mathbf{NP^{NP}}$, and if given DFA is cyclic, even in $\mathbf{NP}$; but not contained in $\mathbf{P}$ unless all problems in $\mathbf{NP}$ are deterministically decidable in quasipolynomial time [112].
Approximability : Approximable within $O(n^{1/2})$, and indeed within $O(\mathrm{opt}^2)$ (Theorem 6.18). If given unary DFA is cyclic, approximable within $O(\log n)$, and indeed within $O(\mathrm{opt}^{3/2} \cdot \log \mathrm{opt})$ [69].

Unary NFA → NFA
Instance : Unary NFA A, integer k.
Solution : Number of states of a smallest NFA equivalent to A.
Comment : Contained in $\mathbf{NP^{NP}}$, but $\mathbf{coNP}$-hard [172].
Approximability : Not approximable within $o(n)$ unless $\mathbf{P} = \mathbf{NP}$ (Theorem 6.22); same applies for transition minimization and smallest equivalent regular expression, and also when given regular expression instead of NFA.

Part III

Converting Finite Automata into Regular Expressions

8 Lower Bounds for the Conversion Problem: Infinite Languages

In this part of the thesis, we shall deal with the problem of converting finite automata into regular expressions. The results of the previous chapter imply that obtaining an equivalent regular expression of minimum size is computationally hard. In this part, we want to address the question mainly from the viewpoint of descriptional complexity. Throughout, our investigations will be centered around the following question:

> Given a finite automaton, determine bounds on the size of a smallest equivalent regular expression in the worst case.

This conversion problem has received by far not that much attention as the converse problem of converting regular expressions into finite automata. For recent references concerning the latter problem, see e.g. [110, 86, 103, 165].Nevertheless, it is arguably of fundamental nature. Indeed, most textbooks on automata theory have a section devoted to both conversion problems, see e.g. [96]. Furthermore, we are aware of applications of this problem in the fields of software maintenance [148] and model checking [42, 40]. Finally, as we shall see in the third part of this work, a deeper understanding of this problem enables us to analyze the effect of the most natural language operations on the size of regular expressions.

We have already mentioned in the introductory part (Section 2.2.5) that regular expressions can be converted into ε-NFAs of linear size, while the result by Ehrenfeucht and Zeiger (Theorem 2.11) states that the conversion in the back direction incurs an inevitable exponential blow-up in size: They found an infinite family of languages that admit n-state finite automata over an alphabet of size $O(n^2)$, but require regular expression size at least $2^{\Omega(n)}$. Unlike for the conversion problem of NFAs into DFAs, this blow-up is not caused by nondeterminism, and the result still holds if we consider converting DFAs into regular expressions.

Nevertheless, it can be argued that the examples given by Ehrenfeucht and Zeiger are somewhat contrived: the transition structure of their witness DFAs forms a complete digraph, and therefore the automata are over alphabets of largely growing size. But, as Sakarovitch [163] notes, the finite automata we are typically interested in do not have a complete digraph as transition structure. These considerations might qualify to sow the seeds of doubt in the reader's mind about the predictive value of the lower bound given by Ehrenfeucht and Zeiger. But we can reassure the reader, in that we shall prove in this chapter that for given a DFA over binary alphabets, a lower bound of $2^{\Omega(n)}$ on required expression size still holds—although we are unable to give a lower bound as strong as $\Omega(2^n)$ when restricting to binary alphabets.

In a previous effort on proving similar lower bounds for languages over fixed alphabets, Waizenegger [177] proposed a particular way of encoding the witness languages used by Ehrenfeucht and Zeiger in a fashion retaining all necessary features required to mimic the original proof. Unfortunately, there is a flaw as the encoding proposed by Waizenegger does not share all of the necessary features, as explained in [65]. Only very recently, Gelade and Neven were able to show that an alteration of the suggested method can be nevertheless made to work [65]. Here we choose an entirely different approach resulting from an independent effort, by relating the descriptional complexity of regular languages to their structural complexity. We shall describe this and the resulting lower bounds below. Recall that the star height of a regular expression measures the nesting depth of star operators in the expression, and that the star height of a regular language L, denoted by $h(L)$, is the minimum star height among all regular expressions describing L (compare Section 2.2.4). We will now forge a link between star height and alphabetic width of regular languages. This relation will allow us to reduce the task of proving lower bounds on alphabetic width to the one of proving lower bounds on star height.

8.1 Digraph Connectivity Measures and Star Height of Regular Languages

As we shall see, the star height of regular languages is related to a certain connectivity measure on digraphs. Before we study this relation, let us recall some basic facts about some connectivity measures on *undirected* graphs first. A very popular measure for the structural complexity of graphs is (undirected) treewidth, first studied (under a different name) by Halin [87]. This concept remained largely unnoticed until it was rediscovered by two independent groups of researchers [6, 159], who noticed that many hard computational problems become tractable when restricted to graphs of small treewidth. The definition reads as follows, compare [48]:

Definition 8.1. Let $G = (V, E)$ be an undirected graph, and assume $\mathcal{V} = \{U_1, U_2, \ldots, U_r\}$ is a collection of subsets of V. A tree $\mathcal{T} = (\mathcal{V}, \mathcal{E})$ with vertex set $\mathcal{V}$ is called a *tree decomposition*, if all of the following conditions hold:

- The collection $\mathcal{V}$ covers the vertex set of the graph G, in the sense that $V = \bigcup_{U \in \mathcal{V}} U$.

- For every edge $(u, v) \in E$, there is a tree node $U \in \mathcal{V}$ such that both u and v are in U.

- If two tree nodes U_1 and U_2 are connected in the tree by a path, then $U_1 \cap U_2$ is a subset of each tree node visited along this path.

The *width* of a tree decomposition $\mathcal{T} = (\mathcal{V}, \mathcal{E})$ is defined as $\max\{\,|U| - 1 \mid U \in \mathcal{V}\,\}$, and the *undirected treewidth* of a graph G is defined as the minimum width among all tree decompositions for G. The undirected treewidth of a digraph is defined as the undirected treewidth of its symmetric closure.

For readers unfamiliar with treewidth, we illustrate this concept by a small example.

Example 8.2. Especially in electrical networks, we often encounter graphs that are recursively built from atomic units using series and parallel composition. An instance of such a series-parallel graph is depicted in Figure 8.1(a).

Series-parallel graphs always admit a tree decomposition of width at most 2, see [19] for a more detailed exposition. Informally, the tree decomposition given in Figure 8.1(b)

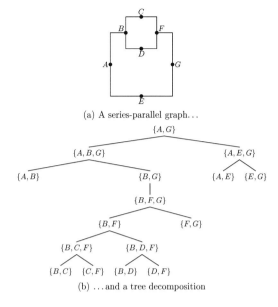

(a) A series-parallel graph...

$\{A, G\}$

$\{A, B, G\}$ $\{A, E, G\}$

$\{A, B\}$ $\{B, G\}$ $\{A, E\}$ $\{E, G\}$

$\{B, F, G\}$

$\{B, F\}$ $\{F, G\}$

$\{B, C, F\}$ $\{B, D, F\}$

$\{B, C\}$ $\{C, F\}$ $\{B, D\}$ $\{D, F\}$

(b) ...and a tree decomposition

Figure 8.1: An example of a series-parallel graph and a tree decomposition of width 2 for it.

exhibits the following pattern: A parallel composition gives rise to a tree node of cardinality 2, whose children are each of size 3. A series composition gives rise to a tree node of cardinality 3, whose children are each of size 2.

Intuitively, the treewidth of a graph measures its structural similarity to a tree. Not by coincidence, trees have treewidth at most 1, whereas a complete graph on n vertices treewidth $n - 1$, which is the maximum possible among graphs on n vertices. We also notice that trees are rather poorly connected: we can always remove a single vertex from the tree such that it falls apart into a bunch of smaller trees, each containing at most half of the original number of vertices. For highly connected graphs, such as complete graphs, this is impossible even if we are allowed to remove a larger portion of the vertices. This nice property of trees is captured by the following definition.

Definition 8.3. Let $G = (V, E)$ be a digraph and let $U \subseteq V$ be a set of vertices. A set of vertices S is a *balanced separator* (respectively *weak balanced separator*) for U if every component (respectively strong component) of $G[U \setminus S]$ contains at most $\frac{1}{2}|U|$ vertices.

For real numbers $0 \leq k \leq |V|$, let $\overrightarrow{s}(G, k)$ denote the maximum of the size of the smallest balanced separator for U, where the maximum is taken over all subsets U of size at most k of V. The *separator number* of G, denoted by $\overrightarrow{s}(G)$, is defined as $\overrightarrow{s}(G, |V|)$.

With the function $s(G, k)$ being the analogue to $\overrightarrow{s}(G, k)$ for weak balanced separators, the *weak separator number* is then defined as $s(G) = s(G, |V|)$.

Robertson and Seymour [160] observed that (di)graphs of low treewidth must necessarily have low separator number:

Lemma 8.4. *Let G be a digraph of undirected treewidth at most k. Then the separator number of G is at most $k + 1$.*

While the concept of treewidth proves most useful for symmetric digraphs (see e.g. [48]), it does not tell us much about the strong connectivity of digraphs in general. For, it is easily observed that there are acyclic digraphs on n vertices that still have undirected treewidth $n - 1$. We thus call to attention a structural complexity measure for digraphs intimately related to the star height of regular languages, called the cycle rank. This notion was suggested by Eggan and Büchi in the course of investigating the star height of regular languages [54].

Definition 8.5. The *cycle rank* of a directed graph $G = (V, E)$, denoted by $cr(G)$, is inductively defined as follows:

1. If G is acyclic, then $cr(G) = 0$.

2. If G is strongly connected and not acyclic, then

$$cr(G) = 1 + \min_{v \in V}\{cr(G - v)\}.$$

3. If G is not strongly connected, then $cr(G)$ equals the maximum cycle rank among all strongly connected components of G.

We continue our investigation of structural properties of digraphs before we turn our attention to the relation between cycle rank and star height. First, we establish a basic fact about cycle rank, which is used throughout the following sections. The second part of the following statement is found in [141, Theorem 2.4.], and the other part is established by an easy induction:

Lemma 8.6. *Let $G = (V, E)$ be a digraph and let $U \subseteq V$. Then we have the inequalities $cr(G) - |U| \le cr(G - U) \le cr(G)$.* $\qquad\square$

Above we have introduced the notion of (weak) balanced separators in digraphs, and noticed that low treewidth implies small separator number. In contrast, we shall now prove a result geared more toward digraphs, namely that small weak separator number implies that the cycle rank cannot be too large. This is an easy extension of the proof from [149] for the case of undirected graphs; see also [18] for an earlier proof of this special case.

Lemma 8.7. *Let $G = (V, E)$ be a digraph with $n \ge 1$ vertices. Then*

$$cr(G) \le 1 + s(G) \log n.$$

Proof. We first prove the following relation: Let $G = (V, E)$ be a digraph with $n \ge 1$ vertices. Then

$$cr(G) \le 1 + \sum_{0 \le k \le \log n - 1} s\left(G, \frac{n}{2^k}\right). \tag{8.1}$$

The proof proceeds by induction on n. The base case $n = 1$ is immediate because $cr(G) \le |V| = 1$. The induction step is as follows: By definition of weak separator number, G has a weak separator S of size at most $s(G, n)$. Let $C_1, C_2, \ldots, C_p$ be the strong components of $G - S$. Each of these has cardinality at most $\frac{n}{2}$. With Lemma 8.6, we obtain

$$cr(G) \leq |S| + \max_{1 \leq i \leq p} cr(G[C_i]) \leq s\left(G, \frac{n}{2^0}\right) + \max_{1 \leq i \leq p} cr(G[C_i]).$$

Since for each $k \leq n$ and for each strong component C_i obviously holds $s(G[C_i], k) \leq s(G, k)$, we have by induction hypothesis

$$\max_{1 \leq i \leq p} cr(G[C_i]) \leq 1 + \sum_{0 \leq k \leq \log(n/2)-1} s\left(G, \frac{n/2}{2^k}\right)$$

$$= 1 + \sum_{0 \leq k \leq \log n - 2} s\left(G, \frac{n}{2^{k+1}}\right)$$

$$= 1 + \sum_{1 \leq k \leq \log n - 1} s\left(G, \frac{n}{2^k}\right).$$

By putting the two inequalities together, this completes the proof of Inequality (8.1). Since for all $1 \leq k \leq n$ holds $s(G, k) \leq s(G)$, we finally have

$$cr(G) \leq 1 + \sum_{0 \leq k \leq \log n - 1} s(G) = 1 + s(G) \log n,$$

and the proof is completed.

□

Combining this with Lemma 8.4, we immediately obtain:

Corollary 8.8. *Let G be a digraph of undirected treewidth at most k. Then the cycle rank of G is at most $1 + (k + 1) \log n$.*

A similar statement, for undirected graphs, is found in [18]. After this short detour into the theory of digraphs, we now return to finite automata. In the following, we will be often concerned with the cycle rank of the digraph underlying the transition structure of finite automata. For a given finite automaton A, let its cycle rank, denoted by $cr(A)$, be defined as the cycle rank of the underlying digraph. The following relation between cycle rank of automata and star height of regular languages became known as Eggan's Theorem [54]:

Theorem 8.9 (Eggan). *The star height of a regular language L equals the minimum cycle rank among all ε-NFAs accepting L.*

The star height of a regular language is apparently a much more difficult concept than alphabetic width, compare [91, 124]. So proving lower bounds on alphabetic width *via* lower bounds on star height appears to be at first sight like trading a hard problem for an even harder one. But early research on the star height problem established a subclass of regular languages for which the star height is determined more easily, namely the family of bideterministic regular languages, which are defined as follows: A deterministic finite automaton is *bideterministic*, if it has a single final state, and if the NFA obtained by reversing all transitions and exchanging the roles of initial and final state is again deterministic—notice that, by construction, this NFA in any case accepts the reversed language. A regular language L is *bideterministic* if there exists a bideterministic finite automaton accepting L. These languages form a proper subclass of the regular languages. The star height of bideterministic languages was shown by McNaughton to be computable in [140], building on his earlier work which was, however, published only later in [141]:

Theorem 8.10 (McNaughton). *Let L be a bideterministic regular language, and let A be the minimal DFA accepting L. Then $h(L) = cr(A)$.*

In fact, the minimality requirement in the above theorem is not needed: An observation made by Angluin [4] is that a bideterministic finite automaton in which all states are useful is already guaranteed to be a minimal DFA. Recall from Chapter 2.2 that a state is useful if both it is reachable from the start state and some final state is reachable from it.

8.2 Star Height and Regular Expression Size

In this section, we show that the alphabetic width of a regular language can be bounded from below in terms of its star height.

We do this by transforming a given regular expression of size n into an equivalent regular expression of star height logarithmic in n. The essential idea of the proof is that every regular expression can be converted into an equivalent ε-NFA of linear size, and the resulting automaton has low undirected treewidth. Now if a digraph has low undirected treewidth, its cycle rank cannot be too large. Here Eggan's Theorem comes into play: An ε-NFA of low cycle rank can always be converted back into an equivalent regular expression of low star height.

At some point, the proof of the following theorem makes use of the fact that the treewidth of a graph is not increased during *edge contractions*. Here, an edge contraction of a graph is performed by deleting an edge while merging the two vertices belonging to the edge into a single vertex; this single vertex inherits the neighborhood of the former two vertices. A proof of this fact is found e.g. in the textbook [48].

Theorem 8.11. *Let $L \subseteq \Sigma^*$ be a regular language. Then*

$$\mathrm{alph}(L) \geq 2^{1/3(h(L)-1)} - 1.$$

Proof. Let r be a regular expression over Σ of alphabetic width $n = \mathrm{alph}(L)$. We will prove the equivalent statement that $h(L) \leq 3\log(n+1) + 1$: The construction given in [110] shows how to transform the expression r into an equivalent ε-NFA A having at most $n + 1$ states. Possibly after removing certain redundant subexpressions from r, such as replacing $(\varepsilon + \emptyset)^*$ with ε, the construction from [110] recursively applies the steps illustrated in Figures 8.2 to 8.6. Throughout the construction the invariant is maintained that the constructed ε-NFA has a single start state with no entering transitions and a single accepting state with no transitions leaving it.

Let G be the digraph underlying the transition structure of the resulting automaton A. We claim that its undirected treewidth is at most 2. It is well known that series-parallel graphs have treewidth at most 2, see [19], and from the perspective of the underlying graph, the construction steps for concatenation and union from Figures 8.4 and 8.5 are nothing else than series and parallel composition. On the contrary, the construction step for the star from Figure 8.6 appears to be problematic at first glance. But, as illustrated in Figure 8.7, the underlying *undirected* graph resulting from this construction can be equivalently obtained by a sequence of series and parallel compositions, followed by a single edge contraction. It is known that edge contractions cannot increase treewidth (see e.g. [48]), so the resulting graph is again of treewidth at most 2.

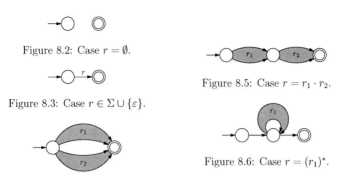

Figure 8.2: Case $r = \emptyset$.

Figure 8.5: Case $r = r_1 \cdot r_2$.

Figure 8.3: Case $r \in \Sigma \cup \{\varepsilon\}$.

Figure 8.6: Case $r = (r_1)^*$.

Figure 8.4: Case $r = r_1 + r_2$.

Figure 8.7: The effect of the star operation on the undirected graph simulated through series-parallel composition followed by edge contraction.

Now with Corollary 8.8, we can relate this to the cycle rank of the automaton and deduce that $cr(A) \leq 1 + 3\log(n+1)$. The final step is to invoke Eggan's Theorem (Theorem 9.9) to get $h(L) \leq cr(A)$.

$\square$

The following two examples indicate that the above bound can be almost attained, at least up to the factor $1/3$ in the exponent:

Example 8.12. Eggan [54] devised the following family of expressions r_n—in place of a formal definition of r_n, we provide the first few instances.

$$r_1 = a_1^*$$
$$r_2 = (a_1^* a_2^* a_3)^*$$
$$r_3 = ((a_1^* a_2^* a_3)^* (a_4^* a_5^* a_6)^* a_7)^*$$
$$r_4 = (((a_1^* a_2^* a_3)^* (a_4^* a_5^* a_6)^* a_7)^* ((a_8^* a_9^* a_{10})^* (a_{11}^* a_{12}^* a_{13})^* a_{14})^* a_{15})^*$$

He then went on to prove that $L(r_n)$ has star height n, thus showing that there exist regular languages of unbounded star height. Unwittingly he thus also provided infinitely many languages L having $\text{alph}(L) \leq 2^{h(L)} - 1$, which numerically gets close to the inequality given in the theorem above.

For similar examples over a small alphabet, we reconsider the "buffer" language L_n from Example 2.5. As noted there, the language L_4 admits the regular expression

$$\big(a\,(a\,(a(ab)^*b)^*b)^*b\big)^*.$$

A straightforward generalization of this type of expression yields $\text{alph}(L_n) \leq 2n$. In contrast, McNaughton [141] proved that $h(L_n) = \lfloor \log(n+1) \rfloor$. Also this result was originally proved with the goal of providing languages of unbounded star height—this time over binary alphabets.

In contrast, there cannot exist an upper bound on the alphabetic width in terms of star height, since all finite languages have star height 0, while for fixed alphabet there are only finitely many languages of bounded alphabetic width.

8.3 Cycle Rank *via* a Cops and Robber Game

Already McNaughton [141] suggested to view the cycle rank of a digraph as the optimum outcome of some "game against the graph." We will give a modern formulation of this idea below, in terms of a cops and robber game. This characterization provides a useful tool in proving lower bounds on the cycle rank of specific families of digraphs. Moreover, many other digraph connectivity measures proposed recently admit a characterization in terms of some cops and robber game, compare e.g. [11, 107, 150]; this allows to compare the cycle rank with these other measures more easily.

The *k cops and strong visible robber game*, as defined by Johnson et al. [116], is given as follows: Let $G = (V, E)$ be a digraph. Initially, the k cops occupy some set of $X \subseteq V$ vertices, with $|X| \leq k$, and the robber is placed on some vertex $v \in V \setminus X$. At any time, some of the cops can reside outside the graph, say, in a helicopter. In each round, the cop player chooses the next location $X' \subseteq V$ for the cops. The stationary cops in $X \cap X'$ remain in their positions, while the others go to the helicopter and fly to their new position. During this, the robber player, knowing the cops' next position X' from wiretapping the police radio, can run at great speed to any new position v', provided there is both a (possibly empty) directed path from v to v', and a (again, possibly empty) directed path back from v' to v in $G - (X \cap X')$, i.e., he has to avoid to run into a stationary cop, and to run along a path in, and to stay within, the same strong component of the remaining graph induced by the non-blocked vertices. Afterwards, the helicopter lands the cops at their new positions, and the next round starts, with X' and v' taking over the roles of X and v, respectively. The cop player wins the game if the robber cannot move any more, and the robber player wins if the robber can escape indefinitely. In this definition, the number k of cops is a parameter of the game.

The *immutable cops* variant of the above game restricts the movements of the cops in the following way: Once a cop has been placed on some vertex of the graph, he has to stay there forever. The *hot-plate* variant of the game restricts allowed the movements of the robber, in that he has to move along a nontrivial path in each move—although it is allowed that this path consists only of a self-loop. These games are robust in the sense that small variations of rules, such as letting the robber player begin, or allowing only the placement of one cop at a time, do not alter the number of required cops.

The following theorem gives a characterization of cycle rank in terms of such a game.

Theorem 8.13. *Let G be a digraph and $k \geq 0$. Then k cops have a winning strategy for the immutable cops and hot-plate strong visible robber game if and only if the cycle rank of G is at most k.*

Proof. We proceed by induction on n, the number of vertices in G. In case $n = 1$, the graph has either no edge, or exactly one edge. Since the robber has to move in each step, no cop, respectively, one cop is required to catch the robber.

To do the induction step for the "if" part, assume G has cycle rank at most k. We will show that k cops have a winning strategy for the immutable hot-plate strong visible robber game by induction on the number n of vertices in G.

Now we consider two cases:

1. If G is not strongly connected itself, the cops play $\emptyset$ in the first move, that is, none of the cops is placed on G. Let c be the first position played by the robber, and let C be the strong component containing c. Then the robber cannot ever leave the subgraph C. Thus it suffices to describe each a winning strategy for k cops on the induced subgraph $G[C]$ for every initial choice of the robber, that is, for each strong component of G. Since G is not strongly connected, each strong component has size at most $n-1$, and by induction assumption, k cops have a winning strategy on each of these, and hence on G.

2. The remaining case is that G is strongly connected. In this case, by definition of cycle rank, there exists some vertex v such that $cr(G-v) = cr(G) - 1$. In this case, we place the first cop on v, and the game continues on $G - v$. Since the latter graph has $n-1$ vertices, the induction assumption implies that the remaining $k-1$ cops have a winning strategy on $G - v$.

To do the induction step for the "only if" part, assume k cops have a winning strategy in the above game on G. Then they also have a winning strategy which plays $\emptyset$ unless the robber has moved for the first time. That is, they have a winning strategy for every subgraph induced by some strong component C of G. The cycle rank of G equals the maximum cycle rank among its strong components, so if G is not strongly connected, then $cr(G) \leq k$ follows by the induction assumption. In the other case, let U be the set of vertices occupied by the cops when the cop player makes a nontrivial move for the first time. Then the game continues on $G - U$, and there is a winning strategy for $k - |U|$ cops on $G - U$. By induction assumption, we have $cr(G - U) \leq k - |U|$. By Lemma 8.6, we have $cr(G) \leq cr(G - U) + |U|$, and thus $cr(G) \leq k$, as desired. $\qquad\square$

Also note that at most one additional cop is needed if we drop the hot-plate restriction: Dropping the hot-plate restriction can be simulated by adding for each vertex a self-loop and playing the game on the resulting digraph with the hot-plate restriction. Then the options for the robber to move remain the same as long as he stays in a strong component of size at least 2. The only thing that changes is that on the new graph, he might be still able to move when he is almost trapped, namely in a strong component, which was trivial in the original graph, but becomes nontrivial in the new digraph. But the cop player can easily compensate this disadvantage with one additional (immutable) cop. Restricting our attention to loop-free digraphs, we thus obtain the following characterization of cycle rank in terms of the game without the hot-plate restriction:

Corollary 8.14. *Let G be a loop-free digraph. Then $k + 1$ cops have a winning strategy for the immutable cops and strong visible robber game if and only if the cycle rank of G is at most k.*

Also observe that, as is immediate from the definition of cycle rank, adding self-loops to G can increase its cycle rank by at most 1.

8.4 Converting DFAs into Regular Expressions

By Theorem 8.13, the cycle rank of a digraph G can be described in terms of the immutable cops and strong visible robber game. The *greedy* strategy for the robber player is to choose in each step the largest strong component he can reach in the remaining graph. We will identify a class of graphs in which the greedy strategy is particularly successful, namely (undirected) expander graphs. Note that in the case of undirected graphs, i.e., symmetric digraphs, every connected component of size at least two is also a nontrivial strong component.

Definition 8.15. Let $G = (V, E)$ be a loop-free undirected graph. For a subset $U \subset V$, the vertex boundary of U, denoted by δU, is defined as

$$\delta U = \{\, v \in V \setminus U \mid \{u, v\} \in E \text{ for some } u \in U \,\}.$$

An (undirected) d-regular graph $G = (V, E)$ with n vertices is called a (n, d, c)-*expander*, for $c > 0$, if each subset $U \subset V$ of vertices satisfies

$$|\delta U| > c \cdot |U|, \text{ if } |U| < n/2, \text{ and } |\delta U| \geq c \cdot (n - |U|), \text{ if } |U| \geq n/2.$$

A now standard probabilistic argument, originally due to Pinsker [156], shows that expander graphs are the rule rather than the exception among d-regular graphs, for all $d \geq 3$.

Theorem 8.16 (Pinsker). *There exists a fixed $c > 0$ such that for any $d \geq 3$ and even integer n, there is an (n, d, c)-expander, which is furthermore d-edge-colorable.*[1]

The proof of the following theorem is similar to that of [15, Theorem 4], where it was shown that each directed expander graph contains a long directed path.

Theorem 8.17. *Let G be a (n, d, c)-expander with $n \geq 3$. Then the cycle rank of G is at least $\frac{c}{d+1}(n-1)$.*

Proof. We show that at least $\frac{c}{d+1} \cdot (n-1) - 1$ cops are needed in the immutable cops and strong visible robber game on G in order to catch the robber. Then the result follows by Corollary 8.14. It is no restriction to require that the set X_0 of initial positions for the cop player is empty, and that the cop player places exactly one new cop in the first and every following round. That is, if X_i denotes the set of positions occupied by the cops in round i, we have $|X_0| = 0$ and $|X_{i+1}| = |X_i| + 1$ for $i \geq 0$. It is convenient to think of the robber's moves as choosing a non-blocked (strongly) connected component C_i in round i, instead of choosing a position $v_i \in C_i$. Because of the expansion property, G is connected, and we have $C_0 = V$. It is also easy to see that $C_{i+1} \subseteq C_i$, for all rounds i.

For $i \geq 0$, consider the $(i + 1)$-th move of the robber. The strategy we use for the robber is a greedy choice, based on the size of the maximum strong component in the remaining graph. A more precise description follows. If the cop player places no cop on component C_i, the robber player stays where he is. So assume x_{i+1}, the position for the $(i + 1)$-th cop, is in C_i. By removing x_{i+1} from the graph $G[C_i]$, the remaining graph falls apart into connected components $C_{i+1}^{(1)}, C_{i+1}^{(2)}, \ldots, C_{i+1}^{(d')}$. Since G is d-regular, we have $1 \leq d' \leq d$. Among these, the robber player chooses the component of maximum size.

---

[1]That is, one can assign to its edges d colors such that no pair of incident edges receives the same color.

Since $\bigcup_{j=1}^{d'} G[C_{i+1}^{(j)}] = G[C_i] - x_{i+1}$, and the largest connected component C_{i+1} has at least average size, we have

$$|C_{i+1}| \geq \frac{|C_i| - 1}{d}. \tag{8.2}$$

For reasons that become obvious only later, we are now interested in locating the vertex boundary of C_{i+1}. It is clear that $\delta C_{i+1} \cap C_{i+1}^{(j)} = \emptyset$ holds for all j, since the subgraphs $G[C_{i+1}^{(j)}]$ are mutually disconnected in $G[C_i] - x_{i+1}$. Neither can there be edges between C_{i+1} and any connected component $C_k^{(j)}$ that was split off in any previous round $k \leq j$, since C_{i+1} is a subset of C_k, the component chosen in round k, the parts $C_k^{(j)}$ and C_k were separated from each other by the kth cop placement.

Now, where is the vertex boundary of δC_{i+1} located? The only candidates remaining are the vertices X_{i+1} occupied by the cops in round $i+1$, and thus $\delta C_{i+1} \subseteq X_{i+1}$. We note for later reference the inequality

$$|\delta C_{i+1}| \leq i + 1. \tag{8.3}$$

We now divide the game into two phases. The first phase lasts as long as $|C_{i+1}| \geq \frac{n}{2}$, or, to put it differently, the second phase starts in round i, if $|C_i| \geq \frac{n}{2}$ and $|C_{i+1}| < \frac{n}{2}$. We will prove that this first phase lasts for quite a few steps. Here the expander inequalities come into play: During the first phase, that is, as long as $|C_{i+1}| \geq \frac{n}{2}$, we have $|\delta C_{i+1}| \geq c \cdot (n - |C_{i+1}|)$. With Inequality (8.3), we obtain thus

$$|C_{i+1}| \geq n - \frac{i+1}{c}, \text{ for } i \text{ in the first phase.} \tag{8.4}$$

We now claim that the first phase lasts at least as long as the following invariant holds:

$$i + 1 \leq c \cdot \frac{|C_i| - 1}{d}. \tag{8.5}$$

This is, although not entirely obvious, not too hard to see: Namely, the inequalities (8.3) and (8.2) hold during both phases. Assuming in addition (8.5), these three can be combined to yield

$$|\delta C_{i+1}| \leq i + 1 \leq c \cdot \frac{|C_i| - 1}{d} \leq c \cdot |C_{i+1}|, \tag{8.6}$$

which negates the expander inequality $|\delta C_{i+1}| > c \cdot |C_{i+1}|$ that necessarily holds during the second phase, where $|C_{i+1}| < n/2$.

Having established the invariant, we give a lower bound on the starting time of the second phase. That is, we determine the largest m such that Inequality (8.5) still holds, thus guaranteeing that the first phase is not yet over after at most m steps. Determining m over the real domain is more convenient, so let $C(x)$ be a continuous, monotonically decreasing, nonnegative function with $C(i) = |C_i|$ for integer values i.

Inequality (8.5) becomes equality for $m + 1 = \frac{c}{d}(C(m) - 1)$, and resolving after $C(m)$ gives $C(m) = \frac{d(m+1)}{c} + 1$. If we plug the value of $C(m)$ into Inequality (8.4), we thus obtain:

$$C(m) \geq n - \frac{m}{c}$$
$$\frac{d(m+1)}{c} + 1 \geq n - \frac{m}{c}$$
$$d(m+1) \geq c \cdot (n-1) - m$$
$$dm + d + m \geq c \cdot (n-1)$$
$$m \geq \frac{c \cdot (n-1) - d}{d+1} > \frac{c \cdot (n-1)}{d+1} - 1.$$

It is easy to see that, in this variant of the game, at least two cops are needed to catch the robber on a connected undirected graph with at least two vertices. Recall that $C(m) \geq \frac{n}{2}$, thus $C(m) \geq 2$ for $n \geq 4$.

To conclude, at the time the robber resides on C_m, the graph is already populated with m cops, and at least two additional cops are needed to catch the robber: thus a winning strategy on G for the cops is ruled out unless at least $m + 2 > \frac{c \cdot (n-1)}{d+1} + 1$ cops are used. Together with Corollary 8.14, we finally conclude that the cycle rank of G is at least $\frac{c}{d+1}(n-1)$.

$\square$

The next lemma shows that an expander graph equipped with an edge coloring can be easily converted into a bideterministic finite automaton that accepts a language of large star height and uses only the edge colors as input alphabet.

Lemma 8.18. *For every d-edge colorable, connected undirected graph G with n vertices of cycle rank k, there exists an n-state deterministic finite automaton A over a d-symbol alphabet such that the star height of $L(A)$ is k.*

Proof. Let $G = (V, E)$ be such a graph, with $V = \{1, 2, \ldots, n\}$. and maximum degree d, equipped with an edge coloring $c : E \rightarrow \{0, 1, \ldots, d\}$ such that no pair of incident edges receives the same color. Given this edge-colored graph, we construct a deterministic finite automaton over the alphabet $\Sigma = \{a_1, a_2, \ldots, a_d\}$ with state set V, start and single final state $v_0 \in V$ (arbitrary), and whose transition relation is defined as follows: $\delta(p, a_i) = q$ if the colored graph G has an i-colored edge $\{p, q\}$. It is not hard to see that this automaton is a bideterministic automaton, and therefore minimal. Furthermore, its underlying digraph is symmetric, and its undirected version is isomorphic to G. By Theorem 8.10, the star height of $L(A)$ equals k.

$\square$

By the existence of 3-regular expanders, this would already allow us to deduce an exponential lower bound for the conversion problem over alphabets of size at least three. To reduce the alphabet size to binary, we make use of a suitable encoding that preserves star height.

Definition 8.19. *Let Γ, Σ be finite alphabets. A homomorphism $f : \Gamma^* \rightarrow \Sigma^*$ preserves star height, if for each regular language L over Γ holds $h(L) = h(f(L))$.*

The existence of homomorphisms to a binary alphabet with this property has been already conjectured by Eggan in the very first paper on star height [54], and later McNaughton [141] proved their existence by means of concrete examples:

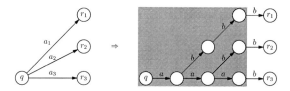

Figure 8.8: Illustrating the replacement of state q with private states. On the right, the states private to q are grouped together in the gray box.

Theorem 8.20. *Let $\Sigma = \{a_1, a_2, \ldots, a_d\}$ be a finite alphabet, $d \geq 1$, and let $\sigma : \Sigma^* \to \{a, b\}^*$ be the homomorphism defined by $\sigma(a_i) = a^i b^{d-i+1}$, for $i = 1, 2, \ldots, d$. Then for every regular language L over Σ, the star height of L equals the star height of $\sigma(L)$.*

This allows for coding down to a binary alphabet, and we obtain:

Theorem 8.21. *For alphabet size $|\Sigma| \geq 2$, there is an infinite family of languages L_n over Σ such that L_n can be accepted by an n-state DFA, but every equivalent regular expression has alphabetic width at least $2^{\Omega(n)}$.*

Proof. By Theorem 8.16, there exists a constant $c > 0$, such that for all even integers n, there exists an $(n, 3, c)$-expander G_n, which is 3-edge colorable. By Theorem 8.17, the cycle rank of this graph is at least $\frac{c}{4}(n-1)$. We can apply Lemma 8.18 to deduce that there exits an n-state DFA A_n over a ternary alphabet, whose accepted language $K_n = L(A_n)$ has star height at least $\frac{c}{4}(n-1)$.

We encode the language family K_n in binary using the star-height-preserving homomorphism σ presented above. The deterministic finite automaton A_n can be easily transformed into a 7n-state deterministic finite automaton A'_n accepting $L_n = \sigma(K_n)$ by replacing each state q with an appropriate set of "private" states for q such that whenever A moves from q to state r_i on input a_i, automaton A' moves from q to state r_i on input $\sigma(a_i)$ using the set of states private to q. The transformation is illustrated in Figure 8.8.

The number of states in A'_n is $7n$, and the star height is preserved under the homomorphism σ, hence with Theorem 8.11 the identity $\mathrm{alph}(L_n) = 2^{\Omega(n)}$ holds. $\qquad\square$

8.5 Converting Planar DFAs into Regular Expressions

In the previous section, we saw that an exponential size blow-up is unavoidable when converting finite automata into regular expressions, even when restricting our attention to the deterministic model and allow only binary alphabets. It is therefore interesting to study structural restrictions that allow shorter regular expressions.

One such restriction is the class of planar finite automata, first studied by Book and Chandra [20] because they arose in certain to circuit layout problems. Ellul et al. [59] later showed that for planar finite automata, we can construct equivalent regular expressions of size at most $|\Sigma| \cdot 2^{O(\sqrt{n})}$. Observe that for general DFAs, no algorithm can achieve a better bound than $2^{O(n)}$, because of the lower bound given in Theorem 8.21. Using the techniques developed above, we can prove that the algorithm found by Ellul et al. is asymptotically optimal, again even for the case of DFAs over alphabets of size two.

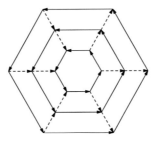

Figure 8.9: A drawing of the digraph G_3. Edges belonging to the radial inward and outward paths are indicated by dashed arrows. When viewed as automaton A_3, the solid (respectively dashed) arrows indicate a-transitions (respectively b-transitions)

Theorem 8.22. *For alphabet size $|\Sigma| \geq 2$, there is an infinite family of languages L_n over Σ such that L_n can be accepted by an n-state planar DFA, but every equivalent regular expression has alphabetic width at least $2^{\Omega(\sqrt{n})}$.*

Proof. By Theorem 8.11 and Theorem 8.10, it suffices to find an infinite family of bideterministic finite automata A_k of size $O(k^2)$ such that the digraph underlying A_k has cycle rank $\Omega(k)$.

The DFAs A_k witnessing the claimed lower bound are inspired by a family of digraphs G_k defined in [116]. These graphs each admit a planar drawing as the union of k concentric, equally directed, $2k$-cycles, which are connected to each other by $2k$ radial directed k-paths, the first k of which are directed inwards, while the remaining k are directed outwards; see Figure 8.9 for illustration.

Formally, for $k \geq 1$, let $G_k = (V, E)$ be the digraph with vertex set $V = \{ u_{i,j} \mid 1 \leq i, j \leq k \} \cup \{ v_{i,j} \mid 1 \leq i, j \leq k \}$, and whose edge set can be partitioned into a set of directed $2k$-cycles C_i, and two sets of directed k-paths P_i and Q_i, with $1 \leq i \leq k$. Here each C_i admits a walk visiting the vertices $u_{i,1}, u_{i,2}, \ldots, u_{i,k}, v_{i,1}, v_{i,2}, \ldots, v_{i,k}$ in order, each P_i admits a walk visiting the vertices $u_{1,i}, u_{2,i}, \ldots, u_{k,i}$ in order, and Q_i admits a walk visiting the vertices $v_{k,i}, v_{k-1,i}, \ldots, v_{1,i}$ in order.

Fix $\{a, b\}$ as a binary input alphabet. If we interpret the edges in G_k belonging to the cycles C_i as a-transitions, the edges belonging to the paths P_i and Q_i as b-transitions, interpret the vertices as states and choose a single initial and a single final state (both arbitrarily), we obtain a finite automaton A_k, with $O(k^2)$ states, whose underlying digraph is G_k. It is easily observed that A_k is bideterministic; thus it only remains to show that for the underlying graph G_k the identity $cr(G_k) = \Omega(k)$ holds.

Together with the game characterization of cycle rank of loop-free digraphs from Corollary 8.14, this falls off from a known result: In fact, it was shown by Johnson et al. in [116] that on the digraph G_k, the robber has a winning strategy against k cops in the cops and strong visible robber game, even if the cops are not immutable and can freely jump between vertices on the graph. $\qquad\square$

9 Lower Bounds for the Conversion Problem: Finite Languages

In this chapter, we shall deal with the problem of converting deterministic finite automata into regular expressions, in the setup restricted to finite languages. After we have seen very strong negative results for the general case of this problem in Chapter 8, studying this restriction appears quite natural. Indeed, the case of finite languages was already addressed by Ehrenfeucht and Zeiger in the very first paper on the descriptional complexity of regular expressions [55]. As pointed out by Ellul et al. [59], these results imply that every n-state DFA accepting a finite language can be converted into an equivalent regular expression of size $n^{O(\log n)}$. Ehrenfeucht and Zeiger also found the following lower bound:

Theorem 9.1. *There is an infinite family of finite languages L_n, such that L_n can be accepted by an n-state DFA over an alphabet of size at most n^2, but every equivalent regular expression has alphabetic width at least $n^{\Omega(\log \log n)}$.*

The first apparent problem with this result is that it leaves a large gap between upper and lower bound, and the authors explicitly asked for tightening this gap. There has been only little progress in this direction since the challenge was raised in 1976: We are only aware of two related results. The first, due to Ellul et al. [59], shows a still nontrivial lower bound for this problem when restricting the alphabet to binary. However, that lower bound is only quadratic in n. The second and less directly related result, due to Moreira and Reis [147], states that finite automata with a very special underlying transition structure, namely series-parallel acyclic digraphs, can be converted into regular expressions of linear size. Both of these studies appear to be still very far from providing a more thorough understanding of the conversion problem in the case of finite languages. The scarcity and weakness of previous results only adds to the impression that it is not too easy to successfully get one's hand on the proposed research problem.

In this chapter, we aim to give a rather definite answer to the challenge suggested by Ehrenfeucht and Zeiger. Namely, we prove a lower bound of $n^{\Omega(\log n)}$. This gives a tight worst-case bound of $n^{\Theta(\log n)}$ for the conversion problem of acyclic DFAs into regular expressions. As a bonus, the languages witnessing this bound over a binary alphabet. Recall that for fixed alphabet size the best previous bound was $\Omega(n^2)$.

Notice that the lower bound technique we devised for regular expression size of infinite languages (Theorem 8.11) fails to predict anything nontrivial in the case of finite languages, since they have star height zero.

We will develop a different lower bound technique for regular expressions describing finite languages. As mentioned above, Ellul et al. [59] proved a quadratic lower bound on the conversion problem, for a finite language over binary alphabet. Their proof proceeds by a reduction to Khrapchenko's classical bound [122] on the size of Boolean formulas for the parity function. Yet their approach appears to be difficult to be taken further at first sight, since their proof relies on proving lower bounds on Boolean formula size, commonly acknowledged to be an enormously difficult mathematical problem. We show how to circumvent this difficulty, by harnessing a somewhat newer technique than Khrapchenko's, which was used to obtain better lower bounds for *monotone* Boolean formulas. This technique is the communication complexity of monotone search problems, introduced by Karchmer and Wigderson [119]. We briefly recall the basic notions of this theory in the following section.

9.1 Communication Complexity

Let X, Y, Z be finite sets and $R \subseteq X \times Y \times Z$ a ternary relation on them. In the search problem R, we have Alice given some input $x \in X$, Bob is given some input $y \in Y$. Initially, no party knows the other's input, and Alice and Bob both want to output some z such that $(x, y, z) \in R$, by communicating as few bits as possible. A *communication protocol* is a binary tree with each internal node v labeled either by a function $a_v : X \to \{0, 1\}$ if Alice transmits at this node, or $b_v : Y \to \{0, 1\}$ if Bob transmits at this node. Each leaf is labeled by an output $z \in Z$. We say that a protocol *solves the search problem* for relation R if for every input pair $(x, y) \in X \times Y$, walking down the tree according to the functions a_v and b_v leads to a leaf labeled with some z satisfying $(x, y, z) \in R$. The overall number of bits transmitted for a given input pair $(x, y) \in X \times Y$ and a given protocol is then equal to the length of the walk just described; and the maximum length among these walks equals the depth of the tree. The *(deterministic) communication complexity* $D(R)$ is now defined as the minimum depth among all communication protocols solving R, and the *protocol partition number* $C^P(R)$ denotes the minimum number of leaves among all protocols solving the search problem for R.

At first glance, it is not clear to what extent the protocol partition number measures the necessary amount of communication. The number of leaves in a protocol tree can be clearly at most exponential in its depth. But there exist protocols whose depth is even linear in the number of leaves. Yet a standard argument about balancing binary trees shows that every such deep protocol can be transformed into a shallow protocol, see e.g. [129, ch. 2]:

Lemma 9.2. *Let X, Y, Z be finite sets and $R \subseteq X \times Y \times Z$ a ternary relation on them. Then $\log C^P(R) \geq 1/3 \cdot D(R)$.*

The constant factor $c = 1/3$ in the above inequality was subsequently improved by Doerr [49] to $c = \log \left(1 / \left(\sqrt{3} - 1 \right) \right) \doteq 0.450$. This improved constant gives $D(R) < 2.223 \log C^P(R)$. While only the latter inequality is stated explicitly in that paper, the expression for c we give above is easily extracted from the proof.

An important fact about the two complexity measures $D(R)$ and $C^P(R)$ is a close correspondence with the complexity of Boolean circuits and Boolean formulas, respectively. We need the following definition: A finite language whose words are all of the same length is called *homogeneous*. For a homogeneous language $\emptyset \subset L \subset \Sigma^n$, the *search problem associated with L* is informally described as follows: Alice is given an input v from L, and Bob is given an input w from the complementary set $\Sigma^n \setminus L$; they want to agree on a position i witnessing that their inputs are different, while communicating as few bits as possible. Formally, the search problem S_L is a ternary relation $S_L \subseteq L \times (\Sigma^n \setminus L) \times \{1, 2, \ldots, n\}$ defined by: $(v, w, i) \in S_L$ iff $v_i \neq w_i$.

Karchmer and Wigderson established the following connection to circuit complexity [119]: Take $\Sigma = \{0,1\}$. If we naturally identify each set $L \subseteq \{0,1\}^n$ with its characteristic n-bit Boolean function, then $D(S_L)$ equals the minimum depth of a Boolean circuit (over the standard basis) computing the characteristic function of L. Moreover, $C^P(S_L)$ equals the minimum number of variable occurrences among all Boolean formulas representing L.

Proving superpolynomial lower bounds on formula size for specific functions turns out to be an extremely difficult open problem. Fortunately, this is no longer true if we consider monotone Boolean formulas [119]. A similar class of search problems can be defined for the latter setup:

Given an alphabet $\Sigma = \{a_1, a_2, \ldots, a_k\}$, we impose an arbitrary but fixed total ordering $a_1 < a_2 < \cdots < a_k$ of its elements. The total order on Σ naturally extends pointwise to a partial order on Σ^n. The *upward closure* of a homogeneous language $L \subseteq \Sigma^n$ (w.r.t. this partial order) is defined as the set

$$\uparrow(L) = \{w \in \Sigma^n \mid u \leq w \text{ for some } u \in L\}.$$

We call a homogeneous language *monotone*, if $L = \uparrow(L)$.

Example 9.3. Consider the binary alphabet $\{0,1\}$, naturally ordered by $0 < 1$. The strings 001 and 100 are incomparable w.r.t. the order $<$ extended to Σ^3, while both are smaller than 101 and greater than 000. The upward closure of $L = \{100, 001\}$ equals $\uparrow(L) = \{001, 100, 011, 101, 110, 111\}$, and thus L is not monotone.

For a monotone homogeneous language $\emptyset \subset L \subset \Sigma^n$, the *monotone search problem* associated with L, denoted by M_L, is defined by $(v, w, i) \in M_L$ iff both $(v, w, i) \in S_L$ and moreover $v_i > w_i$. In this variant of the problem, Alice and Bob want to agree on a position i where not only their inputs are different, but where in addition Alice' input letter has larger rank than Bob's. Note that such a position indeed always exists provided L is monotone, nonempty and not equal to Σ^n. For $\Sigma = \{0,1\}$ with $0 < 1$, the measure $C^P(M_L)$ equals the minimum formula size among all *monotone* Boolean formulas[1] representing L. A similar correspondence holds for $D(M_L)$ and minimum depth of *monotone* Boolean circuits [119].

For more background on communication complexity, the reader might want to consult a textbook on the subject, such as [129].

9.2 Protocol Partition Number and Regular Expression Size

The goal of this section is to relate the alphabetic width of a monotone homogeneous language to the protocol partition number of its associated monotone search problem. To this end, we first introduce a normal form for such regular expressions. To avoid considering degenerate cases, the following definition from [59] forbids certain obvious redundancies.

Definition 9.4. Let r be a regular expression. We say that r is *uncollapsible* if all of the following conditions hold: If r contains the symbol $\emptyset$, then $r = \emptyset$; The expression r contains

---

[1]That is, Boolean formulas without negation, using only the logical operators $\wedge$ and $\vee$.

no subexpression of the form st or ts, with $L(s) = \{\varepsilon\}$; if r contains a subexpression of the form $s + t$ or $t + s$ with $L(s) = \{\varepsilon\}$, then $\varepsilon \notin L(t)$; if r contains a subexpression of the form s^*, then $L(s) \neq \{\varepsilon\}$.

Some very careful readers might have noticed that we have added a fourth condition not present in the original definition from [59]; this condition ensures that uncollapsible regular expressions describing finite languages do not use the star operator. As promised, we now introduce a normal form for regular expressions describing homogeneous languages.

Definition 9.5. A regular expression r describing a homogeneous language is called a *homogeneous expression*, if none of the symbols $\emptyset$, ε and * occur in r, or $L(r)$ is empty and $r = \emptyset$.

Lemma 9.6. *For $n \geq 1$, let $L \subseteq \Sigma^n$ be a homogeneous language. If r is an uncollapsible regular expression describing L, then r is a homogeneous expression.*

Proof. For the case $L(r) = \emptyset$, the statement immediately follows from the definitions. Assume r is uncollapsible and $\emptyset \subset L(r) \subseteq \Sigma^n$. We can rule out that any subexpression s with $L(s) = \emptyset$ occurs in r: Every regular expression denoting the empty language contains the symbol $\emptyset$ at least once. Next, finiteness of the described languages is invariant under the operations $+$ and $\cdot$, but not by the Kleene star: For any regular expression s, the set denoted by s^* is infinite unless $L(s) = \emptyset$ or $\{\varepsilon\}$. We have already ruled out the existence of $\emptyset$ symbols in r. Since r is uncollapsible, it does not contain any subexpression of the form s^* with $L(s) = \{\varepsilon\}$ either. Thus, the language $L(r)$ being finite, r cannot have any subexpression of the form s^*.

Finally, we rule out the possibility that ε occurs in r: As all words in $L(r)$ are of length n, we make the following observation: If r contains a subexpression of the form $s + t$, then there exists $m \leq n$ such that both $L(s)$ and $L(t)$ contain only strings of length m. If $\text{alph}(r) \leq 1$, then clearly r has no ε-subexpression. Assume $\text{alph}(r) > 1$ and ε occurs in r. Since r is uncollapsible, the expression r must contain a subexpression of the form $s + \varepsilon$ with $\varepsilon \notin s$ and $s \neq \emptyset$. But then $s + \varepsilon$ describes a set of strings having different lengths, a property which is inherited to r, since r has no subexpressions describing the empty language. $\square$

The following easy lemma shows that for homogeneous languages, the upward closure operator $\uparrow$ commutes with union and concatenation. This follows immediately from the definition of these notions.

Lemma 9.7. *For homogeneous languages L_1 and L_2,*

$$\uparrow(L_1) + \uparrow(L_2) = \uparrow(L_1 + L_2) \ and \ \uparrow(L_1) \cdot \uparrow(L_2) = \uparrow(L_1 \cdot L_2) \, . \qquad \square$$

We establish next that homogeneous monotone languages can be described by regular expressions in some normal form, and that the conversion into this normal form increases the expression size at most by a factor of $|\Sigma|$.

A homogeneous expression is called a *sum* if it uses $+$ as the only operator, i.e. it is of the form $(a_{i_1} + a_{i_2} + \cdots + a_{i_m})$, with all summands a_{i_j} from Σ. Let r be a homogeneous expression and s a subexpression of r. The subexpression s is called a *maximal sum* in r if s is a sum, but each subexpression t having s as a proper subexpression is not a sum. Note that the maximal sums in an expression each describe a subset of Σ. For a homogeneous expression r, the number of maximal sums in r is denoted by $\mathrm{sum}(r)$. Since any non-redundant sum is of size at most $|\Sigma|$ and contains at least one alphabetical symbol, we get $\mathrm{sum}(L) \leq \mathrm{alph}(L) \leq |\Sigma| \cdot \mathrm{sum}(L)$ for every homogeneous language L. A homogeneous expression r is called *monotone* if each maximal sum s in r describes a monotone language, that is $L(s) = \uparrow(L(s))$ for every maximal sum s.

Lemma 9.8. *For each homogeneous expression r over an ordered alphabet Σ, there exists a monotone expression r' with $L(r') = \uparrow(L(r))$ and $\mathrm{sum}(r') = \mathrm{sum}(r)$.*

Proof. The statement is shown by induction on $\mathrm{sum}(r)$. In the base case $\mathrm{sum}(r) = 1$, r is itself a sum. Let a_i be the minimal letter occurring in r, and let $a_{i+1}, a_{i+2}, \ldots, a_k$ be those letters in Σ greater than a_i. We set $r' := (a_i + a_{i+1} \cdots + a_k)$, and we clearly have $L(r') = \uparrow(L(r))$ as well as $\mathrm{sum}(r') = \mathrm{sum}(r) = 1$, hence the statement holds in the base case.

Now assume $\mathrm{sum}(r) > 1$. Then $r = r_1 \oplus r_2$, where the symbol $\oplus$ stands for one of the operators $+$ or $\cdot$. Observe that $\mathrm{sum}(r) > 1$ implies that r cannot be a sum itself; thus we have $\mathrm{sum}(r) = \mathrm{sum}(r_1) + \mathrm{sum}(r_2)$ and $\mathrm{sum}(r_i) < \mathrm{sum}(r)$ for $i = 1, 2$. By the induction hypothesis, there exist expressions r_i' with $L(r_i') = \uparrow(L(r_i))$ and $\mathrm{sum}(r_i') = \mathrm{sum}(r_i)$. We set $r' := r_1' \oplus r_2'$ and obtain

$$\mathrm{sum}(r') = \mathrm{sum}(r_1') + \mathrm{sum}(r_2') = \mathrm{sum}(r_1) + \mathrm{sum}(r_2) = \mathrm{sum}(r).$$

By Lemma 9.7, we have

$$L(r') = \uparrow(L(r_1)) \oplus \uparrow(L(r_2)) = \uparrow(L(r_1) \oplus L(r_2)) = \uparrow(L(r)),$$

so the claim holds. $\qquad\square$

Now we are ready to derive a technique for bounding the alphabetic width of homogeneous languages in terms of communication complexity:

Lemma 9.9. *For every homogeneous language L with $\emptyset \subset L \subset \Sigma^n$ and $n \geq 1$,*

$$\mathrm{alph}(L) \geq \mathrm{sum}(L) \geq C^P(S_L).$$

Moreover, if L is monotone, then

$$\mathrm{alph}(L) \geq \mathrm{sum}(L) \geq C^P(M_L).$$

Proof. Let r be a regular expression with $L(r) = L$. By Lemma 9.6, we can assume that r is homogeneous. If r is a homogeneous expression, then for every subexpression s of r the language $L(s)$ is homogeneous as well, and we denote by $\mathrm{len}(s)$ the common length of all words in $L(s)$. Note that the case $s = \emptyset$ cannot occur here, the expression r being homogeneous and $L(r) \neq \emptyset$.

We will now, given a homogeneous expression r for L, construct a protocol for S_L using only $\mathrm{sum}(r)$ many leaves.

Recall that Alice is given an input $x \in L$, Bob a $y \notin L$, and they have to find an index i with $x_i \neq y_i$. At each state of the protocol, Alice and Bob keep a subexpression s of r together with an interval $[i, j]$ of length $j - i + 1 = \mathrm{len}(s)$, satisfying the invariant that $x_i x_{i+1} \cdots x_j \in L(s)$ and $y_i y_{i+1} \cdots y_j \notin L(s)$. At the beginning $s = r$ and $[i, j] = [1, n]$, hence the invariant holds.

At a state of the protocol with a subexpression $s = s_0 + s_1$ with $\text{sum}(s) > 1$ and interval $[i, j]$, it must hold that

$$x_i x_{i+1} \cdots x_j \in L(s_0) \text{ or } x_i x_{i+1} \cdots x_j \in L(s_1),$$

but at the same time

$$\text{both } y_i y_{i+1} \cdots y_j \notin L(s_0) \text{ and } y_i y_{i+1} \cdots y_j \notin L(s_1).$$

Thus Alice can transmit $\delta \in \{0, 1\}$ such that $x_i x_{i+1} \cdots x_j \in L(s_\delta)$, and the protocol continues with s updated to s_δ and $[i, j]$ unchanged.

At a state with a subexpression $s = s_0 \cdot s_1$ and interval $[i, j]$, let $\ell := i + \text{len}(s_0) - 1$. Then it must hold that

$$\text{both } x_i x_{i+1} \cdots x_\ell \in L(s_0) \text{ and } x_{\ell+1} x_{\ell+2} \cdots x_j \in L(s_1),$$

but at the same time

$$y_i y_{i+1} \cdots y_\ell \notin L(s_0) \quad \text{(case 0), or } y_{\ell+1} y_{\ell+1} \cdots y_j \notin L(s_1) \quad \text{(case 1)}.$$

This time, Bob can transmit $\delta \in \{0, 1\}$ such that case δ holds, and the protocol continues with s updated to s_δ and $[i, j]$ set to $[i, \ell]$ in case 0 and $[\ell + 1, j]$ in case 1.

At a state with a subexpression s that is a maximal sum in r, it must be the case that $i = j$, and that $x_i \in L(s)$ and $y_i \notin L(s)$, hence in particular $x_i \neq y_i$ and the protocol can terminate with output i.

Obviously, the protocol solves S_L, and the tree of the protocol constructed is isomorphic to the parse tree of r with its maximal sums at the leaves, thus the number of leaves is $\text{sum}(r)$.

If L happens to be monotone, then by Lemma 9.8 we can assume that r is a monotone expression. Then also all subexpressions of r that appear in the above proof are monotone, and in the terminating case it must moreover be the case that $x_i > y_i$, therefore the protocol solves M_L. $\qquad\square$

9.3 Converting DFAs into Regular Expressions: Finite Languages

Having developed the tools for proving lower bounds on the conversion problem for finite languages, it remains to find an appropriate family of witness languages. Our languages are inspired a family of graphs used by Grigni and Sipser in the context of monotone Boolean formulas [73]; however the languages they used can only be shown to admit small 2-*way deterministic finite automata*, an automaton model for the regular languages that is in some cases much more succinct than our ordinary (one-way) finite automata, see [146, 118]. We therefore carefully choose a similar family of (di)graphs such that, with the right encoding, these graphs can be recognized by small DFAs, while essentially the same lower bound argument as in [73] remains applicable.

For given positive integers ℓ and m, we define a family of digraphs $G_{\ell, m}$ with parameters ℓ, m as the set of directed acyclic graphs whose vertex set V is organized in $\ell+2$ layers, with m vertices in each each layer. Hence we assume $V = \{\langle i, j \rangle \mid 1 \leq i \leq m, 0 \leq j \leq \ell + 1\}$.

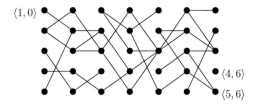

Figure 9.1: A digraph in the family $\mathsf{fork}_{5,5}$. Vertices in the same layer share each a vertical line in the drawing. Membership in $\mathsf{fork}_{5,5}$ can be verified by following the path starting at vertex $\langle 1, 0 \rangle$, in the upper left corner, to the right until we meet the fork at the vertex $\langle 3, 4 \rangle$, in layer 4.

For all digraphs in $G_{\ell,m}$, we require in addition that each edge connects a vertex in some layer j to a vertex in the next layer $j + 1$.

A digraph $G \in G_{\ell,m}$ belongs to the subfamily $\mathsf{fork}_{\ell,m}$, if there exists a simple path starting in $\langle 1, 0 \rangle$ ending eventually in a fork, i.e., a vertex of outdegree at least two. See Figure 9.3 for an example.

The following definition serves to represent subsets of $G_{\ell,m}$ as homogeneous languages over the alphabet $\{0, 1\}$: Fix a digraph $G \in G_{\ell,m}$ for the moment. Let $e(i, j, k) = 1$ if G has an edge from vertex i in layer j to vertex k in layer $j + 1$, and let $e(i, j, k) = 0$ otherwise. Next, for vertex i in layer j, the word

$$f(i, j) = e(i, j, 1)e(i, j, 2) \cdots e(i, j, m)$$

encodes the set of outgoing edges for this vertex. Then for layer j, the word

$$g(j) = f(1, j)f(2, j) \cdots f(m, j)$$

encodes the set of edges connecting vertices in layer j to vertices in layer $j + 1$, for $0 \le j \le \ell$. Finally, the digraph G is encoded by the word

$$w(G) = g(0)g(1) \cdots g(\ell).$$

It is easy to see that each word in the set $\{0, 1\}^{m^2(\ell+1)}$ can be uniquely decoded as a digraph in the set $G_{\ell,m}$.

The goal of this section will be to show that the language

$$\{\, w \in \{0, 1\}^{m^2(\ell+1)} \mid w = w(G) \text{ with } G \in \mathsf{fork}_{\ell,m} \,\}$$

can be accepted by a DFA of size polynomial in both parameters, while this cannot be the case for any regular expression describing this language. Subsequently, we will identify $G \in G_{\ell,m}$ with its encoding $w(G)$, and similarly we will freely use $\mathsf{fork}_{\ell,m}$ to denote the abovementioned set of encodings of the digraphs in $\mathsf{fork}_{\ell,m}$.

Lemma 9.10. *For every pair (ℓ, m) with $\ell, m \geq 1$, the language $\mathsf{fork}_{\ell,m}$ can be accepted by a DFA having at most $3(\ell + 2)m^3$ states.*

Proof. We will construct a DFA whose states are tuples of variables, each over a finite domain. An important observation is that, while reading the input, the only important information to retain across two adjacent layers is the target vertex of the first edge leaving the previous source vertex, and whether that source vertex had outdegree 0, 1, or larger.

First, we introduce the variables, and roughly describe their roles for accepting the language under consideration: The variable j ranges from 0 to $\ell + 1$, and tracks the number of the layer being currently processed; The variable i is a counter ranging from 0 to $m^2 - 1$, which keeps track of the number of bits in the current layer that have already been read; The variable s (respectively t) stores the source (respectively target) vertex of the currently last edge of the simple path which started in $\langle 1, 0 \rangle$ and possibly eventually ends in a fork; and a Boolean flag d, taking on values $\bot$ and $\top$. The flag d represents a judgment about whether the outdegree of $\langle s, j \rangle$ equals zero, based on the part of the input that has been read so far, or whether its outdegree definitely equals one—the case of a fork is handled differently.

The state set of the automaton consists of tuples of the types (s, t, i, j), $(s, i, j, \top)$, $(t, i, j, \bot)$, and (i, j). The start state is $(1, 0, 0, \bot)$. We describe the roles of these states, and the transitions between them in the following:

Fix a layer j for the moment. Assume the automaton is in state $(s, 0, j, \bot)$ after reading the first jm^2 bits of the input. We will maintain the invariant that this happens iff there is a simple path from $\langle 1, 0 \rangle$ to $\langle s, j \rangle$, and no vertex along that path, except possibly the last vertex $\langle s, j \rangle$, is a fork.

On reading the next $(s - 1)m$ input bits, only the counter variable i is increased by one each time, finally leading to state $(s, (s - 1)m, j, \bot)$. These $(s - 1)m$ bits encode possible edges leaving vertices from layer j numbered lower than s, and their values can be disregarded.

The m input bits $x = b_1 b_2 \cdots b_m$, which follow thereafter, are the most interesting ones for this layer, as they encode the possible edges leaving vertex $\langle s, j \rangle$. While reading only zeroes in the prefix of x, only the counter i is increased accordingly. If all bits in the subword x are zero, then there is no edge leaving $\langle s, j \rangle$ in the given digraph, and the automaton enters the dead state $(s, sm, j, \bot)$ after reading the last letter of x.

Otherwise, let b_t be the first nonzero bit in the abovementioned sequence. Then the automaton is in state $(s, (s-1)m + t - 1, j, \bot)$ immediately before reading b_t; on reading b_t the automaton moves to state $(s, t, (s-1)m + t, j)$. In this way, the automaton remembers that the first edge leaving vertex $\langle s, j \rangle$ has $\langle t, j + 1 \rangle$ as target vertex.

Starting from state $(s, t, (s-1)m + t, j)$, while reading zeroes, again only the counter i is increased as long as it does not reach the value sm. When it would reach that value, then we definitely know that there is only one edge leaving vertex $\langle s, j \rangle$, and that this edge has target vertex $\langle t, j + 1 \rangle$. Therefore, the automaton rather goes to state $(t, sm, j, \top)$ in this case. In contrast, if the automaton happens to encounter a second nonzero bit $b_{t'}$ within the subword x, with $t' > t$, we can conclude that there is a second edge leaving vertex $\langle s, j \rangle$, that is, this vertex is a fork. In this case, the automaton can safely accept provided the length of the input word is correct, and it goes to state $((s - 1)m + t', j)$. From that state, it only needs to keep track of the length of the input, thus it increases the counters i and j accordingly with each consumed input bit, until it finally reaches the sole accepting state (m^2, ℓ) of the automaton.

If the automaton is in state $(t, sm, j, \top)$, then it processes the remaining $m^2 - sm$ input bits belonging to layer j while only updating the counter i accordingly. These $m^2 - sm$ bits encode possible edges leaving vertices from layer j numbered higher than s, and their values can be disregarded. Once the counter i would reach the value m^2, it rather goes to state $(t, 0, j + 1, \bot)$, and continues by processing the input bits for the next layer; now t takes over the role of the source vertex.

By construction, the automaton is in state $(t, 0, j+1, \bot)$ after reading the first $(j+1)m^2$ bits of the whole input iff there is a simple path from $\langle 1, 0 \rangle$ to $\langle s, j \rangle$ and no vertex along that path (disregarding the last vertex $\langle s, j \rangle$, whose possible outgoing edges have not been read yet) is a fork. Thus, the invariant mentioned at the outset is maintained. Another invariant that is obviously maintained is that if the first $(j+1)m^2$ input bits already show that the input digraph is in fork$_{\ell,m}$, then the automaton is in state $(0, j+1)$ after reading that input. These observations prove correctness of the construction.

For counting the number of states in layer j, observe that we need no more than $m^2(m-1)$ tuples of the type (s, t, i, j), since for each such tuple, the counter i can take on only values inside the interval $[(s-1)m + 1; sm - 1]$, and we have m possible choices each for fixing s and t. And for tuples of type $(t, i, j, \top)$, $(s, i, j, \bot)$, or (i, j), there are m^2 possible values for i, and m possible values each for s and t. In total, this makes for layer j at most

$$m^2(m-1) + m^3 + m^3 + m^2 = 3m^3$$

states. Summing up over all layers, this gives at most $3(\ell+2)m^3$ states altogether. $\quad\square$

Next, we give a lower bound on the alphabetic width of this language. To this end, we show that the communication complexity of the monotone search problem for the language fork$_{\ell,m}$ is bounded below by the communication complexity of the search problem for a certain relation FORK$_{\ell,m}$. That relation is defined as follows (cf. [129, ch. 5.3]):

Definition 9.11. Let $W := \{1, \dots, m\}^\ell$. The relation FORK$_{\ell,m}$ is a subset of $W \times W \times \{0, 1, \dots, \ell\}$. For two strings $x = x_1 x_2 \cdots x_\ell$ and $y = y_1 y_2 \cdots y_\ell$ in W and an integer $i \in \{0, 1, \dots, \ell\}$ we have $(x, y, i) \in$ FORK$_{\ell,m}$ iff $x_i = y_i$ and $x_{i+1} \neq y_{i+1}$, with the convention that $x_0 = y_0 = 1$, $x_{\ell+1} = m - 1$ and $y_{\ell+1} = m$.

The following lower bound is found in the monograph [129] and is originally due to[2] Grigni and Sipser [73]:

Lemma 9.12. $D(\text{FORK}_{\ell,m}) \geq \lfloor (\log m)/4 \rfloor \cdot \lfloor \log \ell \rfloor$ $\quad\square$

It remains to give a reduction, in the sense of communication protocols, from FORK$_{\ell,m}$ to the monotone search problem for the language fork$_{\ell,m}$.

Lemma 9.13. Let $L = $ fork$_{\ell,m}$. Then $D(M_L) \geq D(\text{FORK}_{\ell,m})$.

Proof. We show that for $L = $ fork$_{\ell,m}$, any protocol that solves M_L can be used to solve FORK$_{\ell,m}$ without any additional communication, which implies the stated lower bound. The reduction is similar to one used, albeit for a different purpose, by Grigni and Sipser [73].

---

[2]In fact, we use the relation as it is presented in the monograph [129], which slightly differs from the one originally investigated by Grigni and Sipser. Although the book [129] only states an asymptotic lower bound of $c \cdot \log \ell \log m$ for some constant c, the proof is the same as for the more precise bound given in the original article [73].

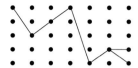

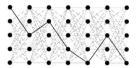

Figure 9.2: The digraph G_x constructed by Alice from her input 32154.

Figure 9.3: The digraph G_y constructed by Bob from his input 32453. The simple non-forking path is drawn in black.

From her input $x \in W$, Alice computes a digraph $G_x \in G_{\ell,m}$ having for every $0 \le i \le \ell$ an edge from $\langle x_i, i \rangle$ to $\langle x_{i+1}, i+1 \rangle$, and an additional edge from $\langle x_\ell, \ell \rangle$ to $\langle m, \ell+1 \rangle$. By construction, $G_x \in \mathsf{fork}_{\ell,m}$. See Figure 9.2 for illustration.

Similarly, from his input $y \in W$, Bob computes a digraph G_y having for every $0 \le i \le \ell$ an edge from $\langle y_i, i \rangle$ to $\langle y_{i+1}, i+1 \rangle$. Additionally, G_y has all the edges from $\langle i, j \rangle$ to $\langle i', j+1 \rangle$ where $i \ne y_j$ and i' is arbitrary. Therefore G_y has a simple path starting in $\langle 1, 0 \rangle$, which however continues until the last layer without ever meeting a fork, and thus $G_y \notin \mathsf{fork}_{\ell,m}$. See Figure 9.3 for an example.

Now running the protocol for M_L on G_x and G_y yields a position k where $(G_x)_k = 1$ and $(G_y)_k = 0$, i.e., an edge that is present in G_x, but not in G_y. By construction, this edge goes from $\langle x_i, i \rangle$ to $\langle x_{i+1}, i+1 \rangle$ for some i, and it must be that $y_i = x_i$ and $y_{i+1} \ne x_{i+1}$, as otherwise the edge would be present in G_y. Thus i is a solution such that $(x, y, i) \in \mathsf{FORK}_{\ell,m}$.

For illustration, the digraph G_x in Figure 9.2 contains two edges not present in the digraph G_y in Figure 9.3, namely from $\langle 2, 2 \rangle$ to $\langle 1, 3 \rangle$ and from $\langle 5, 4 \rangle$ to $\langle 4, 5 \rangle$. The layers 2 and 4, where the respective edges start, are precisely the two possible solutions to the search problem for $\mathsf{FORK}_{5,5}$ on the input pair $x = 32154$ and $y = 32453$. □

Now we are ready to prove the main result of this chapter:

Theorem 9.14. *For alphabet size $|\Sigma| \ge 2$, there is an infinite family of finite languages L_n over Σ such that L_n can be accepted by an n-state DFA, but every equivalent regular expression has alphabetic width at least $n^{(1/144 - o(1)) \log n} = n^{\Omega(\log n)}$.*

Proof. Assume $n = m^6$ for some positive integer m. We use the witness language $L = \mathsf{fork}_{\ell,m}$ with parameter $\ell = \lfloor m^3/3 \rfloor - 2$. Then by Lemma 9.10, the language $L = \mathsf{fork}_{\ell,m}$ is acceptable by a DFA with at most n states, since

$$3(\ell + 2)m^3 = 3\lfloor m^3/3 \rfloor \cdot m^3 \le n.$$

In contrast, with Lemma 9.13, we obtain that

$$\begin{aligned} D(M_L) &\ge (1/4 - o(1)) \cdot \log m \cdot \log(m^3) \\ &= (1/4 - o(1)) \cdot 1/6 \log(m^6) \cdot 1/2 \log(m^6). \end{aligned}$$

Together with the relation between communication complexity and protocol partition number (Lemma 9.2), this implies that

$$C^P(M_L) \ge 2^{1/3 \cdot (1/48 - o(1))(\log n)^2} = n^{(1/144 - o(1)) \log n},$$

and by Lemma 9.9, the measure $C^P(M_L)$ is a lower bound for the alphabetic width of the language $L = L_n$.

$\square$

More than 30 years after the question was raised by Ehrenfeucht and Zeiger in [55], we have finally determined an asymptotically tight bound for the conversion problem in the case of finite languages. While the bound is asymptotically optimal, the factor $1/144 \doteq 0.007$ in the exponent appears rather small. We can increase this constant a bit, if we use Doerr's improvement [49] to Lemma 9.2, with $c = \log\left(1/\left(\sqrt{3} - 1\right)\right) \doteq 0.450$ instead of $c = 1/3$. Then the factor increases somewhat, to slightly above 0.009.

10 Upper Bounds for the Conversion Problem

In theoretical computer science at large, upper and lower bounds on a particular computational problem often naturally fall out of viewing the same phenomenon from different angles. Sometimes we are able to prove lower bounds on the inherent difficulty of a problem once we have understood the limitations that are common to several different algorithms. And sometimes we can design improved algorithms once we have understood the obstacles encountered by diverse lower bound techniques. Whereas the previous chapters were devoted to various lower bounds on the conversion problem, the present chapter explores new directions on the algorithmic side.

There are a few classical algorithms for converting finite automata into regular expressions that look different at first glance [23, 37, 142]. But, as Sakarovitch [163] shows, all of these approaches are more or less reformulations of the same underlying algorithmic idea. All of these algorithms have an upper bound of roughly 4^n on the size of the resulting regular expressions. The desire to obtain shorter regular expressions than this can be traced back to the work by McNaughton and Yamada [142]. They observed that the ordering in which states are processed by their algorithm can affect the size of the resulting regular expression, and they suggested the simple heuristic of placing the states bearing the heaviest traffic last in the ordering. A refinement of this idea was later given by Delgado and Morais [47]. A different heuristic, proposed recently by Han and Wood [88], looks out for possibilities to decompose a given finite automaton into smaller pieces. But none of these yields a provable increase in performance. Such improved upper bounds have been obtained previously only for structurally restricted finite automata: The cases of planar finite automata and of acyclic finite automata were already discussed in Chapter 8.5 and Chapter 9, respectively. When imposing the further restriction on acyclic finite automata that their underlying digraphs are series-parallel acyclic digraphs, then the conversion problem becomes polynomial [147]. The latter result follows since the concatenation and union operators in regular expressions can naturally simulate series and parallel composition, respectively. Summarizing, previous approaches resulted either in heuristics for the general case without guaranteed benefit or in algorithms with provable performance that however holds only under severe structural restrictions. Based on our findings from previous chapters, we will be able to find a proper balance between these two extremes.

In the previous chapters, we encountered some rather strong lower bounds for converting finite automata into regular expressions, which hold already for deterministic finite automata over binary alphabets. Although we were able to prove a lower bound of c^n for some constant $c > 1$, proving a lower bound of $\Omega(2^n)$ as in Theorem 2.11 for unbounded alphabets seems to be by far out of reach: By tracking the size of the constants used in the chain of reductions used for the proof of Theorem 8.21, one can deduce a concrete value for the constant c. For alphabets of size $\ell \geq 3$, we get a lower bound[1] of at least

---

[1]Without going into uninteresting technical details, the inclined reader is informed that here we make

$\Omega\left(2^{\frac{\sqrt{\ell}(n-1)}{3\cdot 2\cdot(\ell+1)^2}}\right)$, for infinitely many values of n. Using a binary encoding that increases the size of the input deterministic finite automaton to $m = 7n$ whilst preserving star height, the very same lower bound (but still in terms of $n = \frac{1}{10}m$) is proved for binary alphabets. Thus we obtain $c \doteq 1.013$ for alphabet size at least 3, and $c \doteq 1.002$ for binary alphabets. This estimation is possibly loose, since it is in turn obtained from a sequence of estimates, which are in part also likely to be unsharp.

At least it looks as if we could increase the constant c in the lower bound somewhat after we enlarge the alphabet size: If we increase the alphabet size, our deterministic finite automata can mimic an expander graph of larger degree, which is the main technical mechanism (see Theorem 8.17). This hints to the alphabet size of DFAs as a potential source of complexity and hence also to a possible line of attack in algorithm design.

What else can we distill from the presented lower bound techniques? On the one hand, the lower bound technique we developed in Chapter 8 shows that bideterministic finite automata which have large cycle rank require huge regular expressions. Here, the restriction to bideterministic finite automata appears to be merely a technicality, whereas the real source of complexity appears to be the property of being very well-connected, i.e. having large cycle rank. On the other hand, we have seen in Chapter 9 that even restricting our attention to finite automata whose cycle rank is zero, or, equivalently, to finite languages, is not sufficient to render the conversion problem tractable. Although we have encountered some structural restrictions on the transition structures that allow for shorter regular expressions, such as planar finite automata (Chapter 8.5) and acyclic finite automata (Chapter 9), we were able to contrast both restrictions with superpolynomial lower bounds.

In this chapter we will identify a parameter very similar to cycle rank that admits a very nice parameterization in the sense that it captures a large family of tractable instances for the conversion problem. The main goal of this chapter will be however to show that, in fact, that the bound of $\Omega(2^n)$ established by Ehrenfeucht and Zeiger (Theorem 2.11) requires larger alphabets: alone the restriction to DFAs over a fixed binary alphabet suffices to get into the realm of $O(1.742^n)$, which is substantially below the lower bound that Ehrenfeucht and Zeiger proved for alphabet size n^2.

10.1 The State Elimination Scheme

In the following we need a refinement of the notion of the computation relation of an ε-NFA as defined in Chapter 2. Namely, for a subset U of the state set Q of a finite automaton A and an input word $w \in \Sigma^*$, we say that A can go on input w from state j *through* U to state k, if it has a computation on input w taking A from state j to k without going through any state outside U. Here, by "going through a state," we mean both entering and leaving. More formally, A can go on input w from j through U to k if one of the following three cases applies:

- $j = k$ and $w = \varepsilon$, or

- $w \in \Sigma \cup \{\varepsilon\}$ and A has a transition $j \xrightarrow{w} k$, or

---

use of the fact from spectral graph theory that, using definitions and notation from [34], for the vertex expansion of ℓ-regular Ramanujan graphs G holds $g_G \geq h_G \geq \lambda_1/2 \geq \frac{\sqrt{\ell}}{2(\ell+1)}$, in particular for $\ell = 3$.

- $w = xa$ for some $x \in \Sigma^*$ and some $a \in \Sigma$ and there is a state r in U such that both A has a transition $r \xrightarrow{a} k$ and A can go on input x from j through U to r.

With the roles of j, k and U fixed as above, we now define the language L_{jk}^U as the set of input words on which the automaton A can go from j through U to k. An essential observation, on which all known algorithms for converting finite automata into regular expressions rely, is the following—a proof can be found e.g. in the seminal work by McNaughton and Yamada on the topic [142].

Lemma 10.1. *Let A be an ε-NFA with state set Q. Let j, k be states in Q, let U be a subset of Q and $i \in Q \setminus U$. Then*

$$L_{jk}^{U \cup \{i\}} = L_{jk}^U \cup L_{ji}^U \left(L_{ii}^U \right)^* L_{ik}^U.$$

Now we present an algorithm scheme that became known as *state elimination*: Without loss of generality, we will assume that the given ε-NFA A is *normalized* in the sense that A has state set $Q \cup \{s, t\}$ where s is the start state and has no ingoing transitions, and t is the sole accepting state and has no outgoing transitions. The algorithm scheme is as follows: We maintain a working set U and matrix whose entries are regular expressions denoting the languages L_{jk}^U. The algorithm proceeds in rounds: Beginning with $U = \emptyset$, we incrementally increase the set U by adding a new state $i \in Q \setminus U$ in each round. The round consists of computing the new entries denoting the languages $L_{jk}^{U \cup \{i\}}$ according to Lemma 10.1. Since the automaton is normalized, we finally obtain a regular expression describing L_{st}^Q, a set equal to $L(A)$ because A is normalized.

As observed by Brzozowski and McCluskey [23], the following simplifications can be made along the way: First, since we are only interested in a regular expression describing L_{st}^Q we never need to compute any expression denoting L_{jk}^U if j or k are in U. That is, after the state i has been added to the set U, we can discard both the row named i and the column with name i from the matrix, hence the name "state elimination." Second, if some of the languages L_{jk}^U, L_{ji}^U, L_{ii}^U, and L_{ik}^U are empty or equal to $\{\varepsilon\}$, then the resulting regular expression can be simplified by applying some obvious reduction rules.

Lemma 10.2. *Let A be a normalized ε-NFA with state set $Q \cup \{s, t\}$. Then there exists an equivalent regular expression of size at most $|\Sigma| \cdot 4^{|Q|}$.*

Proof. Let U be any subset of Q and $j, k \in \{s, t\} \cup Q \setminus U$. We prove by induction on $|U|$ that $\mathrm{alph}(L_{jk}^U) \leq |\Sigma| \cdot 4^{|U|}$. Taking $U = Q$, $j = s$ and $k = t$, this clearly implies the statement, since $L(A) = L_{st}^Q$.

The induction is rooted at $U = \emptyset$: In this case, we have $L_{jk}^\emptyset \subseteq \Sigma \cup \{\varepsilon\}$, and hence $\mathrm{alph}(L_{jk}^\emptyset) \leq |\Sigma| = |\Sigma| \cdot 4^0$. The induction step, going from U to $U \cup \{i\}$ for some $i \in Q \setminus U$, is done by calling Lemma 10.1, since by induction hypothesis each of the languages L_{jk}^U, L_{ji}^U, L_{ii}^U and L_{ik}^U has alphabetic width at most $|\Sigma| \cdot 4^{|U|}$. $\qquad\square$

Remark. The state elimination scheme described above essentially follows the works by McNaughton and Yamada [142], and including the refinements observed by Brzozowski and McCluskey [23]. We note that apart from the observations already mentioned above, also the idea of normalizing the automata by adding a new pair of states with no incoming, respectively outgoing, transitions, is an innovation present only in the later work [23]. McNaughton and Yamada initially used the fact that $L(A) = \bigcup_{f \in F} L_{sf}^Q$. The (modest)

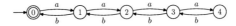

Figure 10.1: A minimal DFA accepting L_4.

from \ to	s	t	0	1	2	3	4
s	ε	$\emptyset$	ε	$\emptyset$	$\emptyset$	$\emptyset$	$\emptyset$
t	$\emptyset$	ε	$\emptyset$	$\emptyset$	$\emptyset$	$\emptyset$	$\emptyset$
0	$\emptyset$	ε	ε	a	$\emptyset$	$\emptyset$	$\emptyset$
1	$\emptyset$	$\emptyset$	b	ε	a	$\emptyset$	$\emptyset$
2	$\emptyset$	$\emptyset$	$\emptyset$	b	ε	a	$\emptyset$
3	$\emptyset$	$\emptyset$	$\emptyset$	$\emptyset$	b	ε	a
4	$\emptyset$	$\emptyset$	$\emptyset$	$\emptyset$	$\emptyset$	b	ε

Table 10.1: The initial matrix with regular expression entries for L_4.

gain offered by the idea of normalizing is illustrated by the bound from Lemma 10.2, which saves a factor of $|Q|$ compared to a similar analysis by Ellul et al. [59] of the McNaughton-Yamada-algorithm.

Example 10.3. We return to the DFA considered in Example 2.5, which is for the convenience of the reader again depicted in Figure 10.1. There we gave the two regular expressions

$$(ab)^* + (ab)^* aa \left(ab + aa(ba)^* bb + bb(ab)^* aa + ba\right)^* bb(ab)^*,$$

and

$$\left(a\left(a\left(a(ab)^* b\right)^* b\right)^* b\right)^*$$

and claimed that both denote the language L_4.

Indeed, both expressions are, after normalizing the automaton, obtained by state elimination. The first expression is obtained by eliminating the states 1, 3, 0, 4, and finally state 2, while the second expression is obtained by eliminating the states in the order $4, 3, 2, 1, 0$. Relevant parts of the computation for the first expression is illustrated in Table 10.1, Table 10.2, and Table 10.3; the analogous computation for the second expression is left as an easy exercise to the reader.

The state elimination scheme we just saw should be called an *algorithm scheme* rather than an algorithm, since there remains some degree of indeterminacy: The working set U has to increased in each round by adding a new state to it. Thus the order in which the states are eliminated one after another forms a parameter of an algorithm scheme, and every such *elimination ordering* gives rise to a different instance of the algorithm scheme. What is most important though is that different elimination orderings can often yield results of largely varying quality. Already in 1960, McNaughton and Yamada observed that the choice of an elimination ordering can greatly influence the size of the resulting regular expression [142].

from \ to	s	t	0	2	4
s	ε	$\emptyset$	ε	$\emptyset$	$\emptyset$
t	$\emptyset$	ε	$\emptyset$	$\emptyset$	$\emptyset$
0	$\emptyset$	ε	$\varepsilon + ab$	aa	$\emptyset$
2	$\emptyset$	$\emptyset$	bb	$\varepsilon + ab + ba$	aa
4	$\emptyset$	ε	$\emptyset$	b	$\varepsilon + ba$

Table 10.2: The matrix obtained after eliminating 1 and 3.

from \ to	s	t	2
s	ε	$(ab)^*$	$(ab)^* aa$
t	$\emptyset$	ε	$\emptyset$
2	$\emptyset$	$bb(ab)^*$	$\varepsilon + ab + ba + aa(ab)^* bb + bb(ab)^* aa$

Table 10.3: The matrix obtained after eliminating 1, 3, 0, and 4.

10.2 Undirected Cycle Rank and Elimination Orderings

We start our investigation of these orderings with some bad news: Namely, there are deterministic finite automata for which state elimination always gives an enormous regular expression, independent of the ordering.

Example 10.4. The following example is essentially due to Ehrenfeucht and Zeiger [55]. We construct a DFA whose underlying digraph is a complete digraph on n vertices; for simplicity, we add two additional states and a few transitions such that the automaton is normalized (but still deterministic). More precisely, let $Q = \{1, 2, \ldots, n\}$. The state set of the resulting DFA is $Q \cup \{s, t\}$, with s and t being the start and sole accepting state, respectively. The DFA has for all pairs of internal states $j, k \in Q$ a transition $j \overset{a_{jk}}{\rightarrow} k$, and in addition the transitions $s \overset{a_{sj}}{\rightarrow} j$ as well as $j \overset{a_{jt}}{\rightarrow} t$ for each internal state j in Q. A simple induction along the lines of the proof of Lemma 10.2 shows that state elimination results in a regular expression of size at least 4^n, independent of the elimination ordering.

Indeed the language $L(A)$ is hard to describe by means of *any* regular expression, not just those that can be obtained by state elimination: It follows from the work by Ehrenfeucht and Zeiger that this language has alphabetic width at least 2^{n-1}.

This imposes severe limitations on what we can expect, in the worst case, from the state elimination scheme. Nevertheless, as mentioned above, a few heuristics to choose good elimination orderings have been proposed in the literature [47, 88, 142]. But for none of these heuristics any quantitative bounds are known. Before we study the quest for good elimination orderings in more detail, we introduce a few more notions.

An ordering on Q naturally induces an ordering on every subset $U \subseteq Q$. For the definition of the languages L_{jk}^U, the ordering on U is clearly irrelevant; abusing notation, we will write r_{jk}^U for the regular expression obtained from eliminating the ordered sequence or set U—in case U is a set, then we imply an arbitrary but fixed ordering for U. Using this convention, r_{jk}^{ε} and $r_{jk}^{\emptyset}$ will both have the same meaning, since the empty sequence is the sole ordering for the empty set.

As already mentioned in the previous section, we can often make some obvious simplifications along the way when the regular expression is built. The following definition will allow us to abstract from inessential differences between regular expressions.

Definition 10.5. Two regular expressions r and s are called *similar*, in symbols $r \cong s$, if r and s can be transformed into each other by repeatedly applying one of the following rules to their subexpressions:

- $r + r \cong r$,

- $(r + s) + t \cong r + (s + t)$,

- $r + s \cong s + r$,

- $r + \emptyset \cong r \cong \emptyset + r$,

- $r \cdot \emptyset \cong \emptyset \cong \emptyset \cdot r$,

- $r \cdot \varepsilon \cong r \cong \varepsilon \cdot r$, and

- $\emptyset^* \cong \varepsilon \cong \varepsilon^*$.

The first three rules above define the notion of similarity introduced by Brzozowski [21], and the remaining ones have been added because of their usefulness in the context of converting regular expressions into finite automata.

Equipped with these notions, we now proceed to the first main technical lemma of this chapter.

Lemma 10.6. *Let A be a normalized ε-NFA with state set $\{s,t\} \cup Q$, and let G be the digraph underlying the transition structure of A. Assume $U \subseteq Q$ can be partitioned into two sets T_1 and T_2 such that the induced subgraph $G[U]$ falls apart into mutually disconnected components $G[T_1]$ and $G[T_2]$. Let j and k be vertices with $j, k \in \{s,t\} \cup Q \setminus U$. Then for the expression $r_{jk}^{T_1 \cdot T_2}$ obtained by elimination of the the vertices in T_1 followed by elimination of the vertices in T_2 holds*

$$r_{jk}^{T_1 \cdot T_2} \cong r_{jk}^{T_1} + r_{jk}^{T_2}. \tag{10.1}$$

Proof. We prove the statement by induction on $|T_1| + |T_2|$. The induction is rooted at $|T_1| + |T_2| = 0$. For the case T_2 is empty, we have in general $r_{jk}^{T_1 T_2} = r_{jk}^{T_1} \cong r_{jk}^{T_1} + r_{jk}^{\varepsilon}$, as desired.

For the induction step, let $|T_1| + |T_2| = n$, with $T_2 \neq \emptyset$. Let τ be the last element in T_2, that is, $T_2 = T\tau$ for some prefix T of T_2. Then

$$r_{jk}^{T_1 T_2} \cong r_{jk}^{T_1 T} + r_{j\tau}^{T_1 T} \cdot \left(r_{\tau\tau}^{T_1 T}\right)^* \cdot r_{\tau k}^{T_1 T}. \tag{10.2}$$

Since $|T_1| + |T| = n - 1$, for the first of the four subexpressions on the right-hand side the induction hypothesis applies: $r_{jk}^{T_1 T} \cong r_{jk}^{T_1} + r_{jk}^{T}$. For the last three subexpressions, we claim that $r_{j\tau}^{T_1 T} \cong r_{j\tau}^{T}$, as well as $\left(r_{\tau\tau}^{T_1 T}\right)^* \cong \left(r_{\tau\tau}^{T}\right)^*$, and $r_{\tau k}^{T_1 T} = r_{\tau k}^{T}$. We only prove the first and the second similarity congruence, because the third is proved symmetrically to the first.

It suffices to prove $r_{j\tau}^{T_1} \cong r_{j\tau}^{\varepsilon}$, since both sides of the congruence $r_{j\tau}^{T_1T} \cong r_{j\tau}^{T}$ are obtained from the mentioned one by eliminating T, and state elimination preserves similarity of expressions. If $L_{j,\tau}^{\varepsilon}$ is nonempty, then these words are already described by $r_{j\tau}^{\varepsilon}$. It only remains to show that no further words are introduced by eliminating T_1. So, for simplicity of exposition, we may as well assume that $L_{j,\tau} = \emptyset$ and prove the congruence for this case. This can be done as follows: Consider the subdigraph $G[U]$. By assumption of the lemma, $\tau \in T_2$ is not reachable from any vertex in T_1, thus the automaton cannot go from from j to τ through any state in T_1 on any input at all, and since there is no direct connection from j to τ either, the language $L_{j\tau}^{T_1}$ is empty. Every regular expression describing the empty set is similar to the expression $\emptyset$, hence $r_{j\tau}^{T_1} \cong \emptyset$, provided $L_{j\tau}^{\varepsilon} = \emptyset$. This completes the proof of the congruence for this subexpression.

Similar to above, the second congruence will follow once we have established that $r_{\tau\tau}^{T_1} \cong r_{\tau\tau}^{\varepsilon}$. This is easy to see since any computation path from τ to τ through T_1 (other than a path given by the empty input ε or by a single self-loop directly returning back to τ itself) would witness that τ is connected to the subgraph T_1; but since τ is in T_2 this would contradict our assumption.

Plugging these three subexpression congruences into Congruence 10.2, we obtain

$$r_{jk}^{T_1T_2} \cong r_{jk}^{T_1} + \left[r_{jk}^{T} + r_{j\tau}^{T} \left(r_{\tau\tau}^{T} \right)^* r_{\tau k}^{T} \right],$$

and the latter is of course similar to $r_{jk}^{T_1} + r_{jk}^{T_2}$, by definition of the state elimination scheme. $\qquad \square$

Remark. To prevent potential misunderstandings, we recall that, by our notational convention, Congruence 10.1 assumes an *arbitrary but fixed ordering* on T_1T_2, which naturally induces an ordering on all of its subsets, including T_1 and T_2. Equivalently, one can assume each an arbitrary but fixed ordering for the two subsets T_1 and T_2. Then these jointly define an ordering on T_1T_2.

The next theorem identifies a parameterized restriction on the transition structure of finite automata that gives rise to a large class of tractable instances of the conversion problem. This parameter is the cycle rank of the *undirected* graph underlying the automaton; recall the definition of cycle rank from Definition 8.5. In the following, the *undirected cycle rank* of a digraph G will refer to the cycle rank of the symmetric digraph $\overleftrightarrow{G}$; similar to our convention in Chapter 8, by the undirected cycle rank of a finite automaton A, we refer to the undirected cycle rank of the underlying (di)graph. Note that undirected cycle rank appears in the literature under many different names, such as ordered chromatic number [120], vertex ranking [17], tree-depth [149], or minimum elimination tree height, see e.g. [18].

Theorem 10.7. *Let A be an ε-NFA with n states, and let c be a positive integer. If A has undirected cycle rank at most c, then*

$$\mathrm{alph}(L(A)) \leq |\Sigma| \cdot 4^c \cdot n.$$

The theorem is indeed a special case of the following slightly more general technical lemma, which we will prove instead:

Lemma 10.8. *Let A be a normalized ε-NFA with state set $\{s, t\} \cup Q$, let c be a positive integer, and let G be its underlying (di)graph. If $U \subseteq Q$ is such that $G[U]$ has undirected cycle rank at most c, then there is an elimination ordering for U which yields, for each pair j, k of states not in U, regular expressions r_{jk}^{U} of size at most $|\Sigma| \cdot 4^c \cdot |U|$.*

Proof. We prove the statement by induction on the number of states in the set U. In the base case $U = \{u\}$, the undirected cycle rank of $G[U]$ is at most $c = 1$, and it is readily verified that in both cases holds

$$\text{alph}\left(r_{jk}^U\right) \leq 4 \cdot |\Sigma| \leq |\Sigma| \cdot 4^c \cdot |U|;$$

recall that we require that the bound c is at least 1.

For the induction step, we consider two cases: If the graph $G[U]$ is disconnected, then it falls apart into the components $C_1, C_2, \ldots, C_\ell$, each having at most $|U| - 1$ vertices. By induction hypothesis, for each such component C, there is an ordering for C such that for each pair of states j, k not in U, the regular expression r_{jk}^C resulting from this ordering satisfies

$$\text{alph}\left(r_{jk}^C\right) \leq |\Sigma| \cdot |C| \cdot 4^c. \tag{10.3}$$

Here we can use the same constant c as for U, since the cycle rank of U is at least as large as the cycle rank of C. Fix such an ordering for each of the components $C_1, C_2, \ldots, C_\ell$, and take the sum of these expressions, that is, $\sum_{i=1}^\ell r_{jk}^{C_i}$. By applying Lemma 10.6 as often as needed, we see that the regular expression $r_{jk}^{C_1 C_2 \cdots C_\ell}$, which is obtained by eliminating according to the ordering $C_1 C_2 \cdots C_\ell$, is similar to the sum $\sum_{i=1}^\ell r_{jk}^{C_i}$—recall that when applying Lemma 10.6, we assume arbitrary but fixed internal orderings on each set C_i. Using Inequality 10.3, the latter expression has alphabetic width at most

$$\sum_{i=1}^\ell |\Sigma| \cdot |C_i| \cdot 4^c = |\Sigma| \cdot |U| \cdot 4^c.$$

Otherwise, by the definition of cycle rank there must be a vertex u in $G[U]$ such that $G[U \setminus \{u\}]$ has undirected cycle rank at most $c - 1$. By induction hypothesis, there is an ordering on $U \setminus \{u\}$ such that for each pair of states j, k not in $U \setminus \{u\}$, the regular expression $r_{jk}^{U \setminus \{u\}}$ resulting from this ordering satisfies

$$\text{alph}\left(r_{jk}^{U \setminus \{u\}}\right) \leq |\Sigma| \cdot (|U| - 1) \cdot 4^{c-1}. \tag{10.4}$$

Finally, eliminating u as last state can incur a size increase by a factor of at most 4, which shows the desired inequality in the second case.

□

Unfortunately, determining the undirected cycle rank is **NP**-complete in general, as proved first by Pothen (cf. [17]). Nevertheless, the above theorem has some interesting algorithmic consequences: For instance, it is known [120] that planar graphs on n vertices have undirected cycle rank in $O(\sqrt{n})$. In Chapter 8.5, we mentioned that Ellul et al. devised an algorithm for converting an n-state planar finite automaton into an equivalent regular expression of size in $2^{O(\sqrt{n})}$. Combined with the above result, it is not too difficult to prove that an expression of size within this bound can be indeed obtained by state elimination in time $2^{O(\sqrt{n})}$, in place of the more complicated algorithm presented in [59]. We shall see one further application immediately; still more applications will be presented later on in Chapter 12, where we investigate language operations on regular expressions.

from \ to	000	001	010	011	100	101	110	111
000	ε	a_1	a_2	$\emptyset$	a_3	$\emptyset$	$\emptyset$	$\emptyset$
001	b_1	ε	$\emptyset$	a_2	$\emptyset$	a_3	$\emptyset$	$\emptyset$
010	b_2	$\emptyset$	ε	a_1	$\emptyset$	$\emptyset$	a_3	$\emptyset$
011	$\emptyset$	b_2	b_1	ε	$\emptyset$	$\emptyset$	$\emptyset$	a_3
100	b_3	$\emptyset$	$\emptyset$	$\emptyset$	ε	a_1	a_2	$\emptyset$
101	$\emptyset$	b_3	$\emptyset$	$\emptyset$	b_1	ε	$\emptyset$	a_2
110	$\emptyset$	$\emptyset$	b_3	$\emptyset$	b_2	$\emptyset$	ε	a_1
111	$\emptyset$	$\emptyset$	$\emptyset$	b_3	$\emptyset$	b_2	b_1	ε

Table 10.4: The initial matrix with regular expression entries. The rows and columns for the states s and t are omitted (all corresponding entries are equal to either ε or $\emptyset$).

10.3 Converting DFAs into Regular Expressions: An Upper Bound

Although we cannot assume that DFAs in general have small undirected cycle rank, we can still try to look for large induced subgraphs that have small undirected cycle rank. The reason is here that after eliminating the vertex set U of an induced subgraph having undirected cycle rank c, the generated intermediate expressions are of size $4^c \cdot |U|$, rather than $4^{|U|}$. This advantage is more prominent if U is very large, while $c \ll |U|$: Ideally, we want to find an induced subgraph of very low cycle rank, but which is so huge that it contains already constant fraction of all vertices. If $|U| = \gamma \cdot n$, for some γ bounded away from zero, then eliminating the remaining $(1 - \gamma)n$ states can increase the size of the intermediate expressions "only" by a factor of $4^{(1-\gamma)n}$. If the intermediate expressions resulting from eliminating the "first, easier half" are of size (say) $2^{o(n)}$, we will finally end up with a regular expression of size $2^{o(n)} \cdot 4^{(1-\gamma)n} = o(4^n)$. We will elaborate this basic idea in more detail in the following. To gain a bit more intuition, we shall take a look at a relatively simple example first:

Example 10.9. For illustrating the above said, consider the following language:

$$(a_1 b_1)^* \ \text{ш} \ (a_2 b_2)^* \ \text{ш} \ (a_3 b_3)^*$$

This language can be accepted by a DFA over the state set $\{0, 1\}^3$, and whose partial transition function is given such that input a_i sets the i-th bit left of the rightmost bit of the current state from 0 to 1, and input b_i resets the i-th bit, again counting from right to left, of the current state from 1 to 0. All other transitions are undefined. Formally, we can set out a matrix with regular expression entries as shown in Table 10.4.

The start state is 000, which is also the single final state. Notice that the graph underlying this automaton is the 3-dimensional cube, with 8 vertices; and generalizing this example to $d \geq 3$, the underlying graph would be the d-dimensional hypercube, with 2^d many vertices. Normalizing this automaton amounts to adding two new states s and t

and adding ε-transitions from s to the old start state and from the latter state to the new final state t.

It is well known that the d-dimensional hypercube admits a huge induced subgraph of very low undirected cycle rank: The hypercube is 2-colorable, and thus has an independent set that contains at least half of the vertices. Notice that an independent set always has cycle rank at most 1. For instance, if we eliminate first the sequence $U = 001, 010, 100, 111$, we end up with a residual matrix having entries as shown in Table 10.5. Not surprisingly, for the resulting regular expressions holds

$$r_{jk}^{U} \cong r_{jk}^{001} + r_{jk}^{010} + r_{jk}^{100} + r_{jk}^{111},$$

which we could also have seen equivalently by applying Lemma 10.6 as often as needed.

Notice that, while the matrix now appears to have many more nontrivial entries, the largest entry has alphabetic width only 6, although we already eliminated half of the original number of states. Continuing the elimination with the matrix from Table 10.5 we will end up with a regular expression of size at most $6 \cdot 4^{|Q \setminus U|} \leq 1536$, *even for the worst ordering* of the remaining states in $Q \setminus U$. Of course, we can again look for a large independent set in the residual matrix. Yet a look at Table 10.5 shows that, in our small example, all independent sets in the residual graph are only of size 1.

While the bound 1536 may appear large at first glance, recall that the upper bound predicted by Lemma 10.2 would be as huge as $4^8 = 65536$. Also notice that the two bounds both are overestimations of the actual resulting expression size.

The above example suggests to look out for large independent sets in the underlying graph, and to eliminate these first. We cannot expect a large independent set in the graph underlying the DFA if the alphabet size is not fixed: Consider again the DFAs exhibiting worst-case behavior, which we saw in Example 10.4. There the number of edges is quadratic in the number of states, and the underlying graph has no independent sets of size greater than 1. But once we require constant alphabet size, the undirected graph underlying the DFA is sparse, i.e., it can have only a linear number of edges. A classical theorem in extremal graph theory due to Turán [176] states that sparse graphs do always contain huge independent sets:

Theorem 10.10 (Turán). *If G is an n-vertex graph of average degree $\overline{d}$, then G admits an independent set having at least $n/(\overline{d} + 1)$ many vertices.*

By generalizing the analysis carried out in Example 10.9 to the case of an independent set U of size $|U| = n/(\overline{d}+1)$, this already enables us to generate regular expressions of size $O(\gamma^n)$, for some constant $\gamma < 4$ depending on the alphabet size. We shall not determine the precise constant here, since we shall present an improved bound immediately.

Recall that our basic idea is that we want to look for huge induced subgraphs whose elimination is cheap in the sense that the intermediate expressions are of size $2^{o(n)}$. For independent sets, which have cycle rank at most 1, this intermediate size is indeed at most $O(n)$, as implied by Lemma 10.8. Thus we can safely look for induced subgraphs with more complex structure allowed. Alon et al. [2] found a generalization of Turán's theorem. Although they used the concept of degeneracy, and not treewidth, a special case of their result can be phrased in terms of treewidth as follows:

Theorem 10.11 (Alon, Kahn & Seymour). *If G is an n-vertex graph of average degree at most $\overline{d}$, with $\overline{d} \geq 2$, then G admits an induced subgraph of treewidth at most 1 that has at least $2n/(\overline{d} + 1)$ many vertices.*

from \ to	000	011	101	110
000	$\varepsilon + a_1b_1 + a_2b_2 + a_3b_3$	$a_1a_2 + a_2a_1$	$a_1a_3 + a_3a_1$	$a_2a_3 + a_3a_2$
011	$b_1b_2 + b_2b_1$	$\varepsilon + a_3b_3 + b_1a_3 + b_2a_2$	$a_3b_2 + b_2a_3$	$a_3b_1 + b_1a_3$
101	$b_1b_3 + b_3b_1$	$a_2b_3 + b_3a_2$	$\varepsilon + a_2b_2 + b_1a_1 + b_3a_3$	$a_2b_1 + b_1a_2$
110	$b_2b_3 + b_3b_2$	$a_1b_3 + b_3a_1$	$a_1b_2 + b_2a_1$	$\varepsilon + a_1b_1 + b_2a_2 + b_3a_3$

Table 10.5: The residual matrix with regular expression entries, after elimination of the independent set $U = 001, 010, 100, 111$. The rows and columns for the states s and t are again omitted (in this particular example, all corresponding entries are still equal to either ε or $\emptyset$).

We point out that independent sets are exactly the induced subgraphs of treewidth zero. The following recent result, due to Edwards and Farr [53], provides a nice analog to Turán's Theorem and to the theorem just stated:

Theorem 10.12 (Edwards/Farr). *If G is an n-vertex graph of average degree at most $\overline{d}$, with $\overline{d} \geq 2$, then G admits an induced subgraph of treewidth at most 2 that has at least $3n/(\overline{d}+1)$ many vertices.*

This reinterpretation of the above theorems as in terms of treewidth appears to be new, as treewidth is not mentioned in any of the references [2, 53, 176]. Now we are ready to state the main result of this chapter.

Theorem 10.13. *Let A be an n-state DFA over an alphabet Σ. Then there is an elimination ordering which yields a regular expression for $L(A)$ having size at most*

$$4 \cdot |\Sigma| \cdot n^7 \cdot 4^{\alpha n},$$

with $\alpha = 1 - 3/(2 \cdot |\Sigma| + 1)$. In particular, for $|\Sigma| = 2$, this bound is in $O(1.742^n)$.

Proof. Assume the given DFA has state set Q. In a first step, we normalize the DFA by adding a new initial state s and a single new final state t and connecting them with Q appropriately. Note that while normalizing might increase the number of edges in the undirected graph G underlying the automaton, this process does not affect the average degree of the induced subgraph $G[Q]$, since all new edges begin or end outside the set Q. Since every state in Q has at most $|\Sigma|$ many transitions connecting it to some other state in Q, the average number of transitions entering some state in Q and also coming from some state in Q is at most $|\Sigma|$. Altogether, the average degree of $G[Q]$ is at most $2 \cdot |\Sigma|$, both before and after the normalization.

To find a good elimination ordering, we choose to eliminate first the vertex set U of a huge induced subgraph of treewidth at most 2 from $G[Q]$. Here Theorem 10.12 guarantees that we can choose U to be of cardinality at least $(1-\alpha)n$. Recall that undirected graphs of treewidth at most k have separator numberat most $k + 1$ (Lemma 8.4), a fact we exploited already in Chapter 8. We can use Lemma 8.7 to bound the cycle rank c of the undirected graph $G[U]$ above, in terms of the separator number. In this way, we get $c \leq 1 + 3 \log |U|$. Now by Lemma 10.8, the set U can be ordered in a way such that for all j, k not in U holds $\mathrm{alph}(r_{jk}^U) \leq 4^c \cdot |U|$.

Now we continue with eliminating the remaining states, by choosing an arbitrary ordering for the states in $\overline{U} = Q \setminus U$. During the second phase, eliminating a state in $\overline{U}$ can increase the size of the intermediate expressions by a factor of at most 4 each time, so we have:

$$\mathrm{alph}\left(r_{st}^Q\right) \leq 4^c \cdot |U| \cdot 4^{\overline{U}}.$$

With $c \leq 1 + 3 \log |U|$, we obtain

$$4^c = 2^{2 \cdot (1 + 3 \log |U|)} \leq 4 \cdot |U|^6.$$

Combined with the inequality $|\overline{U}| = n - |U| \leq \alpha n$, we thus get an upper bound of

$$\mathrm{alph}\left(r_{st}^Q\right) \leq |\Sigma| \cdot 4 \cdot |U|^6 \cdot |U| \cdot 4^{\alpha n} \leq 4 \cdot |\Sigma| \cdot n^7 \cdot 4^{\alpha n}.$$

For $|\Sigma| = 2$, we have $4^\alpha = 4^{2/5} \doteq 1.7411$, and so $n^7 \cdot 4^{2/5 \cdot n} \in O(1.742^n)$. $\square$

Some readers may find that there is no apparent reason to stop at this point. We could of course further generalize the above approach and look for large induced *planar* subgraphs. Admittedly, it can be proved that eliminating an induced planar subgraph still yields intermediate regular expressions of size $2^{o(n)}$. Yet it appears to be difficult to guarantee essentially larger size of the induced subgraphs with such a generalization while retaining sufficiently low undirected cycle rank. In this direction, Alon et al. [2] show that the notion of degeneracy allows for larger induced subgraphs. But we do not believe that there is a sufficiently tight relation between the degeneracy of a graph and its undirected cycle rank. In fact, the original version of Theorem 10.12 is actually stated in terms of planar induced subgraphs, among which the treewidth can become even as large as $\Omega(\sqrt{n})$ [160]; these just happen to be in fact even of treewidth at most 2. The mentioned paper [53] discusses this issue at greater depth.

11 Summary of Results on the Conversion Problem

Previous to this work, only few lower bounds regarding the necessary size blow-up when converting from finite automata into regular expressions were known. We collect all previous and new upper and lower bounds in Table 11.1. The table also includes a result by Gelade and Neven from [65] that they proved around the same time, independently of this work and by means of different proof techniques.

As the table illustrates, we managed to give lower bounds for alphabet size two in all investigated scenarios. In each of the cases, the respective bound is tight, up to the constant factor implied by the Ω-Notation. As the hidden constants appear in the exponents, it is interesting to search for more precise estimates. This issue was, at least in part, addressed in Chapter 10, where we showed algorithmically that the blow-up for converting DFAs over *binary* alphabets into regular expressions can reach at most $O(1.742^n)$. Similar improvements to the upper bounds might be possible in the cases of planar or acyclic DFAs, indicating a possible line of further research. Our new upper bound nicely contrasts with the classical lower bound of $\Omega(2^n)$ obtained by Ehrenfeucht and Zeiger for given DFAs over *unbounded* alphabets (Theorem 2.11). This clearly illustrates the need for proving such lower bounds also for languages over alphabets of constant size.

What is not represented in the table is the parameterization of the conversion problem in terms of cycle rank. Theorem 10.7 shows that the conversion problem is nicely parameterized by the undirected cycle rank k of the graph underlying the finite automaton. Namely, an n-state finite automaton of undirected cycle rank at most k can be converted to a regular expression of size k rather than in n. This is good since k is always smaller than n. The bad thing is, as already mentioned, determining this parameter is **NP**-complete. Luckily, we can get around that problem: In a large variety of cases, we are able to give combinatorial upper bounds on k, which results in *provably* shorter regular expressions.

Finally, as pointed out by Ellul et al. [59], in the case of unary languages, the conversion problem can be solved with only linear increase in size because of the special structure of unary DFAs. A similar observation holds if a unary NFA is given, where the size increase can be at most quadratic.

DFA → RE Conversion	Previous ——— lower bound New		Previous ——— upper bound New	
general	$\Omega(2^n)$, $\quad |\Sigma| = \Omega(n^2)$ [55] $\\ 2^{\Omega(\sqrt{n/\log n})}$, $|\Sigma| \geq 4$ [65]		$4^n \cdot n^{O(1)}$, $|\Sigma| = n^{O(1)}$ [23, 142]	
	$2^{\Omega(n)}$, $\quad |\Sigma| \geq 2$ (Thm. 8.21)		$O(1.742^n)$, $|\Sigma| = 2$ (Thm. 10.13)	
planar	$2^{\Omega(\sqrt{n})}$, $\quad |\Sigma| \geq 2$ (Thm. 8.22)		$2^{O(\sqrt{n})}$, $\quad |\Sigma| = n^{O(1)}$ [59]	
acyclic	$n^{\Omega(\log\log n)}$, $|\Sigma| = \Omega(n^2)$ [55] $\\ n^2$, $\quad |\Sigma| \geq 2$ [59]		$n^{O(\log n)}$, $\quad |\Sigma| = n^{O(1)}$ [55]	
	$n^{\Omega(\log n)}$, $\quad |\Sigma| \geq 2$ (Thm. 9.14)			

Table 11.1: Summary of previous and new lower and upper bounds on converting n-state DFAs to regular expressions. The categories "general", "planar" and "acyclic" indicate the cases of given a DFA, given a DFA whose underlying digraph is planar, and given a DFA whose underlying digraph is acyclic. The last of these of course coincides with the case where a DFA accepting a finite language is given.

Part IV

Language Operations on Regular Expressions

12 Intersection, Interleaving and Complementation

The third main part of this thesis is devoted to the investigation of how efficiently language operations can be implemented on regular expressions. Comparable questions are well understood if (deterministic or nondeterministic) finite automata are used as model of description, see e.g. [93, 181]. But by the time the author started research on this topic, regarding language operations on regular expressions only a few preliminary results were reported by Ellul et al. [59]. Notably, Gelade and Neven obtained results in this direction in a parallel effort,[1] see [64, 65]. We also note that similar questions regarding the *structural* complexity, as opposed to *descriptional* complexity, of regular expressions were already successfully tackled around 1970: At that time, Cohen and Brzozowski [36] studied how some basic language operations can affect the star height of regular languages.

The type of question we are interested in is probably best explained an example, the intersection operation. It is well known that the intersection of two regular languages is again regular, a fact which is usually proved using a product construction on finite automata, see [96]. The naive implementation of this and similar language operations on regular expressions would be to convert the operand expressions into NFAs, realize the operation on finite automata, and convert the result back into a regular expression. The drawback is that, even if the language operation under consideration can be implemented in the NFA model without causing an explosion of the number of states, alone converting a finite automaton into a regular expression may already incur an exponential size blow-up in general, as we saw in Chapter 8.

Regarding the descriptional complexity of regular expressions, the following question raised in [59] thus appears natural:

Given two regular expressions E_1 and E_2, of size at most m and n, describing languages L_1 and L_2, what is the size, as a function of m and n, of a shortest regular expression describing $L_1 \cap L_2$?

Here we are interested in the worst case, that is, we are want to determine the function

$$\mathrm{alph}(\cap, m, n) := \max\{\, \mathrm{alph}(L_1 \cap L_2) \mid \mathrm{alph}(L_1) \leq m, \mathrm{alph}(L_2) \leq n \,\}.$$

Of course, intersection is not the only interesting language operation preserving regularity, and we will also study a few other operations. Here, the choice of operations to study is naturally guided by their relevance for practical applications, as well as their adequacy as a testing ground both for general algorithmic design principles and for lower bound techniques.

---

[1]Part of the results presented below were obtained independently of [64, 65] and by different methods, while another part of our constructions is inspired by those works. What still adds to possible confusion is that Gelade's follow-up paper [64] in turn builds on our results presented beforehand in [79]. We will explain whenever this occurs and give proper credit whenever we are using other authors' ideas, and we will also acknowledge priority where appropriate.

Notice that the function alph($\cap, m, n$), as introduced above, tacitly assumes that we allow alphabet sizes growing along with the size of the operands. An interesting point is here to determine to what extent the alphabet size can affect the function defined above, and it also appears quite natural to study this question when restricted to small alphabets. To avoid ambiguity on the one hand, and heavy notation on the other hand, we will explicitly address the alphabet size in all of our results stated below.

12.1 Alphabetic Width of Intersection and Interleaving

We begin this section by exhibiting a family of language pairs whose intersection necessarily causes an exponential increase in regular expression size. These languages have an appealingly simple structure, and their star height was already studied, although not completely determined, in Eggan's seminal paper on star height of regular languages [54].

Theorem 12.1. *For $m, n \in \mathbb{N}$, define $K_m = \{ w \in \{a, b\}^* \mid |w|_a \equiv 0 \mod m \}$ and $L_n = \{ w \in \{a, b\}^* \mid |w|_b \equiv 0 \mod n \}$. Then we have $h(K_m \cap L_n) = m$, if $m = n$, and $h(K_m \cap L_n) = \min(m, n) + 1$, otherwise.*

Proof. The stated upper bound on the star height is proved already in [54, Corollary 2, pp. 394f.], so it remains to derive a matching lower bound. It is straightforward to construct deterministic finite automata with m states (respectively with n states) describing the languages K_m and L_n, respectively. By applying the standard product construction on these automata, we obtain a deterministic finite automaton A accepting the language $K_m \cap L_n$. It is not hard to see that the automaton A is a minimal deterministic finite automaton, and furthermore that it is bideterministic. Therefore Theorem 8.10 shows $h(K_m \cap L_n) = cr(A)$.

The digraph underlying automaton A is the directed discrete $(m \times n)$-torus. This digraph can be described as the Cartesian graph product of two directed cycles, see Figure 12.1 for illustration.

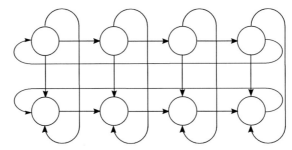

Figure 12.1: Drawing of the discrete directed $(m \times n)$-torus in the case where $m = 2$ and $n = 4$.

The entanglement[2] of this digraph was determined by Berwanger and Grädel [12] based on a similar cops and robber game. We use basically the same argument to give a lower

---

[2]The *entanglement* is a digraph connectivity measure, somewhat similar to cycle rank, introduced recently by Berwanger and Grädel. We shall not further elaborate upon that concept here; the interested reader is referred to [12].

bound on the cycle rank of this digraph *via* the game characterization given in Theorem 8.13. By symmetry, assume the torus has m rows and n columns, with $m \leq n$. At any stage of the game, we say that a row (column, respectively) is *free* if each of the vertices in the row (column, respectively) is neither yet occupied, nor announced to be occupied in the current move of the cops. In the kth move of the cops, there are at least $m - k$ free rows and $n - k$ free columns. As long as $k < m$, the robbers' strategy is to reside on the subgraph induced by the rows and columns that are currently free. For $k < m$, each free row or column is strongly connected itself, and each pair of free columns is strongly connected to each other *via* the (nonempty) set of free rows. The strategy always yields a valid game position, and this already shows the desired lower bound in the case $m = n$. In the case $m > n$, as soon as the last free row is threatening to be occupied, the robber can still flee to one of the remaining free columns. Thus an additional cop is needed, since each free column itself forms a nontrivial strong subset, even though the columns are no longer strongly connected to each other. □

Together with Theorem 8.11, we immediately obtain some results about the alphabetic width of operations on regular languages.

Corollary 12.2. *There exists a constant $c > 1$ such that for all $m \leq n$ holds*

$$\mathrm{alph}(\cap, m, n) = c^m,$$

and this holds for all alphabets of size at least 2. □

This gives an improvement over a lower bound of $c^{\sqrt{m}}$ for alphabet size m, which was obtained independently by Gelade and Neven around the same time [65]. Also for the interleaving operation we can now readily deduce a lower bound, since the language from Theorem 12.1 can be written as $(a^m)^* \; \mathrm{m} \; (b^n)^*$.

Corollary 12.3. *There exists a constant $c > 1$ such that for all $m \leq n$ holds*

$$\mathrm{alph}(\mathrm{m}, m, n) = c^m,$$

and this holds for all alphabets of size at least 2. □

We now turn to upper bounds. As detailed by Ellul et al. [59], the naive idea of converting the operand expressions over Σ into finite automata, performing a product construction, and converting the result back to a finite automaton gives a preliminary upper bound of

$$|\Sigma| \cdot 4^{(m+1)(n+1)} \leq d^{mn}.$$

Note that for the intersection operation, we can safely assume $|\Sigma| \leq \min\{m, n\}$, so the additional parameter can be hidden by appropriate choice of the constant d. We shall see that this easy upper bound can be substantially improved by choosing an appropriate elimination ordering according to some graph-theoretic properties, similar to the considerations carried out in Chapter 10. We need to introduce a few more notions from graph theory first.

Definition 12.4. Let $G_1 = (V_1, E_1)$ and $G_2 = (V_2, E_2)$ be two digraphs. The categorical product $G_1 \otimes G_2$ is defined as the digraph with vertex set $V_1 \times V_2$ and edge set $\{ ((u_1, u_2), (v_1, v_2)) \mid (u_1, v_1) \in E_1 \text{ and } (u_2, v_2) \in E_2 \}$.

Our notation of the categorical product follows the one given in [126].

Incidentally, this product on graphs bears a striking similarity to the standard product construction on finite automata for realizing the intersection of regular languages, compare [96]. We have experienced in previous chapters, as a prime example in Theorem 10.7, that the connectivity of the (di)graph underlying a finite automaton can largely affect the complexity of the conversion problem into regular expressions. We thus inspect next how the connectivity of digraphs evolves under such graph products.

Theorem 12.5. *Let G_1 and G_2 be two digraphs, each having weak separator number at most k. Assume G_1 and G_2 have m and n vertices, respectively, with $m \leq n$. Then for the cycle rank of the categorical product $G_1 \otimes G_2$ holds:*

$$cr(G_1 \otimes G_2) < k \cdot m \cdot \left(\log \frac{n}{m} + 4\right).$$

Proof. The basic idea is to search recursively for certain weak balanced separators in the product digraph that are implied by weak balanced separators in the factor graphs. If we search for a separator of size at most k in the larger factor (say) G_2, this separator gives rise to a weak balanced separator of size only $k \cdot m$ in the product graph, while halving the maximum size among the strong components of the larger factor graph, and thus also of the product graph. This idea is illustrated in Figure 12.2. We proceed by recursively

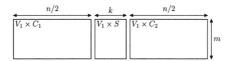

Figure 12.2: Schematic drawing of the product graph $G_1 \otimes G_2$ for the case where G_1 has vertex set V_1 of size m, G_2 has vertex set $V_2 = C_1 \cup C_2 \cup S$ of size n, with C_1 and C_2 separated by S in G_2. Looking for a separator in G_2 induces a much smaller balanced separator for $G_1 \otimes G_2$ if $m \ll n$.

halving the parts of G_2, until the resulting parts become smaller than $|V_1| = m$. Then we look for separators in G_1, and proceed recursively until the size of the parts has sufficiently decreased such that we switch again, to continue working with the parts of G_2 ...

In order to turn this idea into a rigorous proof, we start off with a few observations regarding the categorical product of digraphs: First, the categorical product is commutative in the sense that $G_1 \otimes G_2$ is isomorphic to $G_2 \otimes G_1$. Second, if $S_1 \subseteq V_1$ is a weak balanced separator for G_1, then $S_1 \times V_2$ is a weak balanced separator for $G_1 \otimes G_2$. This can be seen as follows: Each closed walk

$$\left(v_{i_1}^{(1)}, v_{j_1}^{(2)}\right) \to \cdots \to \left(v_{i_2}^{(1)}, v_{j_2}^{(2)}\right) \cdots \to \left(v_{i_1}^{(1)}, v_{j_1}^{(2)}\right)$$

in the product graph $G_1 \otimes G_2$ naturally projects down to a corresponding closed walk

$$v_{i_1}^{(1)} \to \cdots \to v_{i_2}^{(1)} \to \cdots \to v_{i_1}^{(1)}.$$

in G_1. In the counterpositive, if G_1 has the property that every closed walk in G_1 visiting both $v_{i_1}^{(1)}$ and $v_{i_2}^{(1)}$ passes through S, then $G_1 \otimes G_2$ has the property that every closed walk in

$G_1 \otimes G_2$ visiting both a vertex of the form $\left(v_{i_1}^{(1)}, w^{(2)}\right)$ and a vertex of the form $\left(v_{i_2}^{(1)}, x^{(2)}\right)$, with $w^{(2)}, x^{(2)} \in V_2$, necessarily also visits a vertex from $S \times V_2$.

In particular, if $G_1 - S$ has the strong components $C_1, C_2, \ldots, C_r$, then the sets $C_1 \times V_2, C_2 \times V_2, \ldots, C_r \times V_2$ are subsets of pairwise different strong components in the product graph. If S is a weak balanced separator for G_1, none of the strong components in $G_1 - S$ can have size larger than $\frac{1}{2}m$; accordingly none of the strong components in $(G_1 \otimes G_2)[(V_1 \setminus S) \times V_2]$ can have size larger than $\frac{1}{2}m \cdot n$, and thus $S_1 \times V_2$ is a weak balanced separator for the product graph.

Third, for $U_1 \subseteq V_1$ and $U_2 \subseteq V_2$, the subgraph of $G_1 \otimes G_2$ induced by $U_1 \times U_2$ is the same as the categorical product of the induced subgraphs $G_1[U_1]$ and $G_2[U_2]$. In symbols, we have the equation

$$(G_1 \otimes G_2)[U_1 \times U_2] = (G_1[U_1]) \otimes (G_2[U_2]). \tag{12.1}$$

Combining this with our second observation, we see that if S is a balanced separator for $U_1 \subseteq V_1$ in G_1, then $S \times U_2$ is a balanced separator for $U_1 \times U_2$ in the product graph $G_1 \otimes G_2$.

At this point, we have collected enough information to put forward a recurrence. To this end, for real numbers $0 \leq \beta \leq m$ and $0 \leq \eta \leq n$, let $cr(\beta, \eta)$ denote the maximum cycle rank among the induced subgraphs $G[U_1 \times U_2]$, where the maximum is taken subject to $U_1 \subseteq V_1, |U_1| \leq \beta$ and $U_2 \subseteq V_2, |U_2| \leq \eta$. Then, clearly we have $cr(G_1 \otimes G_2) = cr(m, n)$.

Now the function $cr(\beta, \eta)$ can be bounded above using the following recurrence, as we explain below:

$$cr(\beta, \eta) \leq \begin{cases} 1 & \text{for } \beta, \eta < 2, \\ cr(\eta, \beta) & \text{for } 2 \leq \eta < \beta, \\ k\beta + cr\left(\beta, \frac{\eta}{2}\right) & \text{otherwise.} \end{cases} \tag{12.2}$$

The base case of the recurrence is justified by the fact that the cycle rank of any digraph is of course bounded above by its number of vertices. The second case is correct because the categorical product is commutative, and taking products commutes with taking induced subdigraphs of its factors in the sense of Equation (12.1). Correctness of the third case of the recurrence is explained as follows: Consider an induced subdigraph G' of the form $G' = G_1[U_1] \otimes G_2[U_2]$, with $U_1 \leq \beta$ and $U_2 \leq \eta$, and $\beta \leq \eta$. As the digraph $G_2[U_2]$ admits a weak balanced separator S of size at most k, the product G' admits a weak balanced separator of size at most $k \cdot |U_1| \leq k \cdot \beta$. Since removing a set of vertices of size $|U_1 \times S|$ from G' can decrease its cycle rank at most by that number, we have

$$cr(G') \leq |U_1 \times S| + cr(G' - S) \leq k \cdot \beta + cr(G' \setminus S),$$

and if the strong components of $G_2[U_2 \setminus S]$ are denoted by $C_1, \ldots C_r$, then by the definition of cycle rank

$$cr(G' - S) = \max_{1 \leq i \leq r} cr(G[U_1 \times C_i]),$$

and because each C_i has cardinality at most $\eta/2$, each digraph $G[U_1 \times C_i]$ can have cycle rank at most $cr(\eta/2, \beta)$. Altogether, this shows that the recurrence (12.2) gives a correct upper bound.

For the analysis of this recurrence, assume without loss of generality that $\beta \leq \eta$. We observe first that when evaluating cr, eventually the parameters β and η are decreased in alternating order with each recursive call. Namely, for the parameter range $1 < \beta \leq \eta < 2\beta$, we see by partial unrolling that

$$
\begin{aligned}
cr(\beta, \eta) &\leq k \cdot \beta + cr\left(\beta, \frac{\eta}{2}\right) \\
&\leq k \cdot \beta + cr\left(\frac{\eta}{2}, \beta\right) \\
&\leq k \cdot \beta + \frac{1}{2}k \cdot \eta + cr\left(\frac{\eta}{2}, \frac{\beta}{2}\right) \\
&\leq k \cdot \left(\beta + \frac{1}{2}\eta\right) + cr\left(\frac{\beta}{2}, \frac{\eta}{2}\right) \\
&< 2k \cdot \beta + cr\left(\frac{\beta}{2}, \frac{\eta}{2}\right)
\end{aligned}
$$

In this way, we have halved both parameter values appearing in the recurring expression. By unrolling the recurrence thus obtained and simplifying, we obtain for this range of parameter values:

$$
cr(\beta, \eta) \leq \sum_{0 \leq i < \log \beta} \frac{2k \cdot \beta}{2^i} + cr(1,1) < \sum_{i=0}^{\infty} \frac{2k \cdot \beta}{2^i} = 4k \cdot \beta.
$$

We can thus keep for later reference that

$$
cr(\beta, \eta) < 4k \cdot \beta, \text{ for } 1 < \beta \leq \eta < 2\beta. \tag{12.3}
$$

It remains to reduce the case $\eta \geq 2\beta$ to the balanced case we just discussed. To this end, let $x = \left\lfloor \log\left(\frac{\eta}{\beta}\right) \right\rfloor$ denote the integer part of $\log\left(\frac{\eta}{\beta}\right)$. When applying the recurrence (12.2) for x times, the second parameter always remains larger than the first, until we reach the following inequality:

$$
cr(\beta, \eta) \leq k \cdot \beta \cdot x + cr(\beta, 2^{-x} \cdot \eta). \tag{12.4}
$$

Now let y denote the fractional part of $\log \frac{\eta}{\beta}$. Then $2^{-x-y} = \frac{\beta}{\eta}$, or, equivalently, $2^{-x} \cdot \eta = 2^y \cdot \beta$. Using $0 \leq y < 1$, we get $\beta \leq 2^{-x} \cdot \eta < 2\beta$, and thus we can apply Inequality (12.3) to estimate the remaining recurrent expression on the right-hand-side of Inequality 12.4 and get:

$$
\begin{aligned}
cr(\beta, \eta) &\leq k \cdot \beta \cdot x + cr(\beta, 2^{-x} \cdot \eta) \\
&< k \cdot \beta \cdot x + 4k \cdot \beta \\
&= k \cdot \beta \cdot \left(\log \frac{\eta}{\beta} + 4\right).
\end{aligned}
$$

Since $cr(G_1 \otimes G_2) = cr(m, n)$, the proof is now completed.

$\square$

Now an upper bound for the alphabetic width of the intersection operation can be derived as follows:

Theorem 12.6. *There exists a constant d such that for all $m \leq n$, and for arbitrary alphabets, holds*

$$
\mathrm{alph}(\cap, m, n) \leq n \cdot d^{m \cdot (1 + \log(n/m))}.
$$

Proof. Assume we are given two regular expressions r_1 and r_2, of size m and n, respectively, over a common alphabet Σ. The proof begins in a similar vein as the proof of Theorem 8.11. Again, we make use of the fact that r_1 and r_2 can be converted into equivalent ε-NFAs A_1 and A_2 with

$m + 1$ and $n + 1$ states, respectively by the construction given in the proof of Theorem 8.11. This construction guarantees that the underlying undirected graphs $\overleftrightarrow{G_1}$ and $\overleftrightarrow{G_2}$ have treewidth at most 2. Recall that this implies that the separator number of these graphs is at most 3 by Lemma 8.4.

We apply the usual product construction to A_1 and A_2 to obtain an ε-NFA $A_1 \otimes A_2$ with $(m+1)(n+1)$ states accepting the intersection of $L(r_1)$ and $L(r_2)$. Since the present ε-transitions cause a minor technical issue, we briefly recall the construction. Given two ε-NFAs $A_i = \left(Q^{(i)}, \Sigma, q_0^{(i)}, \delta^{(i)}, F^{(i)}\right)$, for $i = 1, 2$, let

$$A_1 \otimes A_2 = \left(Q_1 \times Q_2, \Sigma, \left(q_0^{(1)}, q_0^{(2)}\right), \delta, F^{(1)} \times F^{(2)}\right),$$

where the transition function δ is defined as follows:

- transitions on letters $a \in \Sigma$ are given by $\left(q^{(1)}, s^{(2)}\right) \in \delta\left(\left(p^{(1)}, r^{(2)}\right), a\right)$ iff both $q^{(1)} \in \delta^{(1)}\left(p^{(1)}, a\right)$ and $s^{(2)} \in \delta^{(2)}\left(s^{(2)}, a\right)$, and

- transitions on the empty word are given by $\left(q^{(1)}, s^{(2)}\right) \in \delta\left(\left(p^{(1)}, r^{(2)}\right), \varepsilon\right)$ iff both $q^{(1)} \in \left\{p^{(1)}\right\} \cup \delta^{(1)}\left(p^{(1)}, \varepsilon\right)$ and $s^{(2)} \in \left\{r^{(2)}\right\} \cup \delta^{(2)}\left(r^{(2)}, \varepsilon\right)$.

It is not hard to prove that $A_1 \otimes A_2$ accepts the intersection $L(A_1) \cap L(A_2)$.

Now we are interested in the undirected cycle rank of the undirected graph underlying this ε-NFA. Observe that the latter is a subgraph of the product $\overleftrightarrow{G_1'} \otimes \overleftrightarrow{G_2'}$, where the digraph G_i' is obtained from G_i, for $i = 1, 2$, by adding a self-loop to each vertex. Adding self-loops to a symmetric digraph does not alter its separator number, and hence the factors G_1' and G_2' still have separator number at most 3.

We are finally in a position that allows us to apply Theorem 12.5, and we deduce that there is some constant d' such that the product graph $\overleftrightarrow{G_1'} \otimes \overleftrightarrow{G_2'}$ has cycle rank at most $d' \cdot m \log \frac{n}{m}$. Since the product graph is again symmetric, we do indeed talk here about the undirected cycle rank. Recall that Theorem 10.7 states that all ε-NFAs of low undirected cycle rank can be converted into sufficiently short regular expressions. In our case, the theorem implies that

$$\text{alph}(L(A_1 \otimes A_2)) \leq |\Sigma| \cdot 4^{d' \cdot m \log(n/m)} (m+1)(n+1)$$

With $|\Sigma| \leq \min\{m, n\} = m$ and $m + 1 \leq 4^{\log m}$ for $m \geq 2$, this can be estimated by

$$\text{alph}(L(A_1 \otimes A_2)) \leq (n+1) \cdot 4^{d' \cdot m \log(n/m) + 2 \log m}$$
$$\leq (n+1) \cdot 4^{3d' \cdot m \log(n/m)},$$

which holds for $n \geq m \geq 2$. Taking also the case $m = 1$ into account, it can be readily seen that we can find a suitable constant d such that the right-hand-side in turn is bounded above by $n \cdot d^{m \cdot (1 + \log(n/m))}$, as desired.

$\square$

Notice that for the parameter range where $n = \Theta(m)$, this bound asymptotically matches the lower bound obtained in Corollary 12.2, in symbols $\text{alph}(m, \Theta(m), \cap) = 2^{\Theta(m)}$. Also, the bounds are very close in general. As it was the case for the lower bounds, a slight alteration of this proof gives again a corresponding bound for the interleaving of two regular languages:

Theorem 12.7. *There exists a constant d such that for all $m \leq n$, and for arbitrary alphabets, holds*

$$\text{alph}(\text{ш}, m, n) \leq n \cdot d^{m \cdot (1 + \log(n/m))}.$$

Proof. As for the intersection operation, assume we are given two regular expressions r_1 and r_2 of size m and n, respectively. We apply a simple trick found in the textbook [168] to simulate, in a sense detailed below, the interleaving operation by means of the intersection operation.

We will consider first the case where the expressions r_1 and r_2 are over disjoint alphabets Σ_1 and Σ_2. Again, we convert first the two expressions into ε-NFAs A_1 and A_2 having $m+1$ and $n+1$ states, respectively, such that both underlying undirected graphs $\overleftrightarrow{G_1}$ and $\overleftrightarrow{G_2}$ have separator number at most 3. Next, we add transitions ensuring that A_1 can consume symbols from Σ_2 without changing its state, and perform a similar construction for A_2. More precisely, for each state $q \in A_1$ and each alphabet symbol $a \in \Sigma_2$, we add transitions $p \xrightarrow{a} p$, and we perform a symmetric construction for A_2 in that we add for each state $q \in A_2$ and each alphabet symbol b in Σ_1 a transition $q \xrightarrow{b} q$. Let the A_1' and A_2' denote the respective ε-NFAs resulting from this construction. It is not difficult to prove that $L(A_1') \cap L(A_2') = L(A_1) \text{ ш } L(A_2)$, see [168].

Notice that going from A_i to A_i', for $i = 1, 2$, is mirrored in the underlying digraphs in the mere addition of self-loops to all vertices. Exactly this technicality was dealt with already in the proof of Theorem 12.6 for the intersection of ε-NFAs, and thus the analysis carried out in that proof applies *mutatis mutandis* to the alphabetic width of the interleaving of two regular expressions that are over disjoint alphabets.

Finally, the case where the alphabets are not disjoint can be easily reduced to the case of disjoint alphabets: We rename the second alphabet $\Sigma_2 = \{a_1, a_2, \ldots, a_\ell\}$ into $\Sigma_2' = \{a_1', a_2', \ldots, a_\ell'\}$ and apply the construction outlined above. Then, in the resulting expression for the interleaved language, we change each occurrence of an alphabet symbol from Σ_2' back into an occurrence of the corresponding symbol from Σ_2. The final result describes the language $L(r_1) \text{ ш } L(r_2)$, as desired. $\square$

12.2 Alphabetic Width of Complementation

Ellul et al. [59] also looked at the complementation of regular expressions. This time, the naive algorithm, which converts first the given expression into an NFA, determinizes, complements the resulting DFA, and finally converts back to a regular expression, gives a doubly exponential upper bound of $2^{2^{O(n)}}$. These authors also found a lower bound of $2^{\Omega(n)}$, and stated the quest for tight bounds as an open research problem. Notice that we cannot completely disregard the alphabet size: for unary alphabets, the exact bound is determined to be $2^{\Theta(\sqrt{n \log n})}$ in the abovementioned work [59].

For alphabet size at least four, Gelade and Neven [65] subsequently proved a truly doubly-exponential lower bound. Their witness language is a 4-symbol encoding of the set of walks in a complete digraph on n vertices. Their proof outline is as follows: On the one hand, they gave a very succinct regular expression describing the complement of this encoded set, and on the other hand gave a direct and technical proof showing that also the set of encoded walks requires large regular expressions, roughly following the proof originally provided by Ehrenfeucht and Zeiger in [55] for the preimage of that encoded set.

Resulting from an independent approach, a roughly doubly-exponential lower bound of $2^{2^{O(\sqrt{n \log n})}}$, for binary alphabets, is reported in [79]; the key to the result is here that the complement of the language $K_n \cap L_n$ from Theorem 12.1 can be expressed very succinctly by a regular expression using the Chinese Remainder Theorem, provided the number n has many distinct prime factors. Since we already know that the language $K_n \cap L_n$ requires large regular expressions, we can simply recycle that lower bound argument.

Thus far, we can conclude that there is a huge jump in descriptional complexity of the complementation operation when moving from unary to binary alphabets. Still, the abovementioned results cannot rule out that there is possibly again a smaller jump when increasing the alphabet size from 2 to 4. The goal of this section will be to prove that this is, as one might have suspected, not the case. Inspired by the results obtained in Chapter 8 for binary alphabets, it is now tantalizing to try to harness again the concept of star-height-preserving homomorphisms, this time to further reduce the alphabet size of the witness language given by Gelade and Neven [65]. But unfortunately their lower bound proof does not offer any clue about the star height of that language, which renders a mixing of proof techniques difficult. At least, it has been known for a long time [35] that the language they encode has large star height:

Theorem 12.8 (Cohen). *Let J_n be the complete digraph on n vertices with self-loops, where each edge (i,j) carries a unique label a_{ij}. Let W_n denote the set of all walks $a_{i_0 i_1} a_{i_1 i_2} \cdots a_{i_{r-2} i_{r-1}} a_{i_{r-1} i_r}$ in J_n, including the empty walk ε. Then $h(W_n) = n$.*

By the way, that result confirmed an early conjecture by Eggan [54]. To obtain a tight lower bound for binary alphabets, here we use basically the same idea as Gelade and Neven did in [65], but make sure that the encoding is a star-height-preserving homomorphism. It is therefore worth to take a closer look at this concept. Recall from Definition 8.19 that a homomorphism ρ preserves star height, if the star height of each regular language L equals the star height of its homomorphic image $\rho(L)$. After McNaughton [141] had found some concrete examples of star-height-preserving homomorphisms (Theorem 8.20), Hashiguchi and Honda [92] later gave an astonishingly simple characterization of this class of homomorphisms. They also obtained a still simpler sufficient criterion, which reads as follows:

Theorem 12.9 (Hashiguchi/Honda). *Let $\rho : \Gamma^* \to \Sigma^*$ be a homomorphism. Assume further that ρ has all of the following properties:*

- *it is injective, that is, ρ is a monomorphism*

- *it is both prefix-free and suffix-free, that is, no word in $\rho(\Gamma)$ is prefix or suffix of another word in $\rho(\Gamma)$, and*

- *it has the non-crossing property, that is, for all $v, w \in \rho(\Gamma)$ holds: If v can be decomposed as $v = v_1 v_2$, with $v_1, v_2 \neq \varepsilon$, and w as $w = w_1 w_2$, with $w_1, w_2 \neq \varepsilon$, such that both cross-wise concatenations $v_1 w_2$ and $w_1 v_2$ are again in $\rho(\Gamma)$, then this implies $v_1 = w_1$ or $v_2 = w_2$.*

Then ρ preserves star height.

We note that we use a reformulation of the non-crossing property. The original definition of the non-crossing property from [92] reads as follows.

For all $v_1, v_2, w_1, w_2 \in \Sigma^+$ holds: If $\{v_1, w_1\} \cdot \{v_2, w_2\} \subseteq \rho(\Gamma)$, then $v_1 = w_1$ or $v_2 = w_2$.

A moment of thought reveals that this condition is equivalent to the one stated above. Our reformulation has the advantage that it is a bit easier to apply in proofs. We also remark that the non-crossing property is somehow reminiscent of the relevant property enjoyed by fooling sets (Lemma 3.2); yet there does not seem to be, at least not at first sight, any deeper connection between the two concepts. Notwithstanding, we are now ready to prove the promised lower bound on the complementation of regular expressions.

Theorem 12.10. *For the complementation operation, we have*

$$\mathrm{alph}(\neg, n) = 2^{2^{\Theta(n)}},$$

and this holds for all alphabets of size at least 2.

Proof. We will first prove the theorem for alphabet size 3, and then use a star-height-preserving homomorphism to further reduce the alphabet size to binary. Let W_{2^n} be the set of all walks in a complete 2^n-vertex digraph, as defined in Theorem 12.8. Letting $E = \{a_{ij} \mid 0 \le i, j \le 2^n - 1\}$ denote the edge set of this digraph, and letting $\Sigma = \{0, 1, \$\}$, we define the homomorphism $\rho : E^* \to \Sigma^*$ by

$$\rho(a_{ij}) = \mathrm{bin}(i)\,\mathrm{bin}(j)\,\mathrm{bin}(i)\,\mathrm{bin}(j)\$,$$

where $\mathrm{bin}(i)$ denotes the usual n-bit binary encoding of the number i, for $0 \le i \le 2^n - 1$.

Our witness language for ternary alphabets is the complement of the set $L_n = \rho(W_{2^n})$, where the complement is taken of course with respect to Σ^*. To establish the theorem for ternary alphabets, we give a regular expression of size $O(n)$ describing the complement of L_n and prove that ρ preserves star height; a lower bound of $2^{2^{\Omega(n)}}$ then follows by combining this with Theorem 12.8 and Theorem 8.11.

Using the same idea as Gelade and Neven in [65] for their encoded set, our small regular expression is a union of some local consistency tests. Every nonempty word in L_n is of the form

$$\mathrm{bin}(i_0)\,\mathrm{bin}(i_1)\,\mathrm{bin}(i_0)\,\mathrm{bin}(i_1)\$ \,(\mathrm{bin}(i_1)\,\mathrm{bin}(i_2))^2\,\$\cdots\$(\mathrm{bin}(i_{k-1})\,\mathrm{bin}(i_k))^2\$,$$

and falls apart into blocks of binary digits, which are each of length $4n$ and separated from each other by occurrences of the symbol \$.

Thus, a word $w \in \Sigma^*$ is not in the language L_n if and only if one of the following cases applies:

- The region around the boundary of some pair of adjacent blocks in w is not of the form $\mathrm{bin}(i)\$\,\mathrm{bin}(i)$.

- Some block does not match the pattern $(\mathrm{bin}(i)\,\mathrm{bin}(j))^2$, in the sense that inside the block some pair of bits at distance $2n$ does not match.

- The word w is not even "well-formed" in the first place, in the sense that it has no prefix in $\{0, 1\}^{4n}\$$, or w contains an occurrence of \$ that is not immediately followed by a word in $\{0, 1\}^{4n}\$$.

At least one of these three cases applies iff the word w matches the following regular expression, which is of size $O(n)$:

$$
\begin{aligned}
r_n =\ & \Sigma^*\$(0+1)^{3n}(0+1)^*0\Sigma^{n+1}1\Sigma^* \\
& + \Sigma^*\$(0+1)^{3n}(0+1)^*1\Sigma^{n+1}0\Sigma^* \\
& + \Sigma^*0(0+1)^{2n}1\Sigma^* \\
& + \Sigma^*1(0+1)^{2n}0\Sigma^* \\
& + (0+1)^{\geq 1} + (\varepsilon + \Sigma^*\$)\left((0+1)^{\leq 4n-1}\$ + (0+1)^{\geq 4n+1}\right)\Sigma^*
\end{aligned}
$$

It remains to show that ρ preserves star height. We have to check ρ against the criteria given in Theorem 12.9. It is easily seen that the encoding is a monomorphism, and since ρ maps every symbol to a word of length $4n+1$, it is both prefix-free and suffix-free. For the non-crossing property, observe that the set $\rho(E)$ coincides with the set of squared words of length $4n$ over the alphabet $\{0,1\}$ that are followed by an occurrence of $\$$, in symbols

$$
\rho(E) = \{\, ww\$ \mid w \in \{0,1\}^*, |w| = 2n \,\}.
$$

Assume now $v_1 v_2$ and $w_1 w_2$ form two squared words of length $4n$ over $\{0,1\}$, with the properties that $v_1 \neq w_1$, $v_2 \neq w_2$ and that none of the subwords v_1, w_1, v_2 and w_2 is empty. If v_1 and w_1 have different lengths, then the length of the word $v_1 w_2\$$ is not equal to $4n+1$. Otherwise, there must be some position j with $1 \leq j \leq 2n$, at which $v_1 v_2$ and $w_1 w_2$ have different letters. Then in the cross-wise concatenation $v_1 w_2$, the letter at the jth position differs from the letter at its $(2n+j)$th position, and hence the latter word is not a square. In both cases, the word $v_1 w_2\$$ is not in $\rho(E)$, thus showing the non-crossing property for ρ. Having established also the last criterion, we see that ρ preserves star height, and this completes the proof for alphabet size at least 3.

To further decrease the alphabet size to binary, we use the star-height-preserving homomorphism σ given in Theorem 8.20, which already proved useful for the conversion problem. Then $\sigma(L_n)$ has star height 2^n, and thus by Theorem 8.11 again has alphabetic width at least $2^{2^{\Omega(n)}}$.

For an upper bound on the alphabetic width of the complement with respect to $\{a,b\}^*$, note first that the words which are in $\sigma(\Sigma^*)$ but not in $\sigma(L_n)$ are exactly those matching the homomorphic image under σ of the expression r_n. This is already almost what we need. For, a word is not in $\sigma(L_n)$ if and only if:

- it represents a valid image under σ but is not in $\sigma(L_n)$, or

- it is not even "well-formed" in the sense that it is not in $\sigma(\Sigma^*)$.

In other words,

$$
\{a,b\}^* \setminus \sigma(L_n) = (\sigma(\Sigma^*) \cap (\{a,b\}^* \setminus \sigma(L_n))) \cup (\{a,b\}^* \setminus \sigma(\Sigma^*)).
$$

A regular expression for the first criterion is given by $\sigma(r_n)$, which is still of size $O(n)$, and the language $(\{a,b\}^* \setminus \sigma(\Sigma^*))$ can be of course described by a regular expression of size $O(1)$ because $|\Sigma| = 3$.

$\square$

Notice how the witness expression r_n we used in the above proof makes heavy use of "nondeterministic guessing." This is of course expected: recall that our lower bound in particular realizes a worst case scenario in the naive construction for complementing regular expressions, which involves determinization of nondeterministic finite automata.

13 Extended Regular Expressions

Because regular languages are known to be closed under quite a few language operations, extending the signature of the regular expression syntax with intersection, complement and/or other operators can sometimes offer more convenient ways of describing regular languages. Yet it has to be mentioned that these extensions can largely affect the computational complexity of basic decision problems, such as checking emptiness or universality of the described language. To illustrate this point, extending the syntax with a complement operator can offer a nonelementary gain in succinctness, see e.g. [59]. To explain the term nonelementary, for $k \geq 1$, let $\mathrm{tow}_k(n)$ be the function defined inductively by $\mathrm{tow}_k(n) = 2^{\mathrm{tow}_{k-1}(n)}$ for $k \geq 1$ and $\mathrm{tow}_1(n) = 2^n$. Informally, $\mathrm{tow}_k(n)$ is thus a "stack of exponentials" of height k. A function $f : \mathbb{N} \to \mathbb{N}$ is called *nonelementary*, if $f(n) = \Omega(f_k(n))$ for each constant $k \geq 1$. However this gain is bought at the price of introducing nonelementary time complexity for testing whether a given extended regular expression is empty [172], a problem efficiently solvable for finite automata and regular expressions [96]. More moderate extensions of the syntax of regular expressions, such as providing a built-in intersection, interleaving, or squaring operator, do not cause such a huge blow-up in complexity.

For instance, the squaring operator r^2 is a shorthand notation $r \cdot r$, the concatenation of r with itself. Stockmeyer and Meyer proved that the equivalence problem for regular expressions with squaring is **EXPSPACE**-complete, whereas the same problem for ordinary regular expressions is **PSPACE**-complete [144]. This smaller difference in complexity stems from a more moderate succinctness gain in representation. On the positive side, an easy reduction shows that the emptiness problem is still efficiently solvable for regular expressions with squaring, while regular expressions with squaring can be exponentially more succinct than ordinary regular expressions, compare e.g. [123].

Example 13.1. The squaring operator provides an elegant way to express large iterated concatenations of a given regular language with itself. Assume r_1 is a regular expression denoting a given a regular language L. For $k > 1$, define $r_k = (r_{k-1})^2$. Notice that r_k denotes the the 2^k-fold iterated concatenation L^{2^k} of the set set L with itself, while its size[1] grows only linearly in k, rather than exponentially. For numbers n that are not powers of 2, a standard "repeated squaring" trick allows to represent languages of the form L^n by similar means. With the hint that every positive integer n can be written as sum of powers of 2, we leave this as an exercise to the inclined reader. This trick also allows for short expressions denoting the languages $L^{\leq n} = (L \cup \{\varepsilon\})^n$, $L^{\geq n} = L^n L^*$ and $L^{[m...n]} = L^m L^{\leq n-m}$.

Apart from the squaring operator, the equivalence problem and similar basic decision problems, such as membership and emptiness problems, were studied rather thoroughly for regular expressions extended with intersection, see , [62, 108, 113, 153, 161]. Somewhat

---

[1]For regular expressions with squaring, alphabetic width is no longer an adequate size measure. Here we have to resort to a different measure, e.g. we can take the reverse polish notation length instead.

more recently, Mayer and Stockmeyer studied these questions for regular expressions extended with interleaving [137].

Concerning the succinctness gain of these extensions, quite a few results are found in the abovementioned references. But all of these compare extensions of regular expressions with nondeterministic finite automata, rather than with ordinary regular expressions. In all of the above cases, the mentioned authors found an exponential gain over nondeterministic finite automata.

After Gelade and Neven recently proved that, perhaps surprisingly, regular expressions extended with intersection can offer a roughly doubly exponential succinctness gain over ordinary regular expressions [65], a systematic study of the descriptional complexity of such extensions was undertaken subsequently by Gelade [64]. Still, apart from the easiest case of adding a squaring operator, the upper and lower bounds did not yet match up to now. The main goal of this chapter will be to tighten these gaps.

13.1 Regular Expressions with Intersection

It is known that extending the syntax with an intersection operator can provide an exponential gain in succinctness over nondeterministic finite automata. For instance, Fürer [62] it shows that the set P_n of palindromes of length n can be described by extended regular expressions with intersection of size $O(n)$. On the other hand, it is well known that the number of states of a nondeterministic finite automaton accepting P_n has $\Omega(2^n)$ states, see [143].

Of course, it appears more natural to compare the gain in succinctness of such extended regular expressions to ordinary regular expressions rather than to finite automata. There, a doubly exponential upper bound readily follows by combining standard constructions, compare [64]. In contrast, a roughly doubly-exponential lower bound of $2^{2^{\Omega(\sqrt{n})}}$, for alphabets of size five, was proved recently by Gelade and Neven [65], and a follow-up paper by Gelade [64] shows that such a bound can be reached already for binary alphabets. Here we finally establish a tight doubly-exponential lower bound, which also holds for binary alphabets.

Theorem 13.2. *There are infinitely many languages L_n admitting regular expressions with intersection of size n, but whose shortest equivalent ordinary regular expressions are of size $2^{2^{\Omega(n)}}$.*

Proof. First, we show that the set of walks $W_{2^n} \subset E^*$, as defined in Theorem 12.8, allows a compact representation using regular expressions with intersection. Define

$$Match = \{a_{i,j} \cdot a_{j,k} \mid 0 \leq i, j, k \leq 2^n - 1\}$$
$$Even = Match^* \cap E \cdot Match^* \cdot E$$
$$Odd = E \cdot Match^* \cap Match^* \cdot E;$$

here and in the following we often omit brackets and agree that the intersection operator has the lowest priority. Observe that the set $Even$ consists of the nonempty walks of even length (i.e. total number of seen edges), and the set Odd those of odd length. We thus have

$$W_{2^n} = Even \cup Odd \cup \{\varepsilon\}.$$

This way of describing W_{2^n} appears to be still a long shot from our actual goal; it uses a large alphabet and does not even reach a linear-exponential gain in succinctness over ordinary regular expressions—a similar observation as the above was indeed also made by Ehrenfeucht and Zeiger in [55] over thirty years ago.

In order to get the desired result, we present a binary encoding τ that preserves star height and at the same time allows a representation of the encoded sets $\tau(Match)$ and $\tau(E)$ by extended regular expressions with intersection, each of size $O(n)$.

Let $\tau : E^* \to \{a, b\}$ be the homomorphism defined by

$$\tau : a_{i,j} \mapsto \text{bin}(i) \cdot \text{bin}(j) \cdot \text{bin}(j)^R \cdot \text{bin}(i)^R, \text{ for } 0 \leq i, j \leq 2^{n-1}.$$

To verify that τ preserves star height, we have to check the properties given in Theorem 12.9. It can be readily seen that τ is a monomorphism, and it is both prefix-free and suffix-free, since all words in $\tau(E)$ are of the same length. The set $\tau(E)$ is just the set of binary palindromes of length $4n$, and, by chance, a proof of the non-crossing property of this set is given already in [67], albeit in a different context. Thus, with Theorem 8.11 and Theorem 12.8, the set $\tau(W_{2^n})$ has alphabetic width at least $2^{2^{\Omega(n)}}$.

It remains to give extended expressions with intersection of size $O(n)$ for the set $\tau(W_{2^n})$. Observe that for all languages $L_1, L_2 \subseteq E^*$ holds

$$\tau(L_1 \cdot L_2) = \tau(L_1) \cdot \tau(L_2),$$
$$\tau(L_1 \cup L_2) = \tau(L_1) \cup \tau(L_2),$$
$$\tau(L_2^*) = \tau(L_2)^*,$$

and, the homomorphism τ being injective, even

$$\tau(L_1 \cap L_2) = \tau(L_1) \cap \tau(L_2).$$

Since furthermore

$$\tau(W_{2^n}) = \tau(Even) \cup \tau(Odd) \cup \{\varepsilon\}$$

and the sets $\tau(Even)$ and $\tau(Odd)$ can be described in terms of $\tau(Match)$ and $\tau(E)$ by virtue of the definition given above, it suffices to give regular expressions with intersection for $\tau(E)$ and $\tau(Match)$ of size $O(n)$ each.

We make use of an observation made by Fürer [62], namely that the set of palindromes of fixed length $2m$ admits a regular expression with intersection of size $O(m)$. A straightforward extension of that construction also gives succinct extended regular expressions with intersection for the family of languages

$$S_{m,n} = \{ vwv^R \in \{0, 1\}^* \mid |v| = m, |w| = n \},$$

where m and n are fixed nonnegative integers. Extending the idea given in [62], an expression $r_{m,n}$ describing this set is defined inductively by letting $r_{0,n} = (0 + 1)^n$ and

$$r_{m,n} = (0 + 1) \cdot r_{m-1,n} \cdot (0 + 1) \cap (0(0 + 1)^*0 + 1(0 + 1)^*1), \text{ for } m > 0.$$

Clearly, $r_{m,n}$ describes the language $S_{m,n}$ and has size at most $c \cdot (m+n)$ for some constant c independent of m and n.

Now in particular, the set

$$\tau(E) = \{ww^R \in \{0, 1\}^* \mid |w| = 2n\}$$

is described by $r_{n,0}$, which is of size $O(n)$. Moreover, observe that for the set $\tau(Match)$ holds

$$\begin{aligned}
\tau(Match) &= \{\, \tau(a_{i,j}) \cdot \tau(a_{j,k}) \mid a_{i,j}, a_{j,k} \in E \,\} \\
&= \{\, uv(uv)^R vw(vw)^R \mid |u| = |v| = |w| = n \,\}, \\
&= \{\, uvv^R u^R vww^R v^R \mid |u| = |v| = |w| = n \,\}, \\
&= \{0,1\}^{2n} \cdot S_{n,n} \cdot \{0,1\}^{3n} \cap \tau(E) \cdot \tau(E).
\end{aligned}$$

The latter set can be again described by a regular expression with intersection of size $O(n)$, and the proof is completed.

$\square$

13.2 Regular Expressions with Interleaving

Another basic language operation known to preserve regularity is the interleaving of languages. Regular expressions extended with interleaving were first studied by Mayer and Stockmeyer, with focus on the computational complexity of word problems. *Inter alia* they proved that regular expressions extended with an interleaving operator can be exponentially more succinct than nondeterministic finite automata [137]. Only very recently, Gelade showed in [64] that regular expressions with interleaving can be roughly doubly exponentially more succinct than regular expressions: For constant alphabet size,[2] converting such expressions into ordinary regular expressions can cause a blow-up in required expression size of $2^{2^{\Omega(\sqrt{n})}}$. This bound is close to an easy upper bound of $2^{2^{O(n)}}$ that follows again from standard constructions, see [64]. We will prove next that if we allow alphabets of growing size, the lower bound can be increased to match this trivial upper bound. The language witnessing that bound is in fact of very simple structure.

Theorem 13.3. *There is an infinite family of languages having regular expressions extended with interleaving of size $O(n)$, over an alphabet of size $O(n)$, while the shortest equivalent ordinary regular expression has size at least $2^{2^{\Omega(n)}}$.*

Proof. We consider the language L_n described by the shuffle regular expression

$$r_n = (a_1 b_1)^* \amalg (a_2 b_2)^* \amalg \cdots \amalg (a_n b_n)^*$$

of size $O(n)$ over the alphabet

$$\Gamma = \{a_1, a_2, \ldots, a_n, b_1, b_2, \ldots, b_n\}.$$

To give a lower bound on the alphabetic width of L_n, we estimate first the star height of L_n. The language L_n can be accepted by a 2^n-state bideterministic finite automaton $A = (Q, \Sigma, \delta, q_0, F)$, whose underlying digraph forms a symmetric n-dimensional hypercube:

---

[2]In [64], it is claimed that a further reduction of the alphabet size to binary is straightforward. However, the idea sketched there, which follows an idea from [137] and is based on applying a certain "shuffle resistant" homomorphism ρ, appears to overlook the obstacle that for many pairs of languages, we will have $L_1 \amalg L_2 \neq \rho(L_1) \amalg \rho(L_2)$. Notice that, in contrast to [137], which deals with finite automata, the intersection of regular expressions is expensive. This problem is addressed in more detail below, where at the same time an improved lower bound is given.

The set of states is $Q = \{0,1\}^n$, the state $q_0 = 0^n$ is the initial state, and is also the only final state, i.e. $F = \{0^n\}$. For $1 \leq i \leq n$, the partial transition function δ is specified by $\delta(p, b_i) = q$ and $\delta(q, a_i) = p$ for all pairs of states (p, q) of the form $(x0y, x1y)$ with $x \in \{0,1\}^{i-1}$ and $y \in \{0,1\}^{n-i}$.

It can be readily verified that this DFA is reduced and bideterministic. Therefore, the star height of L_n coincides with the cycle rank of the n-dimensional symmetric Cartesian hypercube. For a symmetric digraph G, the cycle rank coincides with the undirected cycle rank, which is in turn bounded below by its undirected pathwidth [18], a certain graph connectivity measure similar to treewidth. Many structural properties of the n-dimensional hypercube are known, and among these is the recently established fact [28] that its pathwidth equals

$$\sum_{i=0}^{n-1} \binom{i}{\lceil i/2 \rceil} = \Theta(2^{n-1/2\log n}),$$

where our estimation of this sum uses Stirling's approximation. Using Theorem 8.11, we obtain

$$\mathrm{alph}(L_n) = 2^{\Omega(2^{n-1/2\log n})} = 2^{2^{\Omega(n)}},$$

as desired.

$\square$

For a similar result using binary alphabets, we will encode the above witness language in binary using a star-height-preserving homomorphism. Some extra care has to be taken, however: The ideal situation one might hope for is to find for each $\Gamma = \{a_1, a_2, \ldots a_n\}$ a suitable star-height-preserving homomorphism $\rho : \Gamma \to \{0,1\}$ such that

$$\rho(x \ \mathbf{m} \ y) = \rho(x) \ \mathbf{m} \ \rho(y), \text{ for all } x, y \in \Gamma^*.$$

This aim however appears to be a bit too ambitious. At least for all promising candidates we tried, the right-hand-side of the above equation can contain words not in $\rho(\Gamma)^*$, that is, words which are not even valid codewords. To overcome this difficulty, Warmuth and Haussler [178] identified a particular monomorphism that has the above property once we restrict our attention to codewords. For this reason, they called that homomorphism *shuffle resistant*. Inspired by a slightly stronger property enjoyed by that homomorphism, which was proved later by Mayer and Stockmeyer [137, Prop. 3.1], we define the concept of a shuffle resistant homomorphism in general as follows:

Definition 13.4. Let Γ and Σ be alphabets. A homomorphism $\rho : \Gamma \to \Sigma$ is called *shuffle resistant* iff it is injective and for each extended regular expression r with interleaving over Γ holds

$$\rho(L(r)) = L(\rho(r)) \cap \rho(\Gamma)^*.$$

In our new terminology, the following property is proved in [137, Prop. 3.1] for the homomorphism originally devised by Warmuth and Haussler:

Lemma 13.5. Let $\Gamma = \{a_1, a_2, \ldots, a_n\}$ and $\Sigma = \{a, b\}$. The homomorphism ρ mapping the symbol a_i to $a^{i+1}b^i$ is shuffle resistant.

Incidentally, this homomorphism also preserves star height. The drawback is, however, that for an extended regular expression r with interleaving holds $\mathrm{alph}(h(r)) = \Theta(|\Sigma|\,\mathrm{alph}(r))$, provided all alphabet symbols of Σ occur in r. In order to obtain more economic homomorphisms, we now present a general family of homomorphisms enjoying similar properties.

Lemma 13.6. *Let Γ and Σ be alphabets, and let \$ a symbol not in Σ. If ρ is a monomorphism with $\rho(\Gamma) \subseteq \Sigma^k\$$ for some integer k, then ρ is shuffle resistant.*

Proof. We need to show that for each such homomorphism ρ, the equation $\rho(L(r)) = L(\rho(r)) \cap \rho(\Gamma)^*$ holds for all extended regular expressions r with interleaving over Γ. The outline of the proof is roughly the same as the proof sketch for Lemma 13.5 given by Mayer and Stockmeyer in [137].

The proof is by induction on the operator structure of r, using the stronger inductive hypothesis that

$$L(\rho(r)) \subseteq \rho(L(r)) \cup E, \quad \text{with } E = (\rho(\Gamma))^*\Sigma^{\geq k+1}(\Sigma \cup \$)^* \qquad (13.1)$$

Roughly speaking, the "error language" E specifies that the first error occurring in a word in $L(\rho(r))$ but not in $(\rho(\Gamma))^*$ must consist in a sequence of too many consecutive symbols from Σ.

The base cases are easily established, and also the induction step is easy for the regular operators $\{\cdot, \cup, {}^*\}$. The more difficult part is to show that if two expressions r_1 and r_2 satisfy Equation (13.1), then this also holds for $r = r_1 \shuffle r_2$. To prove this implication, it suffices to show the following claim:

Claim 13.7. For all words u, v in $\rho(\Gamma)^* \cup E$ and for each word z in $u \shuffle v$ the following holds:

   a) if both $u, v \in \rho(\Gamma)^*$ and $z \in (\Sigma^k\$)^*$, then $z \in \rho(\rho^{-1}(u) \shuffle \rho^{-1}(v))$.

   b) otherwise, $z \in E$.

Proof. We prove the claim by induction on the length of z. The base case $|z| = 0$ is clear. For the induction step, assume $|z| > 0$ and consider the prefix y consisting of the first $k+1$ letters of z. Such a prefix always exists if z is obtained from shuffling two nonempty words from $\rho(\Gamma)^* \cup E$ (The cases where u or v is empty are trivial.)

Observe first that it is impossible to obtain a prefix in $\Sigma^{<k}\$$ by shuffling two prefixes u' and v' of the words u and v. Also, a prefix in $\Sigma^{>k}$ always completes to a word $z \in E$.

It remains to consider the case z has a prefix y in $\Sigma^k\$$. To obtain such a prefix, two prefixes u' and v' have to be shuffled, with $(u', v') \in (\Sigma^j) \times (\Sigma^{k-j}\$)$ or $(u', v') \in (\Sigma^j\$) \times (\Sigma^{k-j})$. But since these are prefixes of words in $\rho(\Gamma)^* \cup E$, the index j can take on only the values $j = 0$ and $j = k$. Thus if $y \in \Sigma^k\$$, then y is indeed in $\rho(\Gamma)$, and y is obtained by observing exclusively the first $k+1$ letters of u, or exclusively the first $k+1$ letters of v. Hence at least one of the subcases $y^{-1}z \in (y^{-1}u) \shuffle v$ and $y^{-1}z \in u \shuffle (y^{-1}v)$ holds. We only consider the first subcase, for the second one a symmetric argument applies.

It is not hard to see that we can apply the induction hypothesis to this subcase: Because $y \in \rho(\Gamma)$ and $u \in \rho(\Gamma)^* \cup E$, the word $y^{-1}u$ is again in $\rho(\Gamma)^* \cup E$. Having furthermore $|y^{-1}z| < z$, the induction hypothesis readily implies that claimed statement also holds for the word $z = y(y^{-1}z)$. This completes the proof of the claim. $\qquad\square$

Having established the claim, completing the proof of the statement $L(\rho(r)) \subseteq \rho(L(r)) \cup E$ is a rather easy exercise.

$\square$

Now we are ready to prove the existence of economic shuffle resistant homomorphisms, which map to words over binary alphabets, and which furthermore preserve star height.

Lemma 13.8. *Let Γ be an alphabet. There exists an encoding $\rho : \Gamma \to \{0,1\}^*$ such that*

- *for every symbol $a \in \Gamma$, we have $|\rho(a)| = O(\log |\Gamma|)$,*

- *the encoding ρ is shuffle resistant and preserves star height.*

Proof. Without loss of generality assume $\Gamma = \{a_1, \ldots a_{2^k}\}$ for some $k \in \mathbb{N}$. In a first step, we encode into an alphabet of constant size. Let σ be the monomorphism given by $\sigma(a_i) = \text{bin}(i) \, \text{bin}(i)\$$, with $\text{bin}(i)$ being the usual k-bit binary encoding of the number i. Recall that we already encountered this monomorphism in the proof of Theorem 12.10, where we also saw that it preserves star height. Obviously, σ maps all alphabet symbols to strings of length $O(\log |\Gamma|)$.

In a second step, we use the homomorphism τ from Lemma 13.5 to further decrease the alphabet size from ternary to binary. This homomorphism is shuffle resistant. Furthermore, it also preserves star height, as can be easily verified by checking against the sufficient criteria for star-height-preserving homomorphisms given in Theorem 12.9.

The composed homomorphism $\rho = \tau \circ \sigma$ does the job: We have $\tau(\sigma(a)) = O(\log |\Gamma|)$, and it is readily proved that $\tau \circ \sigma$ is both shuffle resistant and preserves star height by expanding the respective definitions of these notions (Definitions 8.19 and 13.4).

$\square$

This homomorphism allows us to prove that for regular expressions with interleaving, the conversion to ordinary regular expressions induces a $2^{2^{\Omega(n/\log n)}}$ lower bound already for binary input alphabet:

Theorem 13.9. *There is an infinite family of languages over an alphabet of size two admitting extended regular expressions with interleaving of size $O(n)$, while the shortest equivalent ordinary regular expression has size at least $2^{2^{\Omega(n/\log n)}}$.*

Proof. Our witness language will be described by the expression

$$\rho(r_n) = (\rho(a_1)\rho(b_1))^* \text{ ш } (\rho(a_2)\rho(b_2))^* \text{ ш } \cdots \text{ ш } (\rho(a_n)\rho(b_n))^*,$$

obtained by applying the homomorphism ρ from Lemma 13.8 to the expression r_n used in the proof of Theorem 13.3. This expression has size $O(n \log n)$, and to prove the theorem, it will suffice to establish that $L(\rho(r_n))$ has alphabetic width at least $2^{2^{\Omega(n)}}$.

Recall from the proof of Theorem 13.3 that the star height of $L(r_n)$ is bounded below by $2^{\Omega(n)}$. Since ρ preserves star height, the same bound applies to the language $\rho(L(r_n))$. By Theorem 8.11, we thus have

$$\text{alph}(\rho(L(r_n))) \geq 2^{2^{\Omega(n)}}. \tag{13.2}$$

Unfortunately, this bound applies to the language $\rho(L(r_n))$ rather than to $L(\rho(r_n))$. At least, since we know from Lemma 13.8 that ρ is a shuffle resistant homomorphism, these two sets are related by

$$L(\rho(r_n)) \cap \rho(\Gamma)^* = \rho(L(r_n)), \tag{13.3}$$

with $\Gamma = \{a_1, b_1, \ldots, a_n, b_n\}$.

To derive a similar lower bound on $L(\rho(r_n))$, we use the upper bound on the alphabetic width of the intersection operation from Theorem 12.6: Recall that there exists a constant d such that the intersection of two languages denoted by regular expressions of alphabetic width m and n, with $m \leq n$, can be described by a regular expression of size at most $nd^{m \cdot (1+\log(n/m))}$. To this end, let $\alpha(n)$ denote the alphabetic width of $L(\rho(r_n))$. We show first that $\alpha(n) > \text{alph}(\rho(\Gamma)^*)$: Assume the contrary. By Lemma 13.8, the set $\rho(\Gamma)^*$ admits a regular expression of size $O(n \log n)$. Assuming $\alpha(n) \leq \text{alph}(\rho(\Gamma)^*)$, the upper bound from Theorem 12.6 implies that the language $\rho(L(r_n)) = L(\rho(r_n)) \cap \rho(\Gamma^*)$ admits a regular expression of size $2^{O(n \log n)}$. But this clearly contradicts Inequality (13.2).

Thus, $\alpha(n) > \text{alph}(\rho(\Gamma)^*)$. Applying the upper bound on alphabetic width of intersection from Theorem 12.6 to the left-hand-side of Equation (13.3), we obtain:

$$\text{alph}(\rho(L(r_n))) = \text{alph}(L(\rho(r_n)) \cap \rho(\Gamma^*)) \leq 2^{O(n \log n \log \alpha(n))}. \tag{13.4}$$

Combining Inequalities (13.2) and (13.4), there exist positive constants c_1 and c_2 such that, for n large enough, holds

$$2^{2^{c_1 n}} \leq 2^{2^{c_2 n \log n \log \alpha(n)}}.$$

Taking double logarithms on both sides and rearranging terms, we obtain

$$c_1 n - O(\log n) \leq \log \log \alpha(n).$$

Since the left-hand-side grows as fast as $\Omega(n)$, we have $\text{alph}(L(\rho(r_n))) = \alpha(n) = 2^{2^{\Omega(n)}}$, and the proof is completed.

$\square$

14 Quotients and Circular Shift

After this abundance of exponential bounds, we turn our attention to language operations that can be carried out on regular expressions efficiently, that is, which can incur at most polynomial blow-up in size. Our goal will be to show that language operations related to quotients can be implemented directly *via* manipulating regular expressions, perhaps most notably the circular shift, which was defined in Section 2.1. In this way, we altogether avoid the construction of finite automata and thus also the potentially expensive conversion back into a regular expression.

We will carry out the main manipulations first for so-called linear expressions, that is, regular expressions in which each alphabet symbol occurs only once. In a linear expression, each alphabet symbol corresponds to a unique position in the expression and *vice versa*, which renders the manipulation of these expressions more convenient. In a second step, we investigate the interplay of the language operations under consideration with length-preserving homomorphisms, which will allow us to generalize our conclusions about linear expressions to the case of general regular expressions.

Since we focus on descriptional complexity, recall the notion of uncollapsible expressions from Definition 9.4 in Chapter 9, thus restricting our attention to expressions without obvious redundancies. This definition immediately lends itself for a set of reduction rules, whose repeated application eventually yields an uncollapsible expression. It is easily seen that collapsing a regular expression does neither increase its star height nor its alphabetic width. We will need the following relation between star height and alphabetic width of uncollapsible regular expressions:

Lemma 14.1. *If r is an uncollapsible expression, then $h(r) \leq \text{alph}(r)$.*

Proof. First, consider the cases $L(r) = \emptyset$ and $L(r) = \{\varepsilon\}$. It is easy to see from the definition of uncollapsible expressions that we must have $r = \emptyset$ and $r = \varepsilon$, respectively, and the claim holds in these cases. These are the only uncollapsible expressions with alphabetic width 0.

For the case $\text{alph}(r) \geq 1$, we prove the following claim by induction on the total number of occurrences of operators in r: If the uncollapsible expression r is a starred expression, then $h(r) \leq \text{alph}(r)$, otherwise $h(r) \leq \text{alph}(r) - 1$.

If r contains no operators at all, then the statement clearly holds. To do the induction step, assume the statement holds for all regular expressions with at most m occurrences of operators. If r is of the form $(s)^*$, then s is not a starred expression, since r is reduced. Furthermore, $L(s)$ can be neither empty nor equal to $\{\varepsilon\}$, since otherwise $L(r) = \{\varepsilon\}$, and r would not be uncollapsible. Thus by induction assumption, $h(s) \leq \text{alph}(s) - 1$. Since $\text{alph}(r) = \text{alph}(s)$ and $h(r) = h(s) + 1$, the claim also holds in this case. In the cases $r = s + t$ and $r = s \cdot t$, we have $h(r) = \max\{h(s), h(t)\}$. The total number of occurrences of operators in r and s is each strictly less than the number of occurrences in r, so the induction hypothesis applies. However, the induction step does not go through directly in the subcase where both s and t are stars, that is, $s = \hat{s}^*$ and $t = \hat{t}^*$, for subexpressions $\hat{s}$ and $\hat{t}$. Nevertheless, since both s and t are reduced, neither $\hat{s}$ nor $\hat{t}$ can be stars themselves, and we can apply the induction hypothesis to these and obtain

$$h(\hat{s}) + h(\hat{t}) \le \text{alph}(\hat{s}) + \text{alph}(\hat{t}) - 2.$$

Regarding the left-hand-side of this inequality, note that

$$h(r) - 1 = \max\left\{h(\hat{s}), h(\hat{t})\right\} \le h(\hat{s}) + h(\hat{t}).$$

Regarding the right-hand-side of the former inequality, note that

$$\text{alph}(\hat{s}) + \text{alph}(\hat{t}) = \text{alph}(r).$$

This completes the induction step also in this subcase, and the lemma is proved. $\qquad\square$

Notice the difference between the statement in the above lemma and the statement of Theorem 8.11. While the former is about star height and alphabetic width of one and the same *expression*, the latter is a statement about *languages*—there the two measures can take on their respective minimum on different expressions. In the latter case, the star height is at most logarithmic in alphabetic width.

14.1 Quotients and Circular Shift for Linear Expressions

In this section, we establish bounds on the alphabetic width of quotients and circular shift in the special case where the operands are linear expressions, that is, regular expressions in which every alphabet symbol occurs only once. More precisely, let r be a regular expression over the alphabet Σ. We refer to the ith alphabetic letter in r as the ith *position*. A regular expression r over an alphabet Σ is called a *linear expression* if and only if every alphabetic symbol occurs only once in the expression. Without loss of generality we will often assume that the ith position in a linear expression r is the symbol a_i. In this case, there is a straightforward bijection between positions and alphabet symbols, and here we shall often denote the used alphabet by P_r.

For two alphabets Σ and Γ, a homomorphism $h : \Sigma^* \to \Gamma^*$ is *length-preserving*, also: *letter-to-letter* , if it maps all symbols from Γ to symbols from Σ. It is easy to see that each regular expression r is the image of a unique linear expression $\bar{r}$ under a special length-preserving homomorphism: That particular homomorphism maps the symbol a_i to the ith position of r, and will be denoted by ℓ_r, or just ℓ in the case r is understood.

Example 14.2. For the regular expression $r = ((ab)^*a)^*$, the corresponding linear expression is $\bar{r} = ((a_1a_2)^*a_3)^*$, and the length-preserving homomorphism which maps $\bar{r}$ to r is given by $\ell = \{a_1 \mapsto a, a_2 \mapsto b, a_3 \mapsto a\}$. $\qquad\square$

The languages that can be described by linear expressions fall into a particular subclass of regular languages. In what follows, to allow a smooth notational treatment of cases where the empty word is contained in a given language, define the operator $\mathcal{E}$ on languages by $\mathcal{E}(L) = \{\varepsilon\}$, if $\varepsilon \in L$ and $\mathcal{E}(L) = \emptyset$ otherwise. Now a language $L \subseteq \Sigma^*$ is called *local* if it can be written as

$$L = \mathcal{E}(L) \cup (P\Sigma^* \cap \Sigma^*S) \setminus (\Sigma^*N\Sigma^*),$$

for some $P, S \subseteq \Sigma$ and $N \subseteq \Sigma^2$ (The choice of variable names P, S and N stems from the words *prefix*, *suffix* and *non-factor*.) Note that in this definition, we permit the empty word to be a member of a local language. Berstel and Pin showed that linear expressions can only describe local languages [10]:

Theorem 14.3. *For every linear expression r, the language $L(r)$ is local.*

Next we briefly recall the definition of the *canonical derivative* $d_a(r)$ of a linear expression r with respect to an alphabet symbol a, using the reformulation given in [27, Prop. 6]:

Definition 14.4. Let r be an uncollapsible linear expression and let a be a symbol in P_r. Then the canonical derivative $d_a(r)$ is computed recursively by applying the following rules and finally collapsing the expression:

$$d_a(a) = \varepsilon$$

$$d_a(s + t) = \begin{cases} d_a(s) & \text{if } d_a(s) \neq \emptyset \\ d_a(t) & \text{otherwise} \end{cases}$$

$$d_a(s \cdot t) = \begin{cases} d_a(s) \cdot t & \text{if } d_a(s) \neq \emptyset \\ d_a(t) & \text{otherwise} \end{cases}$$

$$d_a(s^*) = d_a(s) \cdot s^*$$

And $d_a(r) = \emptyset$ in all cases not covered above.

To become familiar with this definition, the best is to work through an elementary example:

Example 14.5. Consider again the linear expression $\bar{r} = ((ab)^*c)^*$ from Example 14.2; we now use the alphabet $\{a, b, c\}$ instead of $\{a_1, a_2, a_3\}$ to increase readability. Then

$$d_a(\bar{r}) = d_a((ab)^*c) \cdot ((ab)^*c)^* = d_a((ab)^*) \cdot c \cdot ((ab)^*c)^*$$
$$= d_a(ab) \cdot (ab)^* \cdot c \cdot ((ab)^*c)^* = d_a(a) \cdot b \cdot (ab)^* \cdot c \cdot ((ab)^*c)^*$$
$$= \varepsilon \cdot b \cdot (ab)^* \cdot c \cdot ((ab)^*c)^* = b(ab)^*c\,((ab)^*c)^* \,.$$

A similar computation yields $d_b(\bar{r}) = (ab)^*c\,((ab)^*c)^*$ and $d_c(\bar{r}) = ((ab)^*c)^*$. $\square$

Champarnaud and Ziadi [27] relate the canonical derivatives of a linear expression to the original definition of derivatives for general regular expressions due to Brzozowski [21], and to the continuations introduced by Berry and Sethi [9]. The results from [27] relevant in our context are summarized in the following characterization:

Theorem 14.6. *Let r be a linear expression, let a be a symbol in P_r, and u a word over P_r. If the set $(ua)^{-1}L(r)$ is nonempty, then it is described by the canonical derivative $d_a(r)$.*

Thus for an uncollapsible linear expression r, the canonical derivative $d_a(r)$ describes the language quotient $(P_r^*a)^{-1}L(r)$. Now we generalize the above notion from symbols $a \in P_r$ to sets of symbols $A \subseteq P_r$ as follows:

Definition 14.7. Let r be an uncollapsible linear expression and let A be a set of symbol in P_r. Then the canonical derivative $d_A(r)$ is computed recursively by applying the following rules and finally collapsing the expression:

$$d_A(a) = \varepsilon \quad \text{if } a \in A$$
$$d_A(s + t) = d_B(s) + d_{A \setminus B}(t)$$
$$d_A(s \cdot t) = d_B(s) \cdot t + d_{A \setminus B}(t)$$
$$d_A(s^*) = d_A(s) \cdot s^*$$

with $B = \{\, a \in A \mid d_a(s) \neq \emptyset \,\}$. And $d_A(r) = \emptyset$ in all cases not covered above.

A straightforward structural induction shows that the definition works as expected:

Lemma 14.8. *Let r be a linear expression and A a set of symbols in r. Then $L(d_A(r)) = \bigcup_{a \in A} L(d_a(r))$.* $\qquad\square$

Example 14.9. Again we consider the linear expression $\bar{r} = ((ab)^*c)^*$. Let $A = \{b, c\}$, then the expression $d_A(\bar{r})$ computes as follows:

$$
\begin{aligned}
d_A(\bar{r}) &= d_A((ab)^*c) \cdot ((ab)^*c)^* = (d_b((ab)^*) \cdot c + d_c(c)) \cdot ((ab)^*c)^* \\
&= (d_b(ab) \cdot (ab)^* \cdot c + d_c(c)) \cdot ((ab)^*c)^* \\
&= (d_b(b) \cdot (ab)^* \cdot c + d_c(c)) \cdot ((ab)^*c)^* = (\varepsilon \cdot (ab)^* \cdot c + \varepsilon) \cdot ((ab)^*c)^* \\
&= ((ab)^*c + \varepsilon) \cdot ((ab)^*c)^*.
\end{aligned}
$$

In the last line of the above computation, we applied two different rules for collapsing the expression. Note that this expression is indeed shorter than the expression $d_b(\bar{r}) + d_c(\bar{r})$ we computed in Example 14.5, although one might first be tempted to expect the contrary.

A similar computation yields the equations $d_{\{a,b\}}(\bar{r}) = ((b + \varepsilon)(ab)^*c) \cdot ((ab)^*c)^*$ and $d_{\{a,c\}}(\bar{r}) = (b(ab)^*c + \varepsilon) \cdot ((ab)^*c)^*$, and last but not least we find that $d_{\{a,b,c\}}(\bar{r}) = ((b + \varepsilon)(ab)^*c + \varepsilon) \cdot ((ab)^*c)^*$. $\qquad\square$

Next, we estimate the size of the expressions $d_A(r)$.

Lemma 14.10. *Let r be an uncollapsible linear expression of alphabetic width $n \geq 1$ and star height h, and let A be a subset of P_r. Then the expression $d_A(r)$ has size at most $\frac{n^2 - n}{2} + hn = O(n^2)$.*

Proof. First, recall that Lemma 14.1 implies that the claimed size is in $O(n^2)$. We prove the claim by induction on the depth $d \geq 0$ of the syntax tree of r. In the case $d = 0$, then with $\text{alph}(r) \geq 1$ we must have $r = a$ for some $a \in P_r$, and the claim clearly holds. To do the induction step, we consider three cases.

If r is of the form $s + t$, then $d_A(r)$ is the expression obtained from collapsing $d_B(s) + d_{A \setminus B}(t)$. Let $\text{alph}(s) = k$ and $\text{alph}(t) = n - k$, for some $k \geq 0$. By induction hypothesis we obtain that

$$\text{alph}(d_A(r)) \leq \frac{k^2 - k}{2} + hk + \frac{(n-k)^2 - (n-k)}{2} + h(n - k).$$

By rearranging terms, we get

$$\frac{k^2 - k + (n-k)^2 - (n-k)}{2} = \frac{n^2 - n}{2} + k(k - n) \leq \frac{n^2 - n}{2},$$

and thus $\text{alph}(d_A(r))$ is bounded above by $\frac{n^2-n}{2} + hn$ in this case.

If r is of the form $s \cdot t$, then $d_A(r)$ is the expression obtained from collapsing the expression $d_B(s) \cdot t + d_{A \backslash B}(t)$. Since r is uncollapsible, both s and t have alphabetic width at least 1. Letting $k \geq 1$ denote the alphabetic width of s and $n - k$ the alphabetic width of t, we obtain by induction hypothesis that

$$\text{alph}(d_A(r)) \leq \frac{k^2 - k}{2} + hk + \frac{(n-k)^2 - (n-k)}{2} + h(n-k) + n - k.$$

By a similar computation as for the previous case, the right-hand-side in the above inequality is still bounded above by $\frac{n^2-n}{2} + hn$.

Finally, if r is of the form s^*, then the depth and the star height of s are both smaller than those of r, and by induction assumption

$$\text{alph}(d_A(r)) \leq \text{alph}(d_A(s)) + n \leq \frac{n^2 - n}{2} + (h-1)n + n.$$

This covers all possible cases, and the proof is completed. $\qquad\square$

Remark. Our notion of $d_A(r)$ differs from the one given in [27] in that our definition yields expressions of size $O(n^2)$, while defining d_A as $\sum_{a \in A} d_a(r)$ would be much more redundant. It should be said that the actual size of these expressions is immaterial in the context of [27], but of course it does matter here.

Now we take a closer look at local languages. The following "exchange property" readily follows from the definition of local languages:

Lemma 14.11. *If $L \subseteq \Sigma^*$ is a local language and a is a symbol in Σ, then*

- $u_1 \cdot a \cdot v_1 \in L$ *and* $u_2 \cdot a \cdot v_2 \in L$ *implies* $u_1 \cdot a \cdot v_2 \in L$, *and*

- $ua \in \text{pre}(L)$ *implies* $(ua)^{-1} L = (\Sigma^* a)^{-1} L$. $\qquad\square$

For a local language L and an alphabet symbol a, we may thus define $d_a(L)$ as the language quotient $d_a(L) = (\Sigma^* a)^{-1} L$. Likewise, for a set of symbols A define $d_A(L) = (\Sigma^* A)^{-1} L$. This operator overloading is perfectly consistent with the use of the notation $d_a(r)$ to denote the canonical derivative of a linear expression r with respect to an alphabet symbol a: By Theorem 14.6, we have $L(d_a(r)) = d_a(L(r))$.

The above characterization allows us to provide a neat formula for (left) quotients of local languages:

Lemma 14.12. *Let $L \subseteq \Sigma^*$ be a local language and let $W \subseteq \Sigma^*$ an arbitrary language. Define $A = \{\, a \in \Sigma \mid W \cap \text{pre}(L) \cap \Sigma^* a \neq \emptyset \,\}$. Then*

$$W^{-1} L = \mathcal{E}(W) \cdot L \cup \bigcup_{a \in A} d_a(L) = \mathcal{E}(W) \cdot L \cup d_A(L).$$

Proof. First of all, it follows from the definition of language quotients that $W^{-1} L = (W \cap \text{pre}(L))^{-1} L$. Second, if we decompose the set W as $\mathcal{E}(W) \cup \bigcup_{a \in \Sigma} (W \cap \Sigma^* a)$, we obtain

$$
\begin{aligned}
W^{-1} L &= (\mathcal{E}(W))^{-1} L \cup \bigcup_{a \in \Sigma} (W \cap \Sigma^* a \cap \text{pre}(L))^{-1} L \\
&= \mathcal{E}(W) \cdot L \cup \bigcup_{a \in A} (W \cap \Sigma^* a \cap \text{pre}(L))^{-1} L,
\end{aligned}
\tag{14.1}
$$

since $\bigcup_{a\in\Sigma\setminus A}(W\cap\Sigma^*a\cap\mathrm{pre}(L))^{-1}L=(\emptyset)^{-1}L=\emptyset$. Finally, for $a\in A$, let ua be any word in $W\cap\Sigma^*a\cap\mathrm{pre}(L)$. Then from Lemma 14.11 one can readily deduce that $(ua)^{-1}L=(\Sigma^*a\cap\mathrm{pre}(L))^{-1}L=(\Sigma^*a)^{-1}L=d_a(L)$. Thus $(W\cap\Sigma^*a\cap\mathrm{pre}(L))^{-1}L=d_a(L)$. By putting this into Equation (14.1), the result follows. $\qquad\square$

Example 14.13. We compute the left quotient of the language $L=L(\bar r)$ denoted by the linear expression $\bar r=((ab)^*c)^*$ with respect to the set W denoted by the regular expression $\varepsilon+((a+c)b)^*(a+c)$. To this end, we identify the set $A=\{\,d\in\{a,b,c\}\mid W\cap\Sigma^*d\cap\mathrm{pre}(L)\neq\emptyset\,\}$. No word in W ends with b, but the words a and c are both in W and prefixes of words in L, thus $A=\{a,c\}$ in our case. In general, the set A can be effectively computed provided W is represented in a machine model that effectively allows intersection with regular sets and has a decidable emptiness problem. For example, this is the case for the finite automaton and pushdown automaton models, see [96].

Now by Lemma 14.12 holds $W^{-1}L=\mathcal{E}(W)\cdot L\cup d_{\{a,c\}}(L)$. Here we have $\mathcal{E}(W)\cdot L=L$, and a regular expression denoting $d_{\{a,c\}}(L)$ is given in the previous Example 14.9. Thus, a regular expression denoting the quotient $W^{-1}L$ is given by $\bar r+d_{\{a,c\}}(\bar r)=((ab)^*c)^*+(b(ab)^*c+\varepsilon)\cdot((ab)^*c)^*$. $\qquad\square$

Also for the circular shift of local languages, we obtain a nice characterization:

Lemma 14.14. *Let $L\subseteq\Sigma^*$ be a local language. Then for the circular shift $\circlearrowright(L)$ we have*

$$\circlearrowright(L)=\mathcal{E}(L)\cup\bigcup_{a\in\Sigma}a\cdot d_a(L)\cdot\left(d_a\left(L^R\right)\right)^R.$$

Proof. The circular shift of any language L can by definition be written as $\circlearrowright(L)=\mathcal{E}(L)\cup\bigcup_{a\in\Sigma}L_a$, where

$$L_a=\{\,awv\mid v,w\in\Sigma^*,vaw\in L\,\}.$$

In particular, if L is local, Lemma 14.11 tells us that there cannot be any dependencies between the subwords v and w in the definition of L_a. Thus L_a can be rewritten as

$$L_a=\bigcup_{v\in\Sigma^*\mid va\cdot d_a(L)\subseteq L}a\cdot d_a(L)\cdot v,$$

and since local languages are readily seen to be closed under reversal, redoing the same trick for the reversed language yields $L_a=a\cdot d_a(L)\cdot d_a\left(L^R\right)^R$, as desired. $\qquad\square$

Example 14.15. We also compute the circular shift of the language $L=L(\bar r)$ in our running example. By Lemma 14.14, we can write $\circlearrowright(L)$ as $\mathcal{E}(L)\cup\bigcup_{a\in\Sigma}a\cdot d_a(L)\cdot\left(d_a\left(L^R\right)\right)^R$. The sets $d_a(L)$, $d_b(L)$ and $d_c(L)$ are denoted by the expressions $d_a(\bar r)=b(ab)^*c\,((ab)^*c)^*$, $d_b(\bar r)=(ab)^*c\,((ab)^*c)^*$, and $d_c(\bar r)=((ab)^*c)^*$, respectively, which were computed in Example 14.5. In a similar manner, we obtain for $\bar r^R=(c(ba)^*)^*$ the canonical derivatives $d_a\left(\bar r^R\right)=(ba)^*(c(ba)^*)^*$, $d_b\left(\bar r^R\right)=a(ba)^*(c(ba)^*)^*$, and $d_c\left(\bar r^R\right)=(ba)^*(c(ba)^*)^*$. We have $\mathcal{E}(L)=\varepsilon$, and straightforward rules for implementing the reversal of regular expressions yield $\left((ba)^*(c(ba)^*)^*\right)^R=((ab)^*c)^*(ab)^*$ and $\left(a(ba)^*(c(ba)^*)^*\right)^R=((ab)^*c)^*(ab)^*a$. Thus a regular expression denoting $\circlearrowright(L(\bar r))$ is given by

$$\varepsilon+a\cdot b(ab)^*c\,((ab)^*c)^*\cdot((ab)^*c)^*(ab)^*$$
$$+\,b\cdot(ab)^*c\,((ab)^*c)^*\cdot((ab)^*c)^*(ab)^*a+c\cdot((ab)^*c)^*\cdot((ab)^*c)^*(ab)^*.$$

Finally, we note that in an actual implementation the computational overhead for the two reversal operations carried out here could be saved by defining the concept of "canonical right derivatives" using rules analogous to those for computing canonical (left) derivatives in Definition 14.4. □

These characterizations immediately lend themselves to an implementation of quotient and circular shift operations on linear expressions via canonical derivatives. Using Lemma 14.10, we can estimate the resulting expression size as follows:

Theorem 14.16. *Let r be a linear expression of size n, and let $L = L(r)$. Then for any set of words $W \subseteq P_r^*$, there is a regular expression of size $O(n^2)$ denoting $W^{-1}L$, and a regular expression of size $O(n^3)$ denoting the circular shift $\circlearrowleft(L)$.* □

14.2 Quotients and Circular Shift for General Regular Expressions

The above results allow us to compute from a given linear expression relatively small regular expressions denoting a language quotient or the circular shift of the denoted language. In this section, we investigate the interaction of (length-preserving) homomorphisms with the language operations under consideration to transfer the obtained results to the general case. The easier case is a language operation that commutes with length-preserving homomorphisms. This is the case for the circular shift:

Lemma 14.17. *Let ℓ be a length-preserving homomorphism, and let $L \subseteq \Sigma^*$ be a language. Then*
$$\circlearrowleft(\ell(L)) = \ell(\circlearrowleft(L)).$$

Proof. Since both the homomorphism and circular shift operation commute with taking finite and infinite unions, it suffices to show the claim for the case where L contains a single word $w = a_1 a_2 \ldots a_k$. In the case $k \leq 1$, we have $L = \circlearrowleft(L)$, and the claim is trivially true. So assume $k \geq 2$. Then

$$\begin{aligned}
\ell(\circlearrowleft(\{w\})) &= \{\ell(w)\} \cup \ell(\{a_j \ldots a_k a_1 a_2 \cdots a_{j-1} \mid 2 \leq j \leq k\}) \\
&= \{\ell(w)\} \cup \{\ell(a_j) \ldots \ell(a_k)\ell(a_1)\ell(a_2) \ldots \ell(a_{j-1}) \mid 2 \leq j \leq k\}.
\end{aligned}$$

Now let $x = b_1 b_2 \ldots b_k$, with $b_i = \ell(a_i)$. Then

$$\begin{aligned}
\circlearrowleft(\{\ell(w)\}) &= \{\ell(w)\} \cup \{b_j \ldots b_k b_1 b_2 \ldots b_{j-1} \mid 2 \leq j \leq k\} \\
&= \{\ell(w)\} \cup \{\ell(a_j) \ldots \ell(a_k)\ell(a_1)\ell(a_2) \ldots \ell(a_{j-1}) \mid 2 \leq j \leq k\},
\end{aligned}$$

thus proving the desired equality. □

The next lemma shows how length-preserving homomorphisms interact with taking left derivatives. $\ell^{-1}(w) = \{x \mid \ell(x) = w\}$.

Lemma 14.18. *Let $L \subseteq \Sigma^*$ be a regular language, let $\ell : \Sigma^* \to \Gamma^*$ be a length-preserving homomorphism, and let $w \in \Gamma^*$. Then*

$$w^{-1}\ell(L) = \bigcup_{x \mid \ell(x) = w} \ell\left(x^{-1}L\right).$$

Proof. Since the model of NFAs we use does not allow multiple initial states, thus conforming with the treatment in standard textbooks such as [96], it will be technically easier to prove the equivalent statement for right derivatives, namely that

$$\ell(L)w^{-1} = \bigcup_{x|\ell(x)=w} \ell\left(Lx^{-1}\right).$$

This gives our result if we imagine reading all words from right to left.

Let $A = (Q, \Sigma, \delta, q_0, F)$ be an NFA accepting L. We shall see the above equation by applying standard finite automaton constructions for realizing both the left-hand-side and the right-hand-side of the equation, and getting both times the same result.

For the left-hand-side, we first obtain an NFA B accepting $\ell(L)$ by a standard construction from A: Let $B = (Q, \Gamma, \delta', q_0, F)$ with $\delta'(q, a) = \bigcup_{b \in \ell^{-1}(a)} \delta(q, b)$, for every $q \in Q$ and every $a \in \Gamma$. Obtaining an NFA C accepting $\ell(L)w^{-1}$ is now an easy exercise: Simply redefine the set of accepting states as those from which automaton B can reach a final state on reading input w. For later reference, let F' denote the set of final states of the NFA C.

For the right-hand-side, an NFA D accepting the set $\bigcup_{x|\ell(x)=w} Lx^{-1}$ is obtained from A simply by redefining F' to be the new set of accepting states: Recall that a state q is in F' iff automaton B can go from q to some state in F on input w. This again is the case iff automaton A can go from q to some state in F on some input x with $\ell(x) = w$. To obtain an automaton accepting the image under ℓ of the latter set, we replace in D the transition function δ with δ' and accordingly change the input alphabet to Γ, as before in the construction of the automaton B. In this way we end up again with the automaton $C = (Q, \Gamma, \delta', q_0, F')$. Since the automaton C by construction also accepts the set $\ell(L)w^{-1}$, we have $\ell(L)w^{-1} = \bigcup_{x|\ell(x)=w} \ell\left(Lx^{-1}\right)$, as desired. $\square$

Now we are ready to state the main result of this chapter:

Theorem 14.19. *Let W be a set of words. Then for the operation of taking the quotient with respect to W, we have* $\mathrm{alph}(W^{-1\cdot}, n) = O(n^2)$. *For the circular shift operation, we have* $\mathrm{alph}(\circlearrowleft, n) = O(n^3)$.

Proof. Let $\bar{r}$ be the linear expression for r, and $\ell = \ell_r$ be the homomorphism which maps $\bar{r}$ to r. Since ℓ is length-preserving, every word $w \in \Sigma^*$ is in $\ell(P_{\bar{r}})^*$, and thus, by Lemma 14.18, we have

$$w^{-1}\ell\left(L(\bar{r})\right) = \bigcup_{x|\ell(x)=w} \ell\left(x^{-1}L(\bar{r})\right).$$

This readily generalizes to sets of words, and we obtain

$$W^{-1}\ell\left(L(\bar{r})\right) = \bigcup_{w \in W} \bigcup_{x|\ell(x)=w} \ell\left(x^{-1}L(\bar{r})\right)$$

$$= \ell\left(\bigcup_{x|\ell(x)\in W} x^{-1}L(\bar{r})\right) = \ell\left(\left(\ell^{-1}(W)\right)^{-1} L(\bar{r})\right).$$

Here $\ell^{-1}(W)$ denotes the preimage of the set W under the homomorphism ℓ. Notice that last one of the above expressions is the image under ℓ of a certain quotient of $\bar{r}$.

By Theorem 14.16, the latter language can be described by a regular expression of size $O(n^2)$, and applying the map ℓ does not increase the alphabetic width. This shows that $\text{alph}(W^{-1}L) = O(n^2)$. For the circular shift, recall from Theorem 14.16 that $\circlearrowleft(L(\bar{r}))$ has alphabetic width in $O(n^3)$. By Lemma 14.17, $\circlearrowleft(L(\ell(\bar{r}))) = \ell(\circlearrowleft(L(\bar{r})))$, and, as noted before, applying a length-preserving homomorphism does not increase the alphabetic width. □

Example 14.20. We compute the left quotient of $L(r)$ with respect to the set W, which is denoted by the expression $\varepsilon + (ab)^*a$. Following the proof of Theorem 14.19, the language $W^{-1}L(r)$ is equal to $\ell\left(\left(\ell^{-1}(W)\right)^{-1}L(\bar{r})\right)$, where $\ell = \{a \mapsto a, b \mapsto b, c \mapsto a\}$ is the length-preserving homomorphism which maps $\bar{r}$ to r. An expression denoting $\ell^{-1}(W) = \ell^{-1}(\varepsilon + (ab)^*a)$ is given by $\varepsilon + ((a+c)b)^*(a+c)$. Recall from Example 14.13 that the quotient $\left(\ell^{-1}(W)\right)^{-1}L(\bar{r})$ is denoted by the expression

$$\bar{r} + d_{\{a,c\}}(\bar{r}) = ((ab)^*c)^* + (b(ab)^*c + \varepsilon) \cdot ((ab)^*c)^*.$$

Finally, applying the length-preserving homomorphism ℓ to this expression yields the regular expression $((ab)^*a) + (b(ab)^*a + \varepsilon)((ab)^*a)^*$ for $W^{-1}L(r)$. □

Example 14.21. The circular shift is computed even more easily, at least if we already did it for the corresponding linear expression: From Example 14.15 we deduce that the circular shift of $L(r)$ is simply

$$\begin{aligned}\circlearrowleft(L(r)) = {} & \varepsilon + a \cdot b(ab)^*a \left((ab)^*a\right)^* \cdot \left((ab)^*a\right)^* (ab)^* \\ & + b \cdot (ab)^*a \left((ab)^*a\right)^* \cdot \left((ab)^*a\right)^* (ab)^*a + a \cdot \left((ab)^*a\right)^* \cdot \left((ab)^*a\right)^* (ab)^*,\end{aligned}$$

by applying the length-preserving homomorphism $\ell = \{a \mapsto a, b \mapsto b, c \mapsto a\}$ to the regular expression denoting $\circlearrowleft(L(\bar{r}))$. □

As interesting special cases of our main theorem, consider the language operations INIT and FIN, which are defined as $\text{INIT}(L) = \{x \mid \exists y : xy \in L\}$ and $\text{FIN}(L) = \{y \mid \exists x : xy \in L\}$, respectively. These operations are discussed in the standard textbook [96] on automata theory; indeed they are nothing else than the left and right quotient with Σ^*, respectively. Therefore, we also obtain the following:

Corollary 14.22. *For the operations* INIT *and* FIN *holds* $\text{alph}(\text{INIT}, n) = O(n^2)$ *and* $\text{alph}(\text{FIN}, n) = O(n^2)$. □

Currently, we do not know whether these upper bounds have the right order of magnitude. At least, we can show a quadratic lower bound on the increase of alphabetic width for the circular shift operation. To this end, we make use of certain circular arrangements, which are well known in combinatorics: For an integer $k \geq 1$, a *binary De Bruijn sequence* of order k is a circular sequence γ of length 2^k over the binary alphabet $\{a, b\}$ such that every word in $\{a, b\}^k$ is contained, at some *unique* position, in γ. The following theorem, proved first[1] by Flye Sainte-Marie [61], is a classical result in combinatorics:

Theorem 14.23. *For every $k \geq 1$, a binary De Bruijn sequence of order k exists.*

---

[1]As acknowledged by De Bruijn [43], he later rediscovered essentially the same proof.

By cutting open a circular sequence γ at some specified position and read it clockwise, we obtain a word $w \in \{a, b\}^*$ in the usual sense, of length $|\gamma|$. We call such a word a *cut* of γ. With these notions, we are now sufficiently armed to prove a lower bound on the alphabetic width on circular shift.

Theorem 14.24. *For the circular shift operation, we have* $\mathrm{alph}(\circlearrowright, n) = \Omega(n^2)$, *and this holds for all alphabets of size at least* 2.

Proof. We take $n = 2^k$, for some $k \geq 1$. Let γ be a binary De Bruijn sequence of order k, and let w be a cut of γ. Our witness language is simply $L_n = \{w\}$. Of course, L_n admits a regular expression of alphabetic width at most n. For a lower bound on the alphabetic width of $\circlearrowright(\{w\})$, observe first that this set equals the set of all cuts of γ. Since there are $n = 2^k$ such cuts, each of length n, there is trivially a regular expression of size n^2 for this set. Our aim is to show that we cannot do essentially better.

Since every regular expression of size n can be transformed into a nondeterministic finite automaton having at most $n + 1$ states, it suffices to give a lower bound of $\Omega(n^2)$ on the number of states required by any nondeterministic finite automaton accepting the set $\circlearrowright(\{w\})$ of all cuts of γ. To this end, we make use of a proof technique we discussed in Chapter 3. Namely, the size of any fooling set for a regular language is a lower bound on its nondeterministic state complexity (see Lemma 3.2); recall that a fooling set for language L is a set of pairs (x_i, y_i) of words such that $x_i y_i \in L$ for each i, but for $i \neq j$, at least one of the two cross-wise concatenations $x_i y_j$ and $x_j y_i$ is not in L.

Now, let $w_1 = w$ and for $2 \leq i \leq n$, we recursively define $w_i = vu$, if $uv = w_{i-1}$, where $u \in \{a, b\}$ and $v \in \Sigma^*$—thus, all these words are obtained by cuts of γ at appropriate positions. For example, if we have $w_1 = aaababbb$, then $w_4 = babbbaaa$—see Figure 14.1. Note that all these words are pairwise different because the w_i are cuts of a De Bruijn sequence. For $1 \leq i, j \leq n$, let $x_{i,j}$ denote the prefix of length j of w_i. Similarly, we use $y_{i,j}$ to denote the suffix of length j of w_i. We claim that

$$S = \{ (x_{i,j}, y_{i,n-j}) \mid 1 \leq i \leq n \text{ and } k \leq j \leq n - k \}$$

is a fooling set for the language $\circlearrowright(\{w\})$ of all cuts of γ. Clearly, the word $x_{i,j} y_{i,n-j}$ equals w_i, and every w_i is a cut of γ. We will prove that $x_{i,j} y_{r,s}$ is not a member of $\circlearrowright(\{w\})$, if $r \neq i$ or $s \neq n - j$. Consider first the case $s \neq n - j$. Since $x_{i,j}$ is of length j and $y_{r,s}$ of length s, their concatenation has length different from n and cannot be a cut. Now consider the case $r \neq i$ and $s = n - j$. Recall that w_i is the *unique* cut of γ that begins with $x_{i,k}$. By rotational symmetry, w_i is also the *unique* cut that ends with $y_{i,k}$. For the sake of contradiction, assume now that $x_{i,j} y_{r,n-j}$ is a cut of γ. Since the above word begins with $x_{i,j}$ and $j \geq k$, it has $x_{i,k}$ as prefix, so it must be equal to w_i. By similar means, since the word ends with $y_{r,n-j}$ and $n - j \geq k$, it has $y_{r,k}$ as suffix, so it must be equal to w_r. This implies $w_i = w_r$, a contradiction, since by assumption $i \neq r$.

Thus S is a fooling set for $\circlearrowright(\{w\})$, the set of all cuts of γ, and $|S| = \Omega(n^2)$ is a lower bound for the number of states of any nondeterministic finite automaton accepting the language $\circlearrowright(w)$, as desired. $\qquad \square$

To conclude this chapter, we observe that the lower bound becomes tight when we restrict our attention to finite languages: If $L(r)$ is finite, we can safely assume that r does not make use of the star operator, as observed in Lemma 9.6 in the chapter on the conversion problem for finite languages. Any potential starred subexpression could

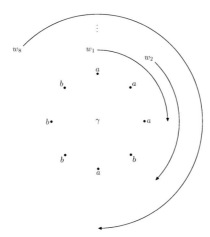

Figure 14.1: The De Bruijn sequence $\gamma = aaababbb$ of order $k = 3$ and length $n = 8$ is shown. The words w_i, for $1 \leq i \leq n$, used in the construction of the fooling set are obtained by cuts of γ at appropriate positions—here $w_1 = aaababbb$ is obtained by cutting γ before 12-o'clock, while $w_4 = babbbaaa$ is obtained by cutting before half past four.

describe only the empty word. In the case of expressions without star, it is not hard to prove, by inspecting Definition 14.4, that all canonical derivatives are of linear size. Plugging this improved estimate into the proof of the $O(n^3)$ bound for the circular shift from Theorem 14.19 results in a quadratic upper bound for the case of finite languages. We thus obtain a tight bound for the regular expression size of circular shift in the case of finite languages:

Corollary 14.25. *Let r be a regular expression of size n denoting a finite language $L \subset \Sigma^*$. Then there is a regular expression of size $O(n^2)$ denoting denoting $\circlearrowleft(L)$. In contrast, there exist infinitely many finite languages L_n over a binary alphabet such that L_n admits a regular expression of alphabetic width n, but every regular expression describing $\circlearrowleft(L_n)$ has alphabetic width at least $\Omega(n^2)$.* □

15 Summary of Results on Language Operations

The last main part of the thesis was devoted to a systematic investigation of the effect of language operations on expression size. We considered two basic types of questions: the first question asks for the effect on required expression size of applying once a given language operation to its operands. The second question concerns a kind of amortized analysis, in that we ask for the succinctness gain over ordinary regular expressions if we enrich the syntax by adding built-in operators for some basic operations on languages. Results regarding the former question are gathered in Table 15.1. A variation on the theme, which we started to explore at the very end of Chapter 14, would be to study these questions in restricted setups. In this regard, Ellul et al. [59] obtained some bounds for the case of unary languages. For more results in this direction, in particular regarding Boolean operations on languages described by linear expressions, the reader is referred to the paper by Gelade and Neven [65].

Regarding the latter question, Table 15.2 reflects our collected knowledge about the succinctness gain when extending regular expressions with the intersection, interleaving, or complementation operations.

Operation	Previous ——— lower bound New	Upper bound
RE ∩ RE	$c^{\sqrt{m}}$, for $|\Sigma| \geq m$ [65] c^{m} , for $|\Sigma| \geq 2$ (Cor. 12.2)	$n \cdot d^{m \cdot (1+\log(n/m))}$ (Thm. 12.6)
RE ⧢ RE	c^{m} , for $|\Sigma| \geq 2$ (Cor. 12.3)	$n \cdot d^{m \cdot (1+\log(n/m))}$ (Thm. 12.7)
¬ RE	$2^{2^{\Omega(n)}}$, for $|\Sigma| \geq 4$ [65] $2^{2^{\Omega(n)}}$, for $|\Sigma| \geq 2$ (Thm. 12.10)	$2^{2^{O(n)}}$ [59]
$W^{-1} \cdot$ RE	—	$O(n^2)$ (Thm. 14.19)
↻ RE	$\Omega(n^2)$, for $|\Sigma| \geq 2$ (Thm. 14.24)	$O(n^3)$ (Thm. 14.19)
INIT(RE)	—	$O(n^2)$ (Cor. 14.22)
FIN(RE)	—	$O(n^2)$ (Cor. 14.22)

Table 15.1: Lower and upper bounds on alphabetic width of language operations on languages of alphabetic width m and n. The symbols c and d refer to some fixed constants with $1 < c, d < \infty$. All binary operations being symmetric, we assume $m \leq n$.

Extension	Previous ——— lower bound New	Upper bound
RE(∩)	$2^{2^{\Omega(\sqrt{n})}}$, for $|\Sigma| \geq 2$ [64] $2^{2^{\Omega(n)}}$, for $|\Sigma| \geq 2$ (Thm. 13.2)	$2^{2^{O(n)}}$ [64]
RE(⧢)	$2^{2^{\Omega(\sqrt{n})}}$, for $|\Sigma| \geq 3$ [64] $2^{2^{\Omega(n)}}$, for $|\Sigma| \geq n$ (Thm. 13.3) $2^{2^{\Omega(n/\log n)}}$, for $|\Sigma| \geq 2$ (Thm. 13.9)	$2^{2^{O(n)}}$ [64]
RE(¬)	nonelementary [172]	

Table 15.2: Lower and upper bounds on required size for transforming extended regular expressions into ordinary regular expressions.

Part V

Outro

16 Conclusion and Further Research

In this thesis, we considered questions regarding how we can deal efficiently with descriptions of regular languages, and where the inherent limitations of the respective mechanism lie. Although by now some parts of the landscape are charted much more completely than at the time this research work started, some questions had to remain unresolved. We shortly recapitulate our main findings and discuss some questions that had to be left open. Here we highlight only a few outstanding questions, in the hope that these are both of interest and also specific enough to stimulate further research in these directions in the near future. A few more questions are found in the respective summaries of each of the three main parts of the thesis.

The first main theme of the thesis was about minimum nondeterministic finite automata. We seized the strengths and limitations of known proof techniques for nondeterministic state complexity and gave a reformulation of these techniques as graph theoretic concepts. Then we looked at different notions of size of NFAs, namely the number of states *versus* the number of transitions. We found that these concepts are essentially different and the NFA minimization problem has to be studied separately for these two flavors. Unfortunately, nondeterministic transition complexity is far less understood. Consequently, classical computational complexity results were found mainly for state minimization. There we saw that the compactness of the input representation can largely influence the computational complexity of the NFA minimization problem if we consider finite languages. Such a phenomenon is known to occur in various computational settings, see, e.g. [63]. But earlier research on the NFA minimization problem [114] showed that the problem remains as hard if the input is specified less succinctly for infinite languages, so we could not expect such a result. Unfortunately, even when restricting to finite languages and specifying the input in the least succinct way that one may find, NFA minimization remains **NP**-hard. There already was evidence that no good approximation algorithms might exist either [70]. We put this evidence on more solid grounds and proved rather high limits on approximability of the variants of the problem under consideration. In this way, we provide a definite (negative) answer to the research question raised in 1993 by Jiang and Ravikumar, and also to most research problems posed more recently by Gramlich and Schnitger regarding other variants of this problem. What remains open yet is the quantitative question of determining more precise bounds: In the case where a unary NFA is given, we already determined the optimal bound under the weakest possible assumption. But in most of the other cases, still some gaps yawn between the upper and lower bounds. Perhaps most astonishing is that the question whether unary NFA minimization is **NP**-hard for given DFA, posed by Jiang et al. [112] almost twenty years ago, is still open.

Concerning the descriptional complexity of regular expressions, we obtained many results, partly with strongly negative algorithmic implications. Undoubtedly, the main result here is that the star height of a regular language can be at most logarithmic in the required regular expression size. While this is already a curious result on its own right, the counterpositive gives a powerful tool in proving lower bounds on regular expression size. This power is illustrated by the many tight bounds obtained not only for the conversion problem but also later, in the third part, on the effect of various language operations. For the problem of converting finite automata into regular expressions, we could prove a tight lower bound of $2^{\Theta(n)}$, where n is the number of states. Such a result had been established by Ehrenfeucht and Zeiger already in the 1970s. Yet the obvious catch in their lower bound was that they used an alphabet of size n^2. We managed to get around this not only by using a different proof technique, but also by crucially relying on a more recent concept from graph theory: Note that the existence of expander graphs was proved by Pinsker only at the time when Ehrenfeucht and Zeiger obtained their results.

Despite of the long list of results obtained by application of the technique based on star height, it tells us absolutely nothing about finite languages. There we devised a different technique, based on communication complexity. We related the sizes of regular expressions and monotone Boolean formulas. This allowed us to transfer results from computational complexity theory and thereby to resolve an old problem posed by Ehrenfeucht and Zeiger [55] concerning the size of regular expressions equivalent to acyclic finite automata. The ingredients in lower bound proofs often also hint at potential algorithmic hooks. This was the case here: We found an improved algorithm for converting DFAs over alphabets of constant size into regular expressions. This algorithm can be implemented as a strategy for state elimination. Notably, this algorithm gives the first improvement over the trivial bound that is known since the early 1960s. While the jump in performance from the previous $O(4^n)$ to $O(1.742^n)$ is already impressive, we feel that both our analysis and our techniques are far from optimal. A few things that come to mind are the following. We derived our bound based on the underlying undirected graph at the beginning of the elimination process. It might be possible to take edge directions and the dynamics of the elimination process better into account. Devising improved algorithms may be a challenging but surely rewarding research goal.

The last part of the thesis was devoted to the evolution of required regular expression size under various language operations. Regular expressions are often used as specification formalism, notably in the context of data exchange over the internet. Thus it was about time to answer the most basic questions regarding their dynamic succinctness properties. Some of these questions were explicitly posed by Ellul et al. [59]. We could provide an answer to several of these questions, including a tight doubly-exponential bound for the complement operation. Interestingly, Gelade and Neven worked at the same time along similar lines but using different techniques [65]. This witnesses that the time was indeed ripe to settle these questions. In several cases we showed that the simplest method of converting to a finite automaton, implementing the language operation under consideration in finite automata, and converting the result back to a regular expression is already optimal. In that last step, a sophisticated choice of the elimination ordering can significantly shorten the resulting regular expression, as we saw for the operations shuffle and intersection. In contrast, we also identified a few other language operations that can be implemented directly on regular expressions. In this way, we can avoid an exponential blow-up in size. There are of course many other interesting language operations waiting to be studied. Another direction is to study these problems for subclasses of regular languages. Often the instances that really arise in practical applications are much more constrained. For example, we determined the cost of the circular shift for finite languages. Some operations on other subclasses of regular languages were studied by Gelade and Neven [65].

Finally, we mention the following research direction, which might be a less obvious offspring of this thesis than the questions outlined above. Inspired by the tradeoff observed when comparing state minimization versus transition minimization for nondeterministic finite automata, we can ask similar questions for regular expressions. We think it is unlikely that every regular language admits a regular expression that is simultaneously of minimum alphabetic width and of minimum star height. This would indicate that there is a tradeoff between structural and descriptional complexity. A promising family of examples might be the languages presented in Example 2.5.

This last problem appears to be related to some difficult questions: For instance, a polynomial upper bound on the size of an equivalent regular expression of minimum star height would locate the famous star height problem in **PSPACE**. While the star height problem is known to be decidable for some time now, analyzing the computational complexity of the problem is still subject to active research, see e.g. [124].

We can also ask some more moderate questions with a similar flavor. For example, in this work, we have proved that the star height is always logarithmic in the alphabetic width of a regular language. It can be shown, using the methods presented in Chapter 10, that we can always obtain an expression of star height this low, while the size of the resulting expression is still polynomial in the minimum required size. Thus it is natural to ask whether we can trade expression size for star height: For instance, can we achieve sublinear star height while allowing only linear increase in expression size?

Thus it appears as if every obtained answer will entail a whole collection of new and intriguing research challenges. This stems from the fact that an improved understanding of a phenomenon often allows us to formulate more sophisticated, and also more detailed, questions about it.

Bibliography

[1] Alfred V. Aho, Ravi Sethi, and Jeffrey D. Ullman. *Compilers: Principles, Techniques, and Tools*. Addison-Wesley, 1986.

[2] Noga Alon, Jeff Kahn, and Paul D. Seymour. Large induced degenerate subgraphs. *Graphs and Combinatorics*, 3(1):203–211, 1987.

[3] Jérôme Amilhastre, Philippe Janssen, and Marie-Catherine Vilarem. FA minimisation heuristics for a class of finite languages. In Oliver Boldt and Helmut Jürgensen, editors, *4th International Workshop on Implementation of Automata*, volume 2214 of *Lecture Notes in Computer Science*, pages 1–12. Springer, 2001.

[4] Dana Angluin. Inference of reversible languages. *Journal of the ACM*, 29(3):741–765, 1982.

[5] Kenneth I. Appel and Wolfgang Haken. *Every planar map is four colorable*, volume 98 of *Contemporary Mathematics*. American Mathematical Society, 1989.

[6] Stefan Arnborg and Andrzej Proskurowski. Linear time algorithms for NP-hard problems restricted to partial k-trees. *Discrete Applied Mathematics*, 23(1):11–24, 1989.

[7] Robert L. Ashenhurst and Susan Graham, editors. *ACM Turing award lectures: the first twenty years: 1966-1985*. ACM Press/Addison-Wesley, 1987.

[8] Giorgio Ausiello, Marco Protasi, Alberto Marchetti-Spaccamela, Giorgio Gambosi, Pierluigi Crescenzi, and Viggo Kann. *Complexity and Approximation: Combinatorial Optimization Problems and Their Approximability Properties*. Springer, 1999.

[9] Gérard Berry and Ravi Sethi. From regular expressions to deterministic automata. *Theoretical Computer Science*, 48(3):117–126, 1986.

[10] Jean Berstel and Jean-Eric Pin. Local languages and the Berry-Sethi algorithm. *Theoretical Computer Science*, 155(2):439–446, 1996.

[11] Dietmar Berwanger, Anuj Dawar, Paul Hunter, and Stephan Kreutzer. DAG-width and parity games. In Bruno Durand and Wolfgang Thomas, editors, *23rd Annual Symposium on Theoretical Aspects of Computer Science*, volume 3884 of *Lecture Notes in Computer Science*, pages 524–536. Springer, 2006.

[12] Dietmar Berwanger and Erich Grädel. Entanglement—A measure for the complexity of directed graphs with applications to logic and games. In Franz Baader and Andrei Voronkov, editors, *11th International Conference on Logic for Programming, Artificial Intelligence, and Reasoning*, volume 3452 of *Lecture Notes in Computer Science*, pages 209–223. Springer, 2005.

[13] Philip Bille and Mikkel Thorup. Faster regular expression matching. In Susanne Albers, Alberto Marchetti-Spaccamela, Yossi Matias, Sotiris Nikoletseas, and Wolfgang Thomas, editors, *36th International Colloquium on Automata, Languages and Programming (Part I)*, volume 5555 of *LNCS*. Springer, 2009. To appear.

[14] Jean-Camille Birget. Intersection and union of regular languages and state complexity. *Information Processing Letters*, 43(4):185–190, 1992.

[15] Andreas Björklund, Thore Husfeldt, and Sanjeev Khanna. Approximating longest directed paths and cycles. In Josep Díaz, Juhani Karhumäki, Arto Lepistö, and Donald Sannella, editors, *31st International Colloquium on Automata, Languages and Programming*, volume 3142 of *Lecture Notes in Computer Science*, pages 222–233. Springer, 2004.

[16] Henrik Björklund and Wim Martens. The tractability frontier for NFA minimization. In Luca Aceto, Ivan Damgård, Leslie Ann Goldberg, Magnús M. Halldórsson, Anna Ingólfsdóttir, and Igor Walkuwiewicz, editors, *35th International Colloquium on Automata, Languages and Programming (Part II)*, volume 5126 of *Lecture Notes in Computer Science*, pages 27–38. Springer, 2008.

[17] Hans L. Bodlaender, Jitender S. Deogun, Klaus Jansen, Ton Kloks, Dieter Kratsch, Haiko Müller, and Zsolt Tuza. Rankings of graphs. *SIAM Journal on Discrete Mathematics*, 11(1):168–181, 1998.

[18] Hans L. Bodlaender, John R. Gilbert, Hjálmtyr Hafsteinsson, and Ton Kloks. Approximating treewidth, pathwidth, frontsize, and shortest elimination tree. *Journal of Algorithms*, 18(2):238–255, 1995.

[19] Hans L. Bodlaender and Babette van Antwerpen-de Fluiter. Parallel algorithms for series parallel graphs and graphs with treewidth two. *Algorithmica*, 29(4):534–559, 2001.

[20] Ronald V. Book and Ashok K. Chandra. Inherently nonplanar automata. *Acta Informatica*, 6(1):89–94, 1976.

[21] Janusz A. Brzozowski. Derivatives of regular expressions. *Journal of the ACM*, 11(4):481–494, 1964.

[22] Janusz A. Brzozowski. Open problems about regular languages. In Ronald V. Book, editor, *Formal language theory—Perspectives and open problems*, pages 23–47. Academic Press, 1980.

[23] Janusz A. Brzozowski and Edward J. McCluskey. Signal flow graph techniques for sequential circuit state diagrams. *IEEE Transactions on Electronic Computers*, EC-12(2):67–76, 1963.

[24] J. Richard Büchi. Weak second-order arithmetic and finite automata. *Zeitschrift für mathematische Logik und Grundlagen der Mathematik*, 6(1–6):66–92, 1960.

[25] Jean-Marc Champarnaud and Fabien Coulon. NFA reduction algorithms by means of regular inequalities. *Theoretical Computer Science*, 327(3):241–253, 2004. Erratum in 347(1-2):437–440, 2005.

[26] Jean-Marc Champarnaud and Jean-Eric Pin. A maxmin problem on finite automata. *Discrete Applied Mathematics*, 23(1):91–96, 1989.

[27] Jean-Marc Champarnaud and Djelloul Ziadi. Canonical derivatives, partial derivatives and finite automaton constructions. *Theoretical Computer Science*, 289(1):137–163, 2002.

[28] L. Sunil Chandran and Telikepalli Kavitha. The treewidth and pathwidth of hypercubes. *Discrete Mathematics*, 306(3):359–365, 2006.

[29] Richard Chang. Bounded queries, approximations, and the Boolean hierarchy. *Information and Computation*, 169(2):129–159, 2001.

[30] Laura Chaubard and Jean-Eric Pin. Open problems on regular languages: an historical perspective. In Jorge M. André, Vitor H. Fernandes, Mário J.J.Branco, Gracinda M. S. Gomes, John Fountain, and John Meakin, editors, *International Conference on Semigroups and Formal Languages—in Honour of the 65th Birthday of Donald B. McAlister*, pages 39–56. World Scientific, 2007.

[31] Noam Chomsky. Three models for the description of language. *IRE Transactions on Information Theory*, IT-2(3):113–124, 1956.

[32] Noam Chomsky. On certain formal properties of grammars. *Information and Control*, 2(2):137–167, 1959.

[33] Marek Chrobak. Finite automata and unary languages. *Theoretical Computer Science*, 47(2):149–158, 1986. Errata in 302(1–3):497–498, 2003, and in [60].

[34] Fan R. K. Chung. *Spectral Graph Theory*, volume 92 of *CBMS Regional Conference Series in Mathematics*. American Mathematical Society, 1997.

[35] Rina S. Cohen. Star height of certain families of regular events. *Journal of Computer and System Sciences*, 4(3):281–297, 1970.

[36] Rina S. Cohen and Janusz A. Brzozowski. General properties of star height of regular events. *Journal of Computer and System Sciences*, 4(3):260–280, 1970.

[37] John H. Conway. *Regular Algebra and Finite Machines*. Chapman and Hall, 1971.

[38] Bruno Courcelle, Damian Niwinski, and Andreas Podelski. A geometrical view of the determinization and minimization of finite-state automata. *Mathematical Systems Theory*, 24(2):117–146, 1991.

[39] Pierluigi Crescenzi. A short guide to approximation preserving reductions. In *12th Annual IEEE Conference on Computational Complexity*, pages 262–273. IEEE Computer Society, 1997.

[40] Berteun Damman, Tingting Han, and Joost-Pieter Katoen. Regular expressions for PCTL counterexamples. In *5th International Conference on the Quantitative Evaluation of Systems*, pages 179–188. IEEE Computer Society, 2008.

[41] Martin Davis. *The universal computer—The road from Leibniz to Turing*. W. W. Norton & Company, Inc., 2000.

[42] Conrado Daws. Symbolic and parametric model checking of discrete-time Markov chains. In Zhiming Liu and Keijiro Araki, editors, *1st International Colloquium on Theoretical Aspects of Computing*, volume 3407 of *Lecture Notes in Computer Science*, pages 280–294. Springer, 2004.

[43] Nicolaas Govert de Bruijn. Acknowledgement of priority to C. Flye Sainte-Marie on the counting of circular arrangements of 2^n zeros and ones that show each n-letter word exactly once. Technical Report 75-WSK-06, Technological University Eindhoven, 1975.

[44] Dominique de Caen, David A. Gregory, and Norman J. Pullman. The Boolean rank of zero-one matrices. In Charles C. Cadogan, editor, *3rd Caribbean Conference on Combinatorics and Computing*, pages 169–173. Department of Mathematics, University of the West Indies, 1981.

[45] Aldo de Luca and Stefano Varricchio. On noncounting regular classes. *Theoretical Computer Science*, 100(1):67–104, 1992.

[46] Françoise Dejean and Marcel Paul Schützenberger. On a question of eggan. *Information and Control*, 9(1):23–25, 1966.

[47] Manuel Delgado and José Morais. Approximation to the smallest regular expression for a given regular language. In Michael Domaratzki, Alexander Okhotin, Kai Salomaa, and Sheng Yu, editors, *9th Conference on Implementation and Application of Automata*, volume 3317 of *Lecture Notes in Computer Science*, pages 312–314. Springer, 2004.

[48] Reinhard Diestel. *Graph Theory*, volume 173 of *Graduate Texts in Mathematics*. Springer, 3rd edition, 2006.

[49] Benjamin Doerr. Communication complexity and the protocol parition number. Technical Report 99-28, Berichtsreihe des Mathematischen Seminars der Universität Kiel, 1999.

[50] Michael Domaratzki, Derek Kisman, and Jeffrey Shallit. On the number of distinct languages accepted by finite automata with n states. *Journal of Automata, Languages and Combinatorics*, 7(4):469–486, 2002.

[51] Michael Domaratzki and Kai Salomaa. Lower bounds for the transition complexity of NFAs. *Journal of Computer and System Sciences*, 74(7):1116–1130, 2008.

[52] Doron Drusinsky. *Modeling and Verification Using UML Statecharts: A Working Guide to Reactive System Design, Runtime Monitoring and Execution-based Model Checking*. Newnes, 2006.

[53] Keith Edwards and Graham E. Farr. Planarization and fragmentability of some classes of graphs. *Discrete Mathematics*, 308(12):2396–2406, 2008.

[54] Lawrence C. Eggan. Transition graphs and the star height of regular events. *Michigan Mathematical Journal*, 10(4):385–397, 1963.

[55] Andrzej Ehrenfeucht and H. Paul Zeiger. Complexity measures for regular expressions. *Journal of Computer and System Sciences*, 12(2):134–146, 1976.

[56] Samuel Eilenberg. *Automata, Languages, and Machines*, volume 59A/B of *Pure and Applied Mathematics—A Series of Monographs and Textbooks*. Academic Press, 1974. Two volumes (Vols. A/B). Vol. B includes 2 chapters by Bret Tilson.

[57] Calvin C. Elgot. Decision problems of finite automata design and related arithmetics. *Transactions of the American Mathematical Society*, 98(1):21–51, 1961.

[58] Keith Ellul. Descriptional complexity measures of regular languages. Master's thesis, University of Waterloo, Ontario, Canada, 2004.

[59] Keith Ellul, Bryan Krawetz, Jeffrey Shallit, and Ming-Wei Wang. Regular expressions: New results and open problems. *Journal of Automata, Languages and Combinatorics*, 10(4):407–437, 2005.

[60] Unary finite automata vs. arithmetic progressions. Anthony widjaja to. *Information Processing Letters*, 2009. To appear.

[61] Camille Flye Sainte-Marie. Question 48. *L'intermédiaire des mathématiciens*, 1:107–110, 1894. Also reproduced as appendix in [43].

[62] Martin Fürer. The complexity of the inequivalence problem for regular expressions with intersection. In Jaco W. de Bakker and Jan van Leeuwen, editors, *7th Colloquium on Automata, Languages and Programming*, volume 85 of *Lecture Notes in Computer Science*, pages 234–245. Springer, 1980.

[63] Michael R. Garey and David S. Johnson. *Computers and Intractability: A Guide to the Theory of NP-Completeness*. A Series of Books in the Mathematical Sciences. W. H. Freeman, 1979.

[64] Wouter Gelade. Succinctness of regular expressions with interleaving, intersection and counting. In Edward Ochmański and Jerzy Tyszkiewicz, editors, *33rd International Symposium on Mathematical Foundations of Computer Science*, volume 5162 of *Lecture Notes in Computer Science*, pages 363–374. Springer, 2008.

[65] Wouter Gelade and Frank Neven. Succinctness of the complement and intersection of regular expressions. In Susanne Albers and Pascal Weil, editors, *25th Annual Symposium on Theoretical Aspects of Computer Science*, volume 08001 of *Dagstuhl Seminar Proceedings*, pages 325–336. Schloss Dagstuhl - Leibniz Center for Informatics, 2008.

[66] Dennis Geller and Saul Stahl. The chromatic number and other functions of the lexicographic product. *Journal of Combinatorial Theory, Series B*, 19(1):87–95, 1975.

[67] Ian Glaister and Jeffrey Shallit. A lower bound technique for the size of nondeterministic finite automata. *Information Processing Letters*, 59(2):75–77, 1996.

[68] Georges Gonthier. Formal proof—The four-color theorem. *Notices of the American Mathematical Society*, 55(1):1382–1393, 2008.

[69] Gregor Gramlich. Probabilistic and nondeterministic unary automata. In Branislav Rovan and Peter Vojtás, editors, *28th International Symposium on Mathematical Foundations of Computer Science*, volume 2747 of *Lecture Notes in Computer Science*, pages 460–469. Springer, 2003.

[70] Gregor Gramlich and Georg Schnitger. Minimizing nfa's and regular expressions. *Journal of Computer and System Sciences*, 73(6):908–923, 2007.

[71] David A. Gregory and Norman J. Pullman. Semiring rank: Boolean rank and nonnegative rank factorizations. *Journal of Combinatorics, Information & System Sciences*, 8(3):223–233, 1983.

[72] David Gries. Describing an algorithm by Hopcroft. *Acta Informatica*, 2(2):97–109, 1973.

[73] Michelangelo Grigni and Michael Sipser. Monotone separation of logarithmic space from logarithmic depth. *Journal of Computer and System Sciences*, 50(3):433–437, 1995.

[74] Hermann Gruber and Markus Holzer. Finding lower bounds for nondeterministic state complexity is hard. In Oscar H. Ibarra and Zhe Dang, editors, *10th International Conference on Developments in Language Theory*, volume 4036 of *Lecture Notes in Computer Science*, pages 363–374. Springer, 2006.

[75] Hermann Gruber and Markus Holzer. Results on the average state and transition complexity of finite automata accepting finite languages (extended abstract). In Hing Leung and Giovanni Pighizzini, editors, *8th Workshop on Descriptional Complexity of Formal Systems*, Computer Science Technical Report NMSU-CS-2006-001, pages 267–275, 2006.

[76] Hermann Gruber and Markus Holzer. Computational complexity of NFA minimization for finite and unary languages. In Remco Loos, Szilárd Zsolt Fazekas, and Carlos Martín-Vide, editors, *1st International Conference on Language and Automata Theory and Applications*, Technical Report 35/07, pages 261–272. Research Group on Mathematical Linguistics, Universitat Rovira i Virgili, 2007.

[77] Hermann Gruber and Markus Holzer. Inapproximability of nondeterministic state and transition complexity assuming P ≠ NP. In Tero Harju, Juhani Karhumäki, and Arto Lepistö, editors, *11th International Conference on Developments in Language Theory*, volume 4588 of *Lecture Notes in Computer Science*, pages 205–216. Springer, 2007.

[78] Hermann Gruber and Markus Holzer. On the average state and transition complexity of finite languages. *Theoretical Computer Science*, 387(2):167–176, 2007.

[79] Hermann Gruber and Markus Holzer. Finite automata, digraph connectivity, and regular expression size. In Luca Aceto, Ivan Damgård, Leslie Ann Goldberg, Magnús M. Halldórsson, Anna Ingólfsdóttir, and Igor Walkuwiewicz, editors, *35th International Colloquium on Automata, Languages and Programming (Part II)*, volume 5126 of *Lecture Notes in Computer Science*, pages 39–50. Springer, 2008.

[80] Hermann Gruber and Markus Holzer. Language operations with regular expressions of polynomial size. In Cezar Câmpeanu and Giovanni Pighizzini, editors, *10th International Workshop on Descriptional Complexity of Formal Systems*, pages 182–193. CSIT University of Prince Edward Island, 2008.

[81] Hermann Gruber and Markus Holzer. Provably shorter regular expressions from deterministic finite automata (Extended abstract). In Masami Ito and Masafumi Toyama, editors, *12th International Conference on Developments in Language Theory*, volume 5257 of *Lecture Notes in Computer Science*. Springer, 2008.

[82] Hermann Gruber and Markus Holzer. Language operations with regular expressions of polynomial size. *Theoretical Computer Science*, 2009. To appear.

[83] Hermann Gruber and Markus Holzer. Tight bounds on the descriptional complexity of regular expressions. In Volker Diekert and Dirk Nowotka, editors, *13th International Conference on Developments in Language Theory*, volume 5583 of *LNCS*, pages 276–287. Springer, 2009. To appear.

[84] Hermann Gruber and Jan Johannsen. Optimal lower bounds on regular expression size using communication complexity. In Roberto Amadio, editor, *11th International Conference Foundations of Software Science and Computation Structures*, volume 4962 of *Lecture Notes in Computer Science*, pages 273–286. Springer, 2008.

[85] Igor Grunsky, Oleksiy Kurganskyy, and Igor Potapov. On a maximal NFA without mergible states. In Dima Grigoriev, John Harrison, and Edward A. Hirsch, editors, *First International Computer Science Symposium in Russia*, volume 3967 of *Lecture Notes in Computer Science*, pages 202–210. Springer, 2006.

[86] Stefan Gulan and Henning Fernau. An optimal construction of finite automata from regular expressions. In Ramesh Hariharan, Madhavan Mukund, and V. Vinay, editors, *28th IARCS Annual Conference on Foundations of Software Technology and Theoretical Computer Science*, volume 08004 of *Dagstuhl Seminar Proceedings*. Schloss Dagstuhl - Leibniz Center for Informatics, 2008.

[87] Rudolf Halin. S-functions for graphs. *Journal of Geometry*, 8(1–2):171–186, 1976.

[88] Yo-Sub Han and Derek Wood. Obtaining shorter regular expressions from finite-state automata. *Theoretical Computer Science*, 370(1-3):110–120, 2007.

[89] Godfrey H. Hardy and Edward M. Wright. *An Introduction to the Theory of Numbers*. Oxford University Press, 1979.

[90] Juris Hartmanis and Richard E. Stearns. On the computational complexity of algorithms. *Transactions of the American Mathematical Society*, 117(5):285–306, 1965.

[91] Kosaburo Hashiguchi. Algorithms for determining relative star height and star height. *Information and Computation*, 78(2):124–169, 1988.

[92] Kosaburo Hashiguchi and Namio Honda. Homomorphisms that preserve star height. *Information and Control*, 30(3):247–266, 1976.

[93] Markus Holzer and Martin Kutrib. Nondeterministic finite automata - Recent results on the descriptional and computational complexity. In Oscar H. Ibarra and Bala Ravikumar, editors, *13th International Conference on Implementation and Applications of Automata*, volume 5148 of *Lecture Notes in Computer Science*, pages 1–16. Springer, 2008.

[94] Markus Holzer and Martin Kutrib. Descriptional and computational complexity of finite automata. In Adrian H. Dediu, Armand-Mihai Ionescu, and Carlos Martín-Vide, editors, *3rd International Conference on Language and Automata Theory and Applications*, volume 5457 of *Lecture Notes in Computer Science*, pages 23–42. Springer, 2009.

[95] John E. Hopcroft. An $n \log n$ algorithm for minimizing the states in a finite automaton. In Zvi Kohavi and Azaria Paz, editors, *The Theory of Machines and Computations*, pages 189–196. Academic Press, 1971.

[96] John E. Hopcroft and Jeffrey D. Ullman. *Introduction to Automata Theory, Languages and Computation*. Addison-Wesley Series in Computer Science. Addison-Wesley, 1979.

[97] Juraj Hromkovič. *Communication Complexity and Parallel Computing*. Texts in Theoretical Computer Science. An EATCS series. Springer, 1997.

[98] Juraj Hromkovič, Holger Petersen, and Georg Schnitger. On the limits of communication complexity technique for proving lower bounds on the size of minimal NFA's. *Theoretical Computer Science*, 2009. To appear.

[99] Juraj Hromkovič and Georg Schnitger. Comparing the size of NFAs with and without epsilon-transitions. *Theoretical Computer Science*, 380(1-2):100–114, 2007.

[100] Juraj Hromkovič and Georg Schnitger. On the hardness of determining small NFA's and of proving lower bounds on their sizes. In Masami Ito and Masafumi Toyama, editors, *12th International Conference on Developments in Language Theory*, volume 5257 of *Lecture Notes in Computer Science*, pages 34–55. Springer, 2008.

[101] Juraj Hromkovič and Georg Schnitger. Ambiguity and communication. In Susanne Albers and Jean-Yves Marion, editors, *26th International Symposium on Theoretical Aspects of Computer Science*, volume 09001 of *Dagstuhl Seminar Proceedings*, pages 553–564. Schloss Dagstuhl - Leibniz Center for Informatics, 2009.

[102] Juraj Hromkovič, Sebastian Seibert, Juhani Karhumäki, Hartmut Klauck, and Georg Schnitger. Communication complexity method for measuring nondeterminism in finite automata. *Information and Computation*, 172(2):202–217, 2002.

[103] Juraj Hromkovič, Sebastian Seibert, and Thomas Wilke. Translating regular expressions into small ε-free nondeterministic finite automata. *Journal of Computer and System Sciences*, 62(4):565–588, 2001.

[104] Juraj Hromkovič. Descriptional complexity of finite automata: Concepts and open problems. *Journal of Automata, Languages and Combinatorics*, 7(4):519–531, 2002.

[105] David A. Huffman. The synthesis of sequential switching circuits. *Journal of The Franklin Institute*, 257(3):161–190, 1954. See [106] for the second part of this article.

[106] David A. Huffman. The synthesis of sequential switching circuits. *Journal of The Franklin Institute*, 257(4):257–303, 1954. See [105] for the first part of this article.

[107] Paul Hunter and Stephan Kreutzer. Digraph measures: Kelly decompositions, games, and orderings. *Theoretical Computer Science*, 399(3):206–219, 2008.

[108] Harry B. Hunt III. The equivalence problem for regular expressions with intersection is not polynomial in tape. Technical Report Report TR 73-161, Department of Computer Science, Cornell University, 1973.

[109] Lucian Ilie, Roberto Solis-Oba, and Sheng Yu. Reducing the size of NFAs by using equivalences and preorders. In Alberto Apostolico, Maxime Crochemore, and Kunsoo Park, editors, *16th Annual Symposium on Combinatorial Pattern Matching*, volume 3537 of *Lecture Notes in Computer Science*, pages 310–321. Springer, 2005.

[110] Lucian Ilie and Sheng Yu. Follow automata. *Information and Computation*, 186(1):140–162, 2003.

[111] Lucian Ilie and Sheng Yu. Reducing NFAs by invariant equivalences. *Theoretical Computer Science*, 306(1-3):373–390, 2003.

[112] Tao Jiang, Edward McDowell, and Bala Ravikumar. The structure and complexity of minimal NFA's over unary alphabet. *International Journal of Foundations of Computer Science*, 2(2):163–182, 1991.

[113] Tao Jiang and Bala Ravikumar. A note on the space complexity of some decision problems for finite automata. *Information Processing Letters*, 40(1):25–31, 1991.

[114] Tao Jiang and Bala Ravikumar. Minimal NFA problems are hard. *SIAM Journal on Computing*, 22(6):1117–1141, 1993.

[115] Galina Jirásková. Note on minimal automata and uniform communication protocols. In Carlos Martín-Vide and Victor Mitrana, editors, *Grammars and Automata for String Processing. From Mathematics and Computer Science to Biology, and Back*, volume 9 of *Topics in Computer Mathematics*, pages 163–170. Taylor and Francis, 2003.

[116] Thor Johnson, Neil Robertson, Paul D. Seymour, and Robin Thomas. Directed tree-width. *Journal of Combinatorial Theory, Series B*, 82(1):138–154, 2001.

[117] Tsunehiko Kameda and Peter Weiner. On the state minimization of nondeterministic finite automata. *IEEE Transactions on Computers*, C-19(7):617–627, 1970.

[118] Christos A. Kapoutsis. Removing bidirectionality from nondeterministic finite automata. In Joanna Jedrzejowicz and Andrzej Szepietowski, editors, *30th International Symposium on Mathematical Foundations of Computer Science*, volume 3618 of *Lecture Notes in Computer Science*, pages 544–555. Springer, 2005.

[119] Mauricio Karchmer and Avi Wigderson. Monotone circuits for connectivity require super-logarithmic depth. *SIAM Journal on Computing*, 3:255–265, 2 1990.

[120] Meir Katchalski, William McCuaig, and Suzanne M. Seager. Ordered colourings. *Discrete Mathematics*, 142(1-3):141–154, 1995.

[121] Sanjeev Khanna, Rajeev Motwani, Madhu Sudan, and Umesh V. Vazirani. On syntactic versus computational views of approximability. *SIAM Journal on Computing*, 28(1):164–191, 1998.

[122] V. M. Khrapchenko. Methods for determining lower bounds for the complexity of Π-schemes (English translation). *Mathematical Notes of the Academy of Sciences of the USSR*, 10:474–479, 1972.

[123] Pekka Kilpeläinen and Rauno Tuhkanen. Regular expressions with numerical occurrence indicators—Preliminary results. In Pekka Kilpeläinen and Niina Päivinen, editors, *8th Symposium on Programming Languages and Software Tools*, pages 163–173. Department of Computer Science, University of Kuopio, Finland, 2003.

[124] Daniel Kirsten. Distance desert automata and the star height problem. *RAIRO – Theoretical Informatics and Applications*, 39(3):455–509, 2005.

[125] Stephen C. Kleene. Representation of events in nerve nets and finite automata. In Claude E. Shannon and John McCarthy, editors, *Automata Studies*, Annals of Mathematics Studies, pages 3–42. Princeton University Press, 1956.

[126] Donald E. Knuth. *The Art of Computer Programming, Volume 4, Fascicle 0: Introduction to Combinatorial Algorithms and Boolean Functions*. Addison-Wesley Professional, 2008.

[127] Donald E. Knuth, James H. Morris Jr., and Vaughan R. Pratt. Fast pattern matching in strings. *SIAM Journal on Computing*, 6(2):323–350, 1977.

[128] Sailesh Kumar, Sarang Dharmapurikar, Fang Yu, Patrick Crowley, and Jonathan S. Turner. Algorithms to accelerate multiple regular expressions matching for deep packet inspection. In Luigi Rizzo, Thomas E. Anderson, and Nick McKeown, editors, *ACM SIGCOMM Conference on Applications, Technologies, Architectures, and Protocols for Computer Communications*, pages 339–350. ACM, 2006.

[129] Eyal Kushilevitz and Noam Nisan. *Communication complexity*. Cambridge University Press, 1997.

[130] Quanzhong Li and Bongki Moon. Indexing and querying XML data for regular path expressions. In Peter M. G. Apers, Paolo Atzeni, Stefano Ceri, Stefano Paraboschi, Kotagiri Ramamohanarao, and Richard T. Snodgrass, editors, *27th International Conference on Very Large Data Bases*, pages 361–370. Morgan Kaufmann, 2001.

[131] Sylvain Lombardy. On the size of the universal automaton of a regular language. In Wolfgang Thomas and Pascal Weil, editors, *24th Annual Symposium on Theoretical Aspects of Computer Science*, volume 4393 of *Lecture Notes in Computer Science*, pages 85–96. Springer, 2007.

[132] Oleg Borisovich Lupanov. A comparison of two types of finite sources. *Problemy kibernetiki*, 9:321–326, 1963. (In Russian).

[133] Michael S. Mahoney. What was the question? The origins of the theory of computation. In Atsushi Akera and William Aspray, editors, *Using History to Teach Computer Science and Related Disciplines*, pages 225–232. Computing Research Association, 2004.

[134] Andreas Malcher. Minimizing finite automata is computationally hard. *Theoretical Computer Science*, 327(3):375–390, 2004.

[135] Wim Martens, Frank Neven, and Thomas Schwentick. Simple off the shelf abstractions for XML schema. *SIGMOD Record*, 36(3):15–22, 2007.

[136] A. N. Maslov. Estimates of the number of states of finite automata. *Soviet Mathematics Doklady*, 11(5):1373–1375, 1970.

[137] Alain J. Mayer and Larry J. Stockmeyer. Word problems—This time with interleaving. *Information and Computation*, 115(2):293–311, 1994.

[138] Warren S. McCulloch. *Embodiments of Mind*. MIT press, 1988.

[139] Warren S. McCulloch and Walter Pitts. A logical calculus of the ideas immanent in nervous activity. *Bulletin of Mathematical Biophysics*, 5:115–133, 1943. Reprinted in [138].

[140] Robert McNaughton. The loop complexity of pure-group events. *Information and Control*, 11(1/2):167–176, 1967.

[141] Robert McNaughton. The loop complexity of regular events. *Information Sciences*, 1(3):305–328, 1969.

[142] Robert McNaughton and Hisao Yamada. Regular expressions and state graphs for automata. *IRE Transactions on Electronic Computers*, EC-9(1):39–47, 1960.

[143] Albert R. Meyer and Michael J. Fischer. Economy of description by automata, grammars, and formal systems. In *12th Annual IEEE Symposium on Switching and Automata Theory*, pages 188–191. IEEE Computer Society, 1971.

[144] Albert R. Meyer and Larry J. Stockmeyer. The equivalence problem for regular expressions with squaring requires exponential space. In *13th Annual IEEE Symposium on Switching and Automata Theory*, pages 125–129. IEEE Computer Society, 1972.

[145] Edward F. Moore. Gedanken experiments on sequential machines. In Claude E. Shannon and John McCarthy, editors, *Automata Studies*, Annals of Mathematics Studies, pages 129–153. Princeton University Press, 1956.

[146] Frank R. Moore. On the bounds for state-set size in the proofs of equivalence between deterministic, nondeterministic, and two-way finite automata. *IEEE Transactions on Computers*, C-20(10):1211–1214, 1971.

[147] Nelma Moreira and Rogério Reis. Series-parallel automata and short regular expressions. *Fundamenta Informaticae*, 91(3-4):611–629, 2009.

[148] Paul H. Morris, Ronald A. Gray, and Robert E. Filman. GOTO removal based on regular expressions. *Journal of Software Maintenance*, 9(1):47–66, 1997.

[149] Jaroslav Nešetřil and Patrice Ossona de Mendez. Tree-depth, subgraph coloring and homomorphism bounds. *European Journal of Combinatorics*, 27(6):1022–1041, 2006.

[150] Jan Obdržálek. DAG-width: Connectivity measure for directed graphs. In *17th Annual ACM-SIAM Symposium on Discrete Algorithms*, pages 814–821. ACM Press, 2006.

[151] James B. Orlin. Contentment in graph theory: Covering graphs with cliques. *Indagationes Mathematicae*, 80(5):406–424, 1977.

[152] Christos H. Papadimitriou. *Computational complexity.* Addison-Wesley, 1994.

[153] Holger Petersen. The membership problem for regular expressions with intersection is complete in LOGCFL. In Helmut Alt and Afonso Ferreira, editors, *19th Annual Symposium on Theoretical Aspects of Computer Science*, volume 2285 of *Lecture Notes in Computer Science*, pages 513–522. Springer, 2002.

[154] Giovanni Pighizzini and Jeffrey Shallit. Unary language operations, state complexity and Jacobsthal's function. *International Journal of Foundations of Computer Science*, 13(1):145–159, 2002.

[155] Jean-Eric Pin. Syntactic semigroups. In Grzegorz Rozenberg and Arto Salomaa, editors, *Handbook of formal languages, Vol. 1: Word, language, grammar*, pages 679–746. Springer, 1997.

[156] Mark Semenovich Pinsker. On the complexity of a concentrator. In *7th International Teletraffic Conference*, pages 318/1–318/4, 1973.

[157] Michael O. Rabin and Dana Scott. Finite automata and their decision problems. *IBM Journal of Research and Development*, 3(2):114–125, 1959.

[158] Neil Robertson, Daniel P. Sanders, Paul D. Seymour, and Robin Thomas. The four-colour theorem. *Journal of Combinatorial Theory, Series B*, 70(1):2–44, 1997.

[159] Neil Robertson and Paul D. Seymour. Graph minors. III. Planar tree-width. *Journal of Combinatorial Theory, Series B*, 36(1):49–64, 1984.

[160] Neil Robertson and Paul D. Seymour. Graph minors. II. Algorithmic aspects of tree-width. *Journal of Algorithms*, 7(3):309–322, 1986.

[161] John Michael Robson. The emptiness of complement problem for semi extended regular expressions requires c^n space. *Information Processing Letters*, 9(5):220–222, 1979.

[162] Grigore Roşu. An effective algorithm for the membership problem for extended regular expressions. In Helmut Seidl, editor, *10th International Conference on Foundations of Software Science and Computational Structures*, volume 4423 of *LNCS*, pages 332–345. Springer, 2007.

[163] Jacques Sakarovitch. The language, the expression, and the (small) automaton. In Jacques Farré, Igor Litovsky, and Sylvain Schmitz, editors, *10th International Conference on Implementation and Application of Automata*, volume 3845 of *Lecture Notes in Computer Science*, pages 15–30, 2005.

[164] Kai Salomaa. Descriptional complexity of nondeterministic finite automata. In Tero Harju, Juhani Karhumäki, and Arto Lepistö, editors, *11th International Conference on Developments in Language Theory*, volume 4588 of *Lecture Notes in Computer Science*, pages 31–35. Springer, 2007.

[165] Georg Schnitger. Regular expressions and NFAs without ε-transitions. In Bruno Durand and Wolfgang Thomas, editors, *23rd Annual Symposium on Theoretical Aspects of Computer Science*, volume 3884 of *Lecture Notes in Computer Science*, pages 432–443, 2006.

[166] Marcel Paul Schützenberger. On finite monoids having only trivial subgroups. *Information and Control*, 8(2):190–194, 1965.

[167] Kyriakos N. Sgarbas, Nikos D. Fakotakis, and George K. Kokkinakis. Incremental construction of compact acyclic NFAs. In *39th Annual Meeting of the Association for Computational Linguistics*, pages 482–489. Association for Computational Linguistics, 2001.

[168] Jeffrey Shallit. *A Second Course in Formal Languages and Automata Theory*. Cambridge University Press, 2009.

[169] Peter W. Shor. A counterexample to the triangle conjecture. *Journal of Combinatorial Theory, Series A*, 38(1):110–112, 1985.

[170] Hans-Ulrich Simon. On approximate solutions for combinatorial optimization problems. *SIAM Journal on Discrete Mathematics*, 3(2):294–310, 1990.

[171] Richard E. Stearns and Harry B. Hunt III. On the equivalence and containment problems for unambiguous regular expressions, regular grammars and finite automata. *SIAM Journal on Computing*, 14(3):598–611, 1985.

[172] Larry J. Stockmeyer and Albert R. Meyer. Word problems requiring exponential time: Preliminary Report. In *5th Annual ACM Symposium on Theory of Computing*, pages 1–9. ACM, 1973.

[173] Ambuj Tewari, Utkarsh Srivastava, and Phalguni Gupta. A parallel DFA minimization algorithm. In Sartaj Sahni, Viktor K. Prasanna, and Uday Shukla, editors, *9th International Conference on High Performance Computing*, volume 2552 of *Lecture Notes in Computer Science*, pages 34–40. Springer, 2002.

[174] Boris A. Trakhtenbrot. Finite automata and the logic of monadic predicates. *Doklady Akademii Nauk SSSR*, 140:326–329, 1961.

[175] Luca Trevisan. *Reductions and (Non-)Approximability*. PhD thesis, University of Rome "La Sapienza", 1997. PhD Theses Series of Electronic Colloquium on Computational Complexity.

[176] Pál Turán. On an extremal problem in graph theory (in Hungarian). *Matematicko Fizicki Lapok*, 48:436–452, 1941.

[177] Volker Waizenegger. On the efficiency of description by regular expressions and finite automata (in German). Diploma thesis, Rheinisch-Westfälische Technische Hochschule Aachen, Fachbereich Informatik, 2000.

[178] Manfred K. Warmuth and David Haussler. On the complexity of iterated shuffle. *Journal of Computer and System Sciences*, 28(3):345–358, 1984.

[179] Sheng Yu. Regular languages. In Grzegorz Rozenberg and Arto Salomaa, editors, *Handbook of formal languages, Vol. 1: Word, language, grammar*, pages 41–110. Springer, 1997.

[180] Sheng Yu. A renaissance of automata theory? *Bulletin of the EATCS*, 72:270–272, 2000.

[181] Sheng Yu. State complexity: Recent results and open problems. *Fundamenta Informaticae*, 64(1-4):471–480, 2005.

[182] David Zuckerman. Linear degree extractors and the inapproximability of max clique and chromatic number. *Theory of Computing*, 3(1):103–128, 2007.

Index

Honda, Namio, 6, 139
Hopcroft, John Edward, 5, 9, 10, 13, 14, 17, 46, 79, 129, 132, 159, 161, 163
Hromkovič, Juraj, 4, 17, 26, 27, 31, 33, 73, 74, 79
Huffman, David Albert, 3, 5
Hunt, Harry Bowen III, 74, 144
Hunter, Paul William, 87
Husfeldt, Thore, 90
hypercube, 147

I

Ilie, Lucian, 74, 79, 85
Ilie, Lucien, 16
incident, 18
independent set, 18, 119, 120
INIT, 163, 168
input expansion, 57
interleaving, 10, 132, 137, 147, 149, 168
intersection, 131, 136, 137, 151, 168
isolated set, *see* matching, $K_{2,2}$-free
iteration, *see* Kleene star

J

Jansen, Klaus, 117, 118
Janssen, Philippe, 33, 49, 66
Jeffrey Outlaw Shallit, 42
Jiang, Tao, 5, 6, 31, 45, 49, 53, 55, 71, 74, 144, 173, 174
Jirásková, Galina, 31
Johnson, David Stifler, 45, 48–50, 56, 58, 65, 70, 173
Johnson, Thor, 87, 94, 95

K

Kahn, Jeffry Ned, 120, 123
Kameda, Tsunehiko, 27, 30, 74
Kann, Viggo, 56
Kapoutsis, Christos Antonios, 4, 103
Karchmer, Mauricio, 98–100
Karhumäki, Juhani, 31
Kari, Jarkko, 43
Katchalski, Meir, 117, 118

Katoen, Joost-Pieter, 79
Kavitha, Telikepalli, 148
Khanna, Sanjeev, 65, 90
Khrapchenko, V. M., 98
Kilpeläinen, Pekka, 143
Kirsten, Daniel, 7, 84, 175
Klauck, Hartmut, 31
Kleene star, 10
Kleene, Stephen Cole, 3, 8
Kloks, Ton Jacobus Johannes, 83, 84, 117, 118, 148
Knuth, Donald Ervin, 5, 132
Kokkinakis, George K., 6, 46
Kratsch, Dieter, 117, 118
Krawetz, Bryan, 4, 7, 8, 14, 94, 97, 98, 100, 112, 118, 125, 129, 130, 132, 138, 143, 167, 175
Kreutzer, Stephan, 87
Kumar, Sailesh, 5
Kurganskyy, Oleksiy, 74
Kushilevitz, Eyal, 99, 100, 107
Kutrib, Martin, 33, 73, 74, 129

L

language
    accepted by a finite automaton, 12
    bideterministic, 84
    cyclic, *see* language, unary cyclic
    finite, 11, 48, 65, 66, 68, 97, 108, 164, 165
    formal, 10
    homogeneous, 99, 102, 104
    local, 155, 158, 159
    monotone, 99, 102
    regular, *see* regular language
    unary, 11, 53, 67, 70, 72, 125, 138, 167
        cyclic, 11, 53, 67
length
    of a word, 9
letter, 9
Li, Quanzhong, 5
linear expression, 153, 155–157, 160, 167
Lombardy, Sylvain, 74
loop, 18, 89, 139
Lupanov, Oleg Borisovich, 5, 16

M

Müller, Haiko, 117, 118
Mahoney, Michael S., 4
Malcher, Andreas, 74
Marchetti-Spaccamela, Alberto, 56
Martens, Wim, 5, 74
Maslov, A. N., 5, 13
matching, 19
$K_{2,2}$-free, 19
perfect, 19
Mayer, Alain Jules, 10, 144, 147–149
McCluskey, Jr., Edward Joseph, 109, 112
McCuaig, William, 117, 118
McCulloch, Warren Sturgis, 3
McDowell, Edward, 5, 31, 53, 71, 174
McNaughton, Robert, 6, 15, 84, 87, 92,
109, 111, 112, 114, 115, 139
Meyer, Albert Ronald da Silva, 5, 16, 33,
45, 53, 70, 74, 143
Michael Domaratzki, 42
minimum elimination tree height, see cy-
cle rank, undirected
monomorphism, 11, 139, 141, 145, 148
monotone
Boolean formula, see Boolean formula,
monotone
language, see language, monotone
search problem, 99, 106, 107
Moon, Bongki, 5
Moore, Edward Forrest, 3, 5
Moore, Frank R., 16, 103
Morais, José, 109
Morais, Rogério, 115
Moreira, Nelma, 97, 109
Morris, James H. Jr., 5
Morris, Paul H., 79
Motwani, Rajeev, 65
Myhill, John R., 13
Myhill-Nerode relation, see equivalence,
Myhill-Nerode

N

Nešetřil, Jaroslav, 83, 117
neighborhood, 18
Nerode, Anil, 13

Neven, Frank, 5, 7, 80, 125, 129, 132,
138–140, 144, 145, 167, 175
NFA, see nondeterministic finite automaton
Nisan, Noam, 99, 100, 107
Niwinsky, Damian, 27
nondeterministic
finite automaton, 12, 144, 147, 161,
164
minimal, 25, 33, 34, 45, 46, 48, 55,
61, 64–66, 68–70, 72, 73
with ε-transitions, 12, 34, 35, 42,
43, 79, 85, 111
message complexity, see biclique edge
cover technique
polynomial time, see **NP**
state complexity, 33
state complexity, 16, 17, 40, 43, 73,
164
transition complexity, 16, 17, 33, 40,
42, 43, 64, 69, 72, 73
nonelementary, 143
normalized
finite automaton, 111, 115
NP, 21, 46, 47
NP-complete, 46, 48, 49, 74, 118
NP^{NP}, 21, 46, 70

O

Obdržálek, Jan, 87
operation
on languages, 10, 129, 153, 167
optimization problem, 56
optimum value, 56
oracle, see Turing machine, oracle
ordered chromatic number, see cycle rank,
undirected
Orlin, James Berger, 20, 49
Ossona de Mendez, Patrice, 83, 117

P

P, 21
P^{NP}, 21
Papadimitriou, Christos, 9, 21, 47
path, 19

pathwidth, 148
performance ratio, 56
period
    of a unary cyclic language, 11, 71
Petersen, Holger, 31, 73, 144
Pighizzini, Giovanni, 67
Pin, Jean-Eric, 4, 66, 155
Pinsker, Mark Semenovich, 89, 90, 174
Pitts, Walter, 3
planar finite automaton, 94, 110, 118
Podelski, Andreas, 27
poly-APX, 57, 65
polynomial
    space, *see* **PSPACE**
    time, *see* **P**
Popatov, Igor, 74
position
    in regular expression, 154
Pothen, Alex, 118
Pratt, Vaughan Ronald, 5
prefix-free, 139, 145
Proskurowski, Andrzej, 80
Protasi, Marco, 56
protocol partition number, 98, 102, 108
PSPACE, 21
PSPACE-complete, 45, 74, 143
Pullman, Norman Jay, 20, 31

Q

quotient, 10, 69, 153, 154, 158, 160, 162,
    168

R

Rabin, Michael Oser, 3, 5, 16
Ramanujan graph, 110
Ramanujan Iyengar, Srinivasa, 110
Ravikumar, Bala, 5, 6, 31, 45, 49, 53, 55,
    71, 74, 144, 173, 174
reduction
    polynomial time, 22, 48
regular expression, 11, 33, 79, 85, 86, 93,
    94, 97, 105, 108, 110, 112, 125,
    129, 138, 144, 153, 167
    extended, 143, 167, 169
    homogeneous, 100, 101

linear, *see* linear expression
minimal, 69, 72
monotone, 101
similar, *see* similarity of regular ex-
    pressions
uncollapsible, 100, 153
with interleaving, 144, 147–150, 167,
    169
with intersection, 144, 145, 167, 169
with squaring, 143
regular language, 11
Reis, Rogério, 97, 109
reversal, 9
Roşu, Grigore, 4
Robertson, George Neil, 49, 80, 81, 87,
    94, 95, 123
Robson, John Michael, 144

S

Sakarovitch, Jacques, 80, 109
Salomaa, Kai, 33, 39, 43, 73
Sanders, Daniel Preston, 49
Schützenberger, Marcel-Paul, 4, 6
Schnitger, Georg, 4–6, 17, 31, 42, 46, 55,
    56, 69, 71, 73, 74, 79, 173, 174
Schwentick, Thomas, 5
Scott, Dana Stewart, 3, 5, 16
Seager, Suzanne M., 117, 118
Seibert, Sebastian, 17, 33, 79
Seibert,Sebastian, 31
separator
    balanced, 81, 122, 137
    weak balanced, 83, 132
separator number, 81, 82
Sethi, Ravi, 5, 156
Seymour, Paul D., 49, 80, 81, 87, 94, 95,
    120, 123
Sgarbas, Kyriakos N., 6, 46
Shallit, Jeffrey Outlaw, 4, 7, 8, 10, 14, 26,
    28, 67, 94, 97, 98, 100, 112, 118,
    125, 129, 130, 132, 137, 138, 143,
    145, 167, 175
Shor, Peter Williston, 4
shuffle, *see* interleaving
similarity
    of regular expressions, 115

Warmuth, Manfred Klaus, 148
weak separator number, 81, 83
Weiner, Peter, 27, 30, 74
Wigderson, Avi, 98–100
Wilke, Thomas, 17, 33, 79
Wood, Derick, 109, 115
word, 9
Wright, Edward Maitland, 70, 71

Y

Yamada, Hisao, 109, 111, 112, 114, 115
Yu, Fang, 5
Yu, Sheng, 4, 5, 16, 74, 79, 85, 129

Z

Zeiger, Howard Paul, 7, 18, 79, 97, 108,
        111, 114, 125, 138, 145, 174
Ziadi, Djelloul, 155, 156, 158
Zuckerman, David, 58, 65